FINDING COMMON GROUND

A GUIDE TO
RELIGIOUS LIBERTY
IN PUBLIC SCHOOLS

WRITTEN AND EDITED BY
CHARLES C. HAYNES
AND
OLIVER THOMAS

JOHN FERGUSON, Associate Editor

FIRST AMENDMENT CENTER
FUNDED BY THE FREEDOM FORUM

D0580126

© 2002 First Amendment Center

FIRST AMENDMENT CENTER
FUNDED BY THE FREEDOM FORUM

1207 18th Avenue South
Nashville, TN 37212
(615) 727-1600
www.firstamendmentcenter.org

Publication No: 01-F09
ISBN 0-9656863-4-5

Educator's discount available for orders of ten or more of this publication.
For more information, call (703) 284-2809.

CONTENTS

ABOUT THE AUTHORS

Charles C. Haynes, Ph.D.

Charles C. Haynes is senior scholar at the First Amendment Center. He is best known for helping schools and communities throughout the United States find common ground on First Amendment issues in public schools.

During the past decade, Haynes has been a principal organizer and drafter of a series of consensus guidelines on religious liberty in public education, endorsed by a broad range of major religious and educational organizations. In January 2000, the U.S. Department of Education distributed three of these guides to every public school in the United States.

Haynes is the author of numerous books and articles, including *Religious Liberty and the Public Schools* (Phi Delta Kappa Educational Foundation, 2001) and *Religion in American History: What to Teach and How* (ASCD, 1990). He is co-author of *Taking Religion Seriously Across the Curriculum* (ASCD, 1998) and *Religion in American Public Life: Living With Our Deepest Differences* (W. W. Norton and Co., 2001). His bi-monthly column *Inside the First Amendment* appears in newspapers nationwide.

An educator for 20 years, Haynes served as executive director of First Liberty Institute at George Mason University in Fairfax, Va., and taught on the college and secondary levels. He presently serves on the board of directors of the Character Education Partnership and the Council for Spiritual and Ethical Education.

Haynes holds a master's degree in religion and education from Harvard Divinity School and a doctorate in theological studies from Emory University.

Oliver Thomas, Esq.

Oliver Thomas is a lawyer, minister, author and school board member. He has written and lectured extensively on the subject of religion and public education and has consulted with hundreds of school districts.

Mr. Thomas has been involved in litigation at every level of state and federal courts including the United States Supreme Court. His clients have included the National Council of Churches and the Baptist Joint Committee.

In addition to representing numerous Evangelical groups, Mr. Thomas co-authored the A.C.L.U. handbook on church-state law. Before returning to his native Tennessee, Mr. Thomas taught at Georgetown University Law Center. He has lectured at such law schools as Harvard and Regent University.

Mr. Thomas is a graduate of the University of Tennessee, University of Virginia and New Orleans Baptist Theological Seminary where he was chosen as the most outstanding divinity graduate.

This guide is designed to provide general information on the subject of religious expression and practices in schools. It is printed with the understanding that the authors are not rendering legal or other professional services. If the reader has specific legal questions, the services of a qualified, licensed attorney should be sought.

FOREWORD

By John Seigenthaler
Founder, First Amendment Center

It has been seven years since the Freedom Forum First Amendment Center initially published *Finding Common Ground,* the landmark guide urging educators to begin taking religious liberty and teaching about religion seriously in public schools.

This new and updated edition is designed to further assist school officials, parents and teachers in keeping pace with evolving law, changing trends and emerging challenges that touch on religious liberty and public education.

Charles Haynes, who created this innovative concept, wrote the original guide convinced that educators had universally misinterpreted U. S. Supreme Court opinions and had effectively stripped religion from text books and classroom discussions. At the time this guide first was published, culture wars over religion in the schools raged in many communities. School board meetings, Parent-Teacher Association gatherings and federal courtrooms often were the battlegrounds.

Many school administrators and teachers worried that *Finding Common Ground* was a radical, even a dangerous idea. They feared that Haynes' vision was naïve and if put into practice would fly in the face of court rulings. They were concerned that it would invite lawsuits and incite further controversy.

In fact, teaching *about* religion was an eminently rational and timely idea. In no sense was it radical. Fears that it would stimulate lawsuits were groundless. Concerns that it would drive people apart were wrongheaded. In fact, once in place the program actually helped resolve many community conflicts, both legal and ideological. In action, Haynes' initiative comported perfectly with a stream of Supreme Court decisions dating back almost four decades to an opinion crafted by Justice Tom Clark.

"A person cannot be fully educated," he wrote for the court in 1963, "without understanding the role of religion in history, culture and politics .... The law, constitutional or otherwise, is no impediment to the realization of this aim."

What had been misunderstood by many educators (and still is misapprehended by too many) was that while Supreme Court rulings barred school-sponsored prayer and religious indoctrination, they had by no means banned teaching *about* religion. The court had decreed that school districts and teachers must be neutral in classroom discussions about religion. Proselytizing or promoting one denomination or faith over others violated the constitutional wall between church and state, the court consistently held. No teacher could encourage students to change religious denominations – or to accept one faith over another.

But Justice Clark understood 40 years ago that it was impossible for any student to be enlightened about world or American history, political science, government, art, law or many other subjects without learning about religion. His thesis remains valid. *Finding Common Ground* has given it vitality and viability by offering specific guidelines for classroom instruction.

So why a new edition of this guide? Neither the law nor school enrollment has been static. Change has been a constant in public education, as courts have ruled, for example, that if a tax-supported school permits extracurricular programs and practices of a secular nature, religious programs and practices must also be given fair and similar treatment. Students, the courts have decreed, are allowed to talk to their fellow students about their own religious beliefs so long as they are not harassing. They are allowed to write about their faith in school essays so long as the work conforms to teacher assignments. As Haynes points out, this offers new challenges and new opportunities for public schools.

There also are challenges and opportunities as school administrators seek to adjust to student populations that are more religiously diverse than at any time in the nation's history. In this new edition of his guide, Haynes provides a reliable compass to direct educators in creating an environment and implementing policies that will make all students—those of every religious faith or none—more comfortable and more welcome in a changing educational climate.

In light of the international unrest and national upheaval that has followed the September 11, 2001 terrorist actions in New York, Washington and elsewhere, it seems worth repeating here the first three paragraphs of the foreword I wrote to the original edition of Finding Common Ground:

> *Almost weekly now, U. S. citizens read in newspapers or see on television reports of 'Muslim terrorist' threats or attacks aimed at some 'enemy of Islam.'*
>
> *The news-media drumbeat has led many of us to the false impression that the Muslim faith is a religion built on a foundation of violence and fanaticism. Nowhere have most of us been taught about the history of Islam or what Muslims today actually believe. We know little about the vision of Muhammad in 610 that began with the revelations known as the Qur'an, accepted by millions of Muslims throughout the world as the word of Allah or God. We are unaware that it is from this experience that the faith of Islam had its beginning.*
>
> *More than 1300 years later American school children, who read and hear about the growing influence of the Islamic world on our lives, learn very little about the Prophet Muhammad or the religious traditions of Muslims.*

If those words had modest meaning in November 1994—and I think they did—they should have bell-ringing resonance since the tragedy that befell the nation that violent

Tuesday morning. It no longer is a question of whether schools *should* teach children about Islam. They *must* teach them—and about other religions as well. It is a responsibility, a duty.

In the days following the terrorist-inspired tragedies, students everywhere came to school with questions about what they had seen and heard and read in the news media. How could a U.S. public school teacher respond to those questions without mentioning religion? Or without putting in context religious extremism by a small group of fanatics? Or without explaining that the Islamic faith of all but a few extremist Muslims would reject the taking of innocent life—any innocent life anywhere?

It is sad but certain that many teachers were forced to deal with those questions from a background of ignorance. Some, no doubt, found themselves answering students' questions by relying mostly on what they had learned from the media.

There were, fortunately, noteworthy exceptions to that drill. In hundreds of schools from California and Utah to New York and New Jersey, teachers whose school systems had embraced the *Finding Common Ground* concept were equipped with answers that were grounded in study and discussion of world religions, including the faith of Muslims. It is probable that many youngsters who had shared in that study and discussion actually were able to help their parents better understand the Islamic religion in the aftermath of the terrorist attacks.

For too long public schools have lived with an unfair reputation of being secular bastions hostile to religion. Religious parents, aware of that public school image, sometimes have opted to send their children to private denominational institutions.

Public schools that now embrace the *Finding Common Ground* model offer students of all faiths and none a unique, enriching academic experience. Seven years ago, it seemed to Charles Haynes that teaching students to understand our deepest religious differences was a way to help save public education. Today, teaching those same lessons may help save far more.

CHAPTER 1

From Battleground
to Common Ground

FIRST AMENDMENT TO THE
UNITED STATES CONSTITUTION

The Religious Liberty clauses of the First Amendment
to the Constitution are a momentous decision, the
most important political decision for religious liberty
and public justice in history. Two hundred years after
their enactment they stand out boldly in a century
made dark by state repression and sectarian conflict.
Yet the ignorance and contention now surrounding
the clauses are a reminder that their advocacy and
defense is a task for each succeeding generation.

—The Williamsburg Charter
1988

*Congress shall make no law respecting an
establishment of religion, or prohibiting the
free exercise thereof;*

—Religious Liberty Clauses,
First Amendment to the
United States Constitution

More than 200 years after their enactment, the first 16 words
of the Bill of Rights undergird the boldest and most successful
experiment in religious freedom in human history. Despite periodic
outbreaks of nativism, anti-Semitism and religious conflict, Americans can be justly proud
that we begin the new century as one nation of many peoples and faiths.

THE CHALLENGE

The challenge for 21st-century America is not
only to sustain this extraordinary arrangement,
but to expand the principles of religious liberty
more fairly and justly to each and every citizen.
This is no small task. Today the United States is
the most religiously diverse society on Earth
and, among developed countries, the most
religious. But exploding religious pluralism
combined with bitter culture wars are making
our public square an increasingly crowded and
often hostile arena.

Nowhere is it more important — or more
difficult — to address our growing ideological
and religious diversity than in the public schools.
Not only are our schools a key battleground in
the culture wars, they are the principal institution
charged with enabling Americans to live with our
deepest differences. If we fail in our schools to

teach and model the rights and responsibilities that flow from the First Amendment, then surely we endanger the future of our daring experiment in religious liberty.

This guide is built on the conviction that finding common ground on many of the issues that divide us is possible within the civic framework provided by the Religious Liberty clauses of the First Amendment to the U.S. Constitution. The key is for all sides to step back from the debate and to give fresh consideration to the democratic first principles that bind us together as a people. Then, in light of our shared civic commitments, we can work for policies and practices in public education that best protect the conscience of every student and parent in our schools.

A NEW CONSENSUS

Here is the good news: Although underreported by the media and still unknown to many school leaders, a new model has emerged for addressing religion and religious liberty in public schools. Over the past decade, religious and educational groups from across the

spectrum have adopted the consensus guidelines included in this guide. Where these agreements have been applied in local districts, they have enabled a growing number of divided communities to move from battleground to common ground.

The measure of just how much consensus we now have was highlighted in early 2000 when every public-school principal in the United States received a packet of comprehensive religious liberty guidelines from President Clinton and the U.S. Department of Education (see Chapters 6, 10, and 12). For the first time in American history, all administrators were given the closest thing possible to a legal safe harbor for addressing perennial conflicts over religion in the schools.

This new consensus on religion in public schools began to emerge as a response to the textbook trials in Alabama and Tennessee in the mid-1980s. Although the constitutional questions were quite different, both cases called attention to the fact that the public-school curriculum largely ignored religious ways of understanding the world. The educational issues raised by the trials were reinforced by several textbook studies. The liberal People for the American Way reached much the same conclusion as the conservative Paul Vitz: Public-school texts included little or nothing about religion.

In the wake of these trials and studies, we convened leading educational and religious organizations in an effort to find common ground on the question of religion in the curriculum. Groups ranging from the National Association for Evangelicals to the Association for Supervision and Curriculum Development agreed that ignoring religion was neither educationally sound nor consistent with the First Amendment. We were convinced that we can (and must) do better in public education.

After a year and a half of discussion and debate, we reached agreement on our first set of guidelines, "Religion in the Public School Curriculum: Questions and Answers." Four months later we forged a second agreement, "Religious Holidays in the Public Schools: Questions and Answers." This was soon followed by a third statement providing consensus guidelines for implementing the Equal Access Act. After a long history of shouting past one another, we had begun to find common ground.

BEYOND TWO FAILED MODELS

These agreements of the late 1980s and early 1990s were important first steps in articulating a civic framework that enables school and communities to move beyond culture-war debates that are often dominated by extremes.

On one end of the spectrum are those who advocate what might be called the "sacred public school," where one religion (theirs) is preferred in school policies and practices. Characteristic of the early history of public education, this approach still survives in some parts of the United States, particularly the rural South. From the "Bible wars" of the 19th century to current fights over posting the Ten Commandments in classrooms, attempts to impose religion in schools have fueled countless lawsuits and bitter fights in communities throughout the nation. Not only is this model unconstitutional, it is also unjust.

In recent decades, however, some on the other end of the spectrum have pushed for a "naked public school," where religion is excluded in the name of the Establishment clause of the First Amendment. The influence of this mistaken view of the First Amendment is apparent in the virtual silence about religion in most of the curriculum and the confusion among many school leaders about the religious-liberty rights of students. But the First Amendment does not mandate that public schools be religion-free zones. This approach is also unjust and, when the rights of students are violated, unconstitutional.

The process of finding consensus during the past decade has yielded a third model – what might be called a "civil public school" – articulated in the various guidelines included in this guide. The shared vision of this model is captured best in "Religious Liberty, Public Education, and the Future of American Democracy," a statement of principles found in Chapter 2. Twenty-four major religious and educational organizations define religious liberty in public schools this way:

> Public schools may not inculcate nor inhibit religion. They must be places where religion and religious conviction are treated with fairness and respect.

> Public schools uphold the First Amendment when they protect the religious liberty rights of students of all faiths or none. Schools demonstrate fairness when they ensure that the curriculum includes study *about* religion, where appropriate, as an important part of a complete education.

These four sentences restate the civic framework of the religious-liberty clauses of the First Amendment — our constitutional commitment to "no establishment" and "free exercise" — as they apply to public education. They describe what schools might look like if we finally lived up to the promise of religious liberty. Rather than simply telling public schools what they may not do, the statement calls for protecting student religious expression and including religious perspectives in the curriculum, while simultaneously rejecting government endorsement or promotion of religion.

YES, BUT HOW?

For many years now, the First Amendment Center has worked with school districts throughout the nation to implement the model of a civil public school. We have found that where communities are committed to coming together in the spirit of the First Amendment, consensus is reached, new policies are drafted, and significant changes take place in the classroom. Significantly, support for these efforts comes from both the "right" and "left" of the political and religious spectrum.

The starting point for local communities must be an agreement on First Amendment ground rules as described in Chapters 2 and 5. In the spirit of the First Amendment, all perspectives have a right to be heard, and each citizen has an obligation to protect the freedom of conscience of all others. Agreeing on civic principles allows the dialogue to begin and enables people of all faiths or none to work toward consensus on the proper role of religion in the public schools.

If the resulting agreements and policies are to inspire broad support in the community, all stakeholders must be fully represented in the discussion. When reaching out to critics of the schools, particularly conservative religious groups, school leaders must look beyond stereotypes to find those representatives most interested in dialogue and consensus. Given the lack of civility in the public square of America today, it is not easy to build bridges of understanding and trust, but it can be done.

While there are extreme voices in the debate, we know from experience that most teachers, parents, administrators and school board members are committed to a principled dialogue, and to fair, open public schools. This includes the vast majority of parents often labeled as members of the "religious right" or the "secular left." Sadly, a few groups on either side thrive on "demonizing" the opposition, often lumping all individuals and groups under one frightening label. Tactics such as these may successfully raise millions of dollars through direct mail, but they destroy the fabric of our life together as citizens. And the media sometimes fuel the conflict by allowing extreme voices to dominate the debate.

To get beyond the labels, trust needs to be carefully rebuilt. Building trust, of course, requires a willingness to listen. But listening is meaningless if parents or others in the community sense that most questions have been answered before the process begins. A number of school-reform advocates, for example, stress the importance of local participation, but then resist the possibility that local communities may not endorse the reform. Some state mandates encourage communities to write "mission statements," but leave little room for local decision-making about the educational mission of the schools.

Listening and trusting are also difficult, if not impossible, in districts unprepared for conflict concerning religion and values in the schools. Every district should have comprehensive policies on these issues, developed and endorsed by a broad spectrum of the community and followed up by teacher and administrator education focused on implementation. Using this guide to take a pro-active — rather than crisis-management — approach to areas of potential controversy is an opportunity for public schools to demonstrate a genuine interest in the concerns of parents, and a concrete commitment to applying religious-liberty principles in public schools.

A COMMON VISION OF THE COMMON GOOD

National consensus statements and guidelines are essential, but they are only starting points in the effort to find lasting common ground. Creating truly civil public schools — schools that take religious liberty seriously – requires school districts willing to do the work of translating these agreements into effective, community-supported policies and practices.

The new consensus represented by the agreements in this guide provides Americans with an historic opportunity. After more than 150 years of shouting past one another about religious liberty in schools, we finally have a model widely agreed-to across our differences. It is now possible to address our differences with civility, reach mutual understanding and forge polices that protect the First Amendment rights of every parent and student.

If we take this opportunity, a common vision of the common good may be realized in public schools and in our communities. The time is now to re-commit ourselves, as American citizens, to the vision of "We the People" — the ongoing and difficult task of building one nation out of many peoples and faiths.

Resources

Al-Hibri, Azizah Y., Jean Bethke Elshtain, Charles C. Haynes (2001). *Religion in American Public Life: Living with Our Deepest Differences*. New York: W.W. Norton and Co.

Hunter, James Davison and Os Guinness, eds. (1990). *Articles of Faith, Articles of Peace: The Religious Liberty Clauses and the American Public Philosophy*. Washington: The Brookings Institution.

Nord, Warren A. (1995). *Religion and American Education: Re-thinking an American Dilemma*. Chapel Hill: University of North Carolina Press.

Nord, Warren A., Charles C. Haynes (1998). *Taking Religion Seriously Across the Curriculum*. Alexandria, Virginia: Association for Supervision and Curriculum Development.

CHAPTER 2

Religious Liberty, Public Education, and the Future of American Democracy:
A Statement of Principles

This Statement of Principles is sponsored jointly by:

American Association of School Administrators

American Center for Law and Justice

American Federation of Teachers

Anti-Defamation League

Association for Supervision and Curriculum Development

Carnegie Foundation for the Advancement of Teaching

Catholic League for Religious and Civil Rights

Central Conference of American Rabbis

Christian Coalition

Christian Educators Association International

Christian Legal Society

Coalition for the Community of Reason

Council on Islamic Education

The First Amendment Center

National Association of Elementary School Principals

National Association of Evangelicals

National Association of Secondary School Principals

National PTA

National Council of Churches of Christ in the U.S.A.

National Education Association

National School Boards Association

People for the American Way Foundation

Phi Delta Kappa

Union of American Hebrew Congregations

Our nation urgently needs a reaffirmation of our shared commitment, as American citizens, to the guiding principles of the Religious Liberty clauses of the First Amendment to the Constitution. The rights and responsibilities of the Religious Liberty clauses provide the civic framework within which we are able to debate our differences, to understand one another, and to forge public policies that serve the common good in public education.

Today, many American communities are divided over educational philosophy, school reform, and the role of religion and values in our public schools. Conflict and debate are vital to democracy. Yet, if controversies about public education are to advance the best interests of the nation, then *how* we debate, and not only *what* we debate, is critical.

In the spirit of the First Amendment, we propose the following principles as civic ground rules for addressing conflicts in public education:

I. Religious Liberty for All

Religious liberty is an inalienable right of every person.

As Americans, we all share the responsibility to guard that right for every citizen. The Constitution of the United States with its Bill of Rights provides a civic framework of rights and responsibilities that enables Americans to work together for the common good in public education.

II. The Meaning of Citizenship

Citizenship in a diverse society means living with our deepest differences and committing ourselves to work for public policies that are in the best interest of all individuals, families, communities and our nation.

The framers of our Constitution referred to this concept of moral responsibility as civic virtue.

III. Public Schools Belong to All Citizens

*Public schools must model the democratic
process and constitutional principles in
the development of policies and curricula.*

Policy decisions by officials or
governing bodies should be made only
after appropriate involvement of those
affected by the decision and with due
consideration for the rights of those
holding dissenting views.

IV. Religious Liberty and Public Schools

*Public schools may not inculcate nor
inhibit religion. They must be places
where religion and religious conviction
are treated with fairness and respect.*

Public schools uphold the First Amendment when they protect the religious liberty
rights of students of all faiths or none. Schools demonstrate fairness when they ensure
that the curriculum includes study *about* religion, where appropriate, as an important
part of a complete education.

V. The Relationship between Parents and Schools

*Parents are recognized as having the primary responsibility for the upbringing of their
children, including education.*

Parents who send their children to public schools delegate to public school educators
some of the responsibility for their children's education. In so doing, parents
acknowledge the crucial role of educators without abdicating their parental duty.
Parents may also choose not to send their children to public schools and have their
children educated at home or in private schools. However, private citizens, including
business leaders and others, also have the right to expect public education to give
students tools for living in a productive democratic society. All citizens must have a
shared commitment to offer students the best possible education. Parents have a special
responsibility to participate in the activity of their children's schools. Children and
schools benefit greatly when parents and educators work closely together to shape
school policies and practices and to ensure that public education supports the societal
values of their community without undermining family values and convictions.

VI. Conduct of Public Disputes

Civil debate, the cornerstone of a true democracy, is vital to the success of any effort to improve and reform America's public schools.

Personal attacks, name-calling, ridicule and similar tactics destroy the fabric of our society and undermine the educational mission of our schools. Even when our differences are deep, all parties engaged in public disputes should treat one another with civility and respect, and should strive to be accurate and fair. Through constructive dialogue we have much to learn from one another.

Conclusion

This Statement of Principles is not an attempt to ignore or minimize differences that are important and abiding, but rather a reaffirmation of what we share as American citizens across our differences. Democratic citizenship does not require a compromise of our deepest convictions.

We invite all men and women of good will to join us in affirming these principles and putting them into action. The time has come for us to work together for academic excellence, fairness and shared civic values in our nation's schools.

3

A History of
Religious Liberty in
American Public Life

Congress shall make

no law respecting an

establishment of religion

or prohibiting the free

exercise thereof; or

abridging the freedom

of speech, or of the

or the right of the people

peaceably to assemble,

and to petition the

Government for a redress

of grievances.

FIRST AMENDMENT TO THE
UNITED STATES CONSTITUTION

The Religion then of every man must be left to the
conviction and conscience of every man; and it is the
right of every man to exercise it as these may dictate.
This right is in its nature an unalienable right.

—James Madison
Memorial and Remonstrance
1785

From the colonial era to the present, religions and religious beliefs have played a significant role in the political life of the United States. Religion has been at the heart of some of the best and some of the worst movements in American history. The guiding principles that the Framers intended to govern the relationship between religion and politics are set forth in Article VI of the Constitution and in the opening 16 words of the First Amendment of the Bill of Rights. Now that America has expanded from the largely Protestant pluralism of the seventeenth century to a nation of some 3,000 religious groups, it is more vital than ever that every citizen understand the appropriate role of religion in public life and affirm the constitutional guarantees of religious liberty, or freedom of conscience, for people of all faiths or none.

The philosophical ideas and religious convictions of Roger Williams, William Penn, John Leland, Thomas Jefferson, James Madison, and other leaders were decisive in the struggle for freedom of conscience. The United States is a nation built on ideals and convictions that have become democratic first principles. These principles must be understood and affirmed by every generation if the American experiment in liberty is to endure.

What Citizens Should Know

The citizen should be able to:

1. Explain the position that religious liberty is a universal human right, the preservation of which depends upon a reciprocal responsibility to respect that right for everyone.

2. Explain how the constitutional principles of religious liberty are the ground rules that enable people of all faiths and none to live together as citizens of one nation.

3. Explain the principles of religious liberty or freedom of conscience as found in the First Amendment of the U.S. Constitution.

4. Explain various interpretations of the constitutional relationship of religion and government in American political life.

5. Explain the significant role religion and religious belief have played in American history and politics.

6. Explain the relationship of religious liberty to the strength and diversity of religious life in the United States.

7. Take, defend, and evaluate positions on constitutional issues regarding religious beliefs and practices.

FRAME OF REFERENCE

Conceptual perspective

I. The central place of faith in the idea of religion.

The radical pluralism of faiths in the United States today makes it difficult to define religion without excluding religions that may not fit a chosen definition. If, however, citizens are to understand the role of religion in American public life and support religious liberty for all, they need to appreciate that faith is of central importance to many Americans.

A. **The centrality of religion in the lives of many Americans.** Without defining what religion is, we can, for purposes of civic understanding, focus on what religion does in the lives of believers. Ultimate beliefs and world views shape the lives of many people because they are regarded as the deepest source of meaning and belonging. In the United States, arguably the most religious of all the industrialized nations, religious beliefs are at the center of life for millions of Americans. These beliefs are not confined to worship and family life; they also shape the political and social views of vast numbers of citizens.

B. **The expansion of religious pluralism.** The United States has moved beyond the largely Protestant pluralism of its early history to a pluralism that includes almost every religious expression in the world. This expanding diversity presents new challenges for American public life.

C. **Religious liberty as freedom of conscience for all, including non-believers.** A growing number of people in the United States express no religious preference at all. Any discussion of pluralism and the role of religion in public life, therefore, must include secularists, humanists, non-believers, and others who do not profess any religious beliefs.

1. *The protection of religion in its broadest sense.* The Supreme Court has accepted the necessity of broad recognition of world views (and the dangers of too narrow a definition of religion) by giving conscientious objector status to those who have "a sincere and meaningful belief which occupies in the life of its possessor a place parallel to that filled by the God of those admittedly qualifying for the exemption ..." (*U.S. v. Seeger,* 1965).

2. *No one excluded from protection.* The important point for citizens to keep in mind is that religious liberty, or freedom of conscience, was intended by the Framers to protect the beliefs of everyone, not just those of recognized faith communities.

II. The American experiment in religious liberty.

Religious liberty in America is a key part of the boldest and most successful experiment in freedom the world has known. The strength and diversity of religion in the United States is due almost entirely to the full protection of religious liberty, or freedom of conscience, guaranteed by the Constitution.

A. Religious liberty as the "first liberty." Religious liberty has been called America's "first liberty" because freedom of the mind is logically and philosophically prior to all other freedoms protected by the Constitution.

B. Definition of religious liberty.

In the American experiment, religious liberty is defined according to the following elements:

1. *Freedom of conscience.* There shall be full freedom of conscience for people of all faiths or none.

2. *Religious liberty, an inalienable right.* Religious liberty is considered to be a natural or inalienable right that must always be beyond the power of the state to confer or remove.

3. *Right to practice any or no religion.* Religious liberty includes the right to freely practice any religion or no religion without governmental coercion or control.

C. Guarantees of religious liberty in the Constitution. The guiding principles supporting the definition of religious liberty are set forth in Article VI of the Constitution and in the opening words of the First Amendment to the Constitution. These principles have become the ground rules by which people of all religions or none can live together as citizens of one nation.

1. *Article VI of the Constitution.* Article VI concludes with these words: "No religious test shall ever be required as a qualification to any office or public trust under the United States." With this bold stroke, the Framers broke with European tradition and opened public office in the federal government to people of all faiths or none.

2. *Religious Liberty clauses.* The First Amendment's Religious Liberty clauses state that "Congress shall make no law respecting an establishment of religion, or prohibiting the free exercise thereof ..." Taken together, these two clauses safeguard religious liberty by protecting religions and religious convictions from governmental interference or control. They ensure that religious belief or nonbelief remains voluntary, free from governmental coercion.

   a. State and local government included. The clauses apply equally to actions of both state and local governments, because the Supreme Court has ruled that the Fourteenth Amendment's dictum that states are not to deprive any person of liberty makes the First Amendment applicable to the states.

   b. Meaning of "no establishment." "No establishment" means that neither a state nor the federal government can establish a particular religion or religion in general. Further, government is prohibited from advancing or supporting religion. This does not mean that the government can be hostile to religion. The government must maintain what the Supreme Court has called "benevolent neutrality," which permits religious exercise

3 A History of
Religious Liberty in
American Public Life

to exist but denies it government sponsorship. The No Establishment clause serves to prevent both religious control over government and political control over religion.

c. Meaning of "free exercise." "Free exercise" is the freedom of every citizen to reach, hold, practice, and change beliefs according to the dictates of conscience. The Free Exercise clause prohibits governmental interference with religious belief and, within limits, religious practice.

(1) The difference between belief and practice. The Supreme Court has interpreted "free exercise" to mean that any individual may believe anything he or she wants, but there may be times when the state can limit or interfere with practices that flow from these beliefs.

(2) The traditional "compelling interest" test. Traditionally, the Court has required a government to demonstrate a compelling interest of the "highest order" before it can burden or otherwise interfere with religious conduct. Even then, the government has to demonstrate that it has no alternative means of achieving its interest that would be less restrictive of religious conduct.

(3) The debate over the "compelling interest" test. A 1990 Supreme Court decision, *Employment Division v. Smith*, states that government no longer has to demonstrate a compelling government interest unless a law is specifically targeted at a religious practice or infringes upon an additional constitutional right, such as free speech. The Religious Freedom Restoration Act, signed into law by President Clinton in 1993, restored the compelling interest test and ensured its application in all cases where religious exercise is substantially burdened. In June 1997, the Supreme Court struck the Act down, holding that Congress overstepped its bounds by forcing states to provide more protection for religious liberty than the First Amendment, as interpreted by the Supreme Court in *Smith*, requires.

(4) In September of 2000, Congress passed the Religious Land Use and Institutionalized Persons Act of 2000. This act is designed to protect religious assemblies and institutions from land use restrictions burdening their property, and to protect the right of institutionalized persons to practice their faith. Several states have also attempted to legislate additional protection for free exercise of religion by enacting state Religious Freedom Restoration Acts.

III. Religion, public life, and politics.

The First Amendment separated church from state but not religion from public life.

A. **The involvement of religious groups in public life.** Many religious groups consider it an article of faith to speak out on issues of moral concern in the public sphere. The Constitution protects the right of religious individuals and organizations to attempt to shape public policy and to exercise their influence. There are presently hundreds of nonprofit groups concerned with religious issues and public life in the United States.

B. **Tax-exempt status dependent on nonpartisanship.** However, religious organizations that are exempt from taxation under Section 501(c)(3) of the Internal Revenue Code may not engage in partisan politics by endorsing or opposing candidates for public office or by spending a substantial amount of their resources lobbying Congress.

C. Religious liberty and political responsibility. In certain cases, the injection of religious views into political debate, though constitutionally protected, may be irresponsible.

1. *Religious views in political debate are protected.* In the American experiment in self-government, disestablishment of religion, or separation of church and state, prevents religious institutions from establishing their faith as the law of the land and from receiving financial support from the state. At the same time, "free exercise" protects the right of religious views to be part of the political debate.

2. *Religious attacks in political debate may be irresponsible.* It is important to remember, however, that some actions taken by religious organizations or individuals in the political arena (for example, attacks against the fitness of people to hold public office because of their religion) may not be unconstitutional but may be politically irresponsible violations of the spirit of religious liberty.

Historical perspective

The relationship of politics and religion has been a central issue in American life since the colonial era. For most of the European settlers who came to North American shores in the seventeenth century from England, France, and Spain—all nations with established churches—a society without an established faith was unimaginable.

The unity and morality of the community, it was believed, depended upon divine sanction of political authority and conformity of the populace in matters of faith. Eventually, however, by separating religion and government and by granting freedom to all religious groups, America launched a new political experiment unprecedented in the world's history.

I. **The religious liberty sought by the Puritans.**

Like many who arrived on these shores in the seventeenth century, the Puritans of Massachusetts Bay came to America seeking religious freedom.

A. **Religious freedom not sought for others.** The freedom they sought, however, was for themselves and not for others. The Puritans felt called by God to establish "new Israel," a Holy Commonwealth based on a covenant between God and themselves as the people of God.

B. **All laws to be grounded in God's law.** Though there were separate areas of authority for church and state in Puritan Massachusetts, all laws of the community were to be grounded in God's law and all citizens were expected to uphold the divine covenant. Massachusetts was to be an example to the world of God's kingdom on earth, "a City upon a hill."

II. Roger Williams and the origins of freedom of conscience in Puritan America.

Very early in the Massachusetts experiment, dissenters arose to challenge the Puritan vision of a holy society. The first dissenter, Roger Williams (c.1603-1683), was himself a Puritan minister but with a very different vision of God's plan for human society. Williams argued that God had not given divine sanction to the Puritan colony. In his view, the civil authorities of Massachusetts had no authority to involve themselves in matters of faith. The true church, according to Williams, was a voluntary association of God's elect. Any state involvement in the worship or God, therefore, was contrary to the divine will and inevitably led to the defilement of the church.

A. "Soul liberty" means freedom of conscience for all. Williams' arguments for religious liberty had two principal parts.

1. Freedom of conscience as God's will. Central to Roger Williams' arguments for separating church and state was his conviction that it was divine will that every individual's conscience remain free to accept or reject the word of God. Williams defined freedom of conscience, which he called "soul liberty," as the freedom of each person to follow his or her own heart in matters of faith without interference or coercion by the state.

2. *Religious intolerance and war.* Citing Europe's long history of wars and divisions, Williams pointed out that coercion in matters of faith inevitably leads to persecution and bloodshed.

B. **Rhode Island's experiment in religious liberty.** Williams found it necessary to seek religious liberty outside of Massachusetts Bay.

1. *The founding of Rhode Island.* Banished from Massachusetts in 1635, Roger Williams founded Rhode Island, the first colony with no established church and the first society in America to grant liberty of conscience to everyone. Jews, Quakers, and others not welcome elsewhere made their home there.

2. *The wider significance of Rhode Island's religious liberty.* Eventually, Williams' conception of soul liberty had an impact far beyond the Rhode Island experiment. In the eighteenth century, dissenting religious groups, particularly the Baptists, were inspired by Williams' ideas to advocate disestablishment and freedom of conscience. Some historians also argue that Williams' writings influenced the Enlightenment philosopher John Locke (1632-1704), a key source for Thomas Jefferson's views concerning religious liberty.

C. **Freedom of conscience as an American conviction.** The Puritans' demand for religious liberty for themselves became, in the vision of Roger Williams, a requirement of religious liberty for all.

1. *Early religious liberty outside Rhode Island.* This revolutionary idea was echoed to a lesser degree (and for only a brief period) in seventeenth-century Maryland and later, more fully, in the eighteenth-century "holy experiment" of Quaker William Penn's colony of Pennsylvania.

2. *Gradual extension of religious liberty.* Gradually, the extension of liberty to include not only one's own group but also others, even those with whom "we" disagree, became a central American conviction. It is this principle of full freedom for people of all faiths and of none that was embodied 150 years later in the First Amendment to the Constitution.

III. **The movement toward religious liberty in the United States.**
The momentous decision by the framers of the Constitution and the Bill of Rights to prohibit religious establishment on the federal level and to guarantee free exercise of religion was related to a number of religious, political, and economic factors in eighteenth-century America. Underlying all of these factors, of course, was the practical difficulty of establishing any one faith in an emerging nation composed of a multiplicity of faiths (mostly Protestant sects), none of which was strong enough to dominate the others.

A. From toleration to free exercise. The period between 1776 and the passage of the First Amendment in 1791 saw critical changes in fundamental ideas about religious freedom.

1. *The Virginia Declaration of Rights.* In May 1776, just prior to the Declaration of Independence, the leaders of Virginia adopted the Virginia Declaration of Rights, drafted by George Mason. The first draft of the Declaration argued for the "fullest toleration in the exercise of religion according to the dictates of conscience." This language echoed the writings of John Locke and the movement in England toward toleration.

2. *Madison's objection: "toleration" versus "free exercise."* Although toleration was a great step forward, a 25-year-old delegate named James Madison (1751-1836) did not think it went far enough. Madison, also deeply influenced by the ideas of the Enlightenment, successfully argued that "toleration" should be changed to "free exercise" of religion. This seemingly small change in language signaled a revolutionary change in ideas. For Madison, religious liberty was not a concession by the state or the established church, but an inalienable or natural right of every citizen.

3. *"Free exercise and the First Amendment."* In 1791, the free exercise of religion proclaimed in the Virginia Declaration became a part of the First Amendment, guaranteeing all Americans freedom of conscience.

B. From establishment to separation. The decisive battle for disestablishment came in the large and influential colony of Virginia, where the Anglican Church was the established faith. Once again, James Madison played a pivotal role by leading the fight that persuaded the Virginia legislature to adopt in 1786 Thomas Jefferson's "Bill for the Establishment of Religious Freedom."

1. *Madison, Jefferson, and the struggle for disestablishment.* Madison and Jefferson argued that state support for a particular religion or for all religions is wrong, because compelling citizens to support through taxes a faith they do not follow violates their natural right to religious liberty. "Almighty God had created the mind free," declared Jefferson's bill. Thus, "to compel a man to furnish contributions of money for the propagation of opinions which he disbelieves and abhors, is sinful and tyrannical."

2. *The "Great Awakening" and the struggle for disestablishment.* Madison and Jefferson were greatly aided in the struggle for disestablishment by the Baptists, Presbyterians, Quakers, and other "dissenting" faiths of Anglican Virginia. The religious revivals of the eighteenth century, often called The Great Awakening (1728-1790), produced new forms of religious expression and belief that influenced the development of religious liberty throughout the colonies. The revivalists' message of salvation through Christ alone evoked a deeply personal and emotional response in thousands of Americans.

3. *Evangelical fervor and religious self-government.* The evangelical fervor of the Awakening cut across denominational lines and undercut support for the privileges of the established church.

   a. Support of religious choice by evangelicals. Religion was seen by many as a matter of free choice and churches as places of self-government. The alliance of church and state was now seen by many as harmful to the cause of religion.

   b. Leadership in Virginia of John Leland. In Virginia this climate of dissent and the leadership of such religious leaders as John Leland, a Baptist, provided the crucial support Madison needed to win the battle for religious liberty in Virginia.

4. *The final demise of religious establishment.* The successful battle for disestablishment in Virginia is a vital chapter in the story of religious liberty in America. By the time of the ratification of the First Amendment in 1791, all of the other Anglican establishments (except in Maryland) were ended. The Congregational establishments of New England lasted longer. Not until 1818 in Connecticut and 1833 in Massachusetts were the state constitutions amended to complete disestablishment.

IV. **The constitutional prohibition of religious tests for office in Article VI.**
The only mention of religion in the Constitution of the United States prior to the
adoption of the First Amendment was the "no religious test" provision of Article VI.
The significance of this often-forgotten provision cannot be exaggerated. At the time
of the Constitutional Convention in 1787, most of the colonies still had religious
establishments or religious tests for office. It was unimaginable to many Americans
that non-Protestants — Catholics, Jews, atheists, and others — could be trusted with
public office.

A. **"No religious test" proposed at the Constitutional Convention.** One aspect of
religious liberty was inserted into the Constitution during its framing in Philadelphia.

1. *The role of Charles Pinckney.* At the Constitutional Convention, Charles
Pinckney (1757-1824), a delegate from South Carolina, proposed that "no
religious test shall ever be required as a qualification to any office or public trust
under the United States." Though he came from a state that had established the
Protestant faith as the state religion, Pinckney represented the new spirit of
religious liberty exemplified in the Enlightenment thinking of Jefferson.

2. *A tool for oppression outlawed.* Remarkably, the "no religious test" provision passed
with little dissent. For the first time in history, a nation had formally abolished
one of the most powerful tools of the state for oppressing religious minorities.

B. **Religious tests imposed in some states.** Most states followed the federal example
and abolished tests for state office. But it was not until 1868 in North Carolina,
1946 in New Hampshire, and 1961 in Maryland that religious tests were
abolished entirely. Maryland had required since 1867 "a declaration of belief in
God" for all officeholders. When the U.S. Supreme Court struck down this
requirement in 1961, freedom of conscience was fully extended to include non-
believers as well as believers. No religious test can be imposed for any office at any
level of government.

C. **Informal religious tests a factor in elections.** Though the Constitution barred
religious tests as a formal qualification for office, many American voters
continued to apply informal religious tests in the political arena, particularly in
presidential elections.

1. *Exclusion of Catholics.* Until the nomination of Al Smith in 1928, all
presidential and vice presidential candidates nominated by the two parties
were Protestants. In 1960, the election of John Kennedy, a Roman Catholic,
broke the informal political barrier that had long excluded non-Protestants
from the presidency.

2. *Religious dissension among Protestants.* Even with Protestant candidates, religion has frequently been an issue. Beginning with attacks on the Deist religious convictions of Thomas Jefferson (Deism is a faith based on reason rather than revelation) and continuing to the recent discussions about which candidate is "born again," questions about the "correctness" of a politician's religion have played an important role in many national elections.

V. **The First Amendment principles of religious liberty.**
In the mind of James Madison and some of the others at the Constitutional Convention, the Constitution established a limited federal government with no authority to act in religious matters. That others were unsure had momentous consequences.

   A. **Reassurance for those fearful of religious intolerance.** Many Americans, including leaders of the Baptists and other religious groups, feared that the Constitution offered an insufficient guarantee of the civil and religious rights of citizens.

      1. *Madison's promise of a bill of rights.* Many of those who suspected the proposed new constitution demanded a bill of rights as their price of moderating their heated opposition to its adoption. To win ratification, Madison promised to propose a bill of rights in the First Congress.

      2. *The enshrinement of religious liberty in the Bill of Rights.* Madison kept his promise, and the Religious Liberty clauses adopted by the first Congress in 1789 became, when ratified by the required number of states in 1791, the opening words of the Bill of Rights.

   B. **Religious liberty and the first principles of American liberty.** Full religious liberty was first applied to acts of the federal government alone. Later it was applied to the states as well.

      1. *The First Amendment and the federal government.* With the passage of the First Amendment, the principles of nonestablishment and free exercise became the first principles of American freedom. The federal government was constitutionally prohibited from establishing or sponsoring religion and prohibited from interfering with the natural right of every citizen to reach, hold, exercise, or change beliefs freely.

      2. *The First Amendment and state governments.* These prohibitions were extended to the states in the twentieth century, following Supreme Court rulings that the Fourteenth Amendment made the First Amendment applicable to the states.

VI. Religious influences in American political life.

Disestablishment was never meant to keep religious beliefs or institutions from influencing public life. From the beginning of American history, religions and religious believers have played a central role in shaping public policy and political debate.

A. *De facto* Protestant establishment. For many Protestants in the nineteenth century, disestablishment meant an end to the coercive power of the state in matters of faith and barred any faith from becoming the legally established religion. But disestablishment did not extinguish the Protestant vision of creating and maintaining a "Christian America." By numbers and influence, Protestantism became the *de facto* established religion of the nation. Many no doubt agreed with Daniel Webster when he argued in 1844 that "general tolerant Christianity is the law of the land."

B. Protestant contributions to social reform. The close ties between Protestant churches and American culture led to many social and political reforms. This can most clearly be seen in the "Second Great Awakening" of the early nineteenth century when some Protestant leaders mounted a crusade to reform and revitalize America. Urban social work, schooling for poor children, the abolitionist movement, supported by Quakers, Methodists, and others, were only a few of the many reform movements inspired in large measure by the religious awakenings.

C. **Nativist reaction to expanding pluralism.** A dark side to the Protestant vision of America became evident in the nineteenth century.

1. *The effects of immigration.* The waves of immigrants coming to these shores in the nineteenth century challenged the Protestant domination of the culture. By 1850 Catholicism was the largest single American denomination, and by the end of the century large numbers of Jews had arrived to become citizens.

2. *The rise of anti-Catholicism and anti-Semitism.* There were only a few Catholics and Jews in America from the earliest days of colonization. This dramatic influx of non-Protestants created fear and anxiety among some Protestants.

    a. Intolerance and the "Know Nothings" at mid-century. An anti-Catholic and anti-foreign nativist movement emerged in the first half of the nineteenth century, culminating in the 1840s and 1850s in the Know-Nothing Party. Catholics were the victims of violence and discrimination in many parts of the nation.

    b. Intolerance at the turn of the century. A resurgence of similar sentiments in the late nineteenth and early twentieth centuries contributed to widespread anti-Semitism, opposition to immigration, and the rise of the Ku Klux Klan.

D. **The positive role of religion in helping shape public policy.** The ugly expressions of religious bigotry in the nativist movement represent some of the worst examples of religious involvement in politics and public policy. But religion has also been at the heart of some of the best movements in American social and political life.

1. *The contribution of African-American churches.* The black churches have played a central role in the political and social history of African-Americans from the colonial period to the present. Indeed, black churches have shaped the lives of all Americans by providing much of the moral and political leadership of the civil rights movement.

2. *The contribution of Judaism and other minority religions.* In the late nineteenth and early twentieth centuries, churches, synagogues, and temples provided vital support for Catholic, Eastern Orthodox, Jewish, and Asian Buddhist immigrants as they adjusted to life in the United States. Religious communities were also at the forefront of many reform movements during the Progressive Era early in this century. Various religious groups, notably Unitarians, Quakers, and Reform Jews, have been particularly visible in the peace movements and in the advocacy of social justice.

3. *Constitutional separation and the role of religion in public life.* In these and in many other ways, religious institutions and believers have significantly influenced public policy in the United States throughout our nation's history.

   a. Benefits of religious moral leadership. Again, disestablishment was not meant to separate religion from public life. Politics and government in America have clearly benefited from the moral leadership and values of many religious traditions and convictions.

   b. Costs of religious zealotry. At the same time, the nation has suffered from violations of the spirit of religious liberty by religious groups who have at various times in our history used the public square to attack the religion of others or to deny others the full rights of citizenship.

Contemporary perspective

More people have died because of their religious convictions in the twentieth century than in any previous century. And there appears to be no end to the tragedy. Of the many wars waged throughout the world in the 1990s, more than two-thirds have religious or ethnic differences as a root cause. From Northern Ireland to Bosnia to Sri Lanka, religious differences contribute daily to death and destruction around the globe.

Even the explosion of freedom in Eastern Europe and the former Soviet Union, by any measure a tremendous advance for democratic principles, has been accompanied by a serious outbreak of religious and ethnic bigotry and division. One of the most frightening developments has been the dramatic rise of anti-Semitism throughout the region. Tensions between Muslims and Christians have resulted in violence in Bosnia, Azerbaijan and Armenia and other places.

How has the United States, the most religiously diverse nation in the world, managed to avoid the "holy wars" so prevalent today and throughout history? This remarkable achievement may be traced directly to the Religious Liberty clauses of the First Amendment. In spite of occasional setbacks and outbreaks of religious bigotry, the American experiment in religious liberty has held.

I. **Religions remain active in American political life.**
Religious liberty has allowed religions in the United States to grow and prosper as in few other places in the world. Not only are a large number of Americans deeply religious, but their religious communities continue to be actively involved in political life. This is evident, for example, in the civil rights and peace movements. Also, since the late 1970s, fundamentalist Christian communities together with other evangelical Christians have become a significant force in American politics, speaking out on a variety of social and moral issues.

II. Confusion about the role of religion in public life threatens religious liberty.

There are disturbing signs that the American experiment in liberty may be in danger from two extremes.

A. Two extremes on the issue of religion and public life. On one end of the political spectrum there are those who seek to establish in law a "Christian America." On the other end are some who seek to exclude religion from public life entirely. Both proposals violate the spirit of religious liberty.

B. Teaching religion versus teaching about religion. The controversy surrounding the role of religion in public life has left many citizens confused about the principles of religious liberty. This confusion is made worse by the absence of teaching about religion and religious liberty in many public schools. Teaching about religion in the schools is often confused with the teaching of religion, or religious advocacy and indoctrination.

  1. Change in some public schools. In the last few years a number of states, most notably California, have mandated more teaching about religion in the schools.

  2. Efforts by U.S. Department of Education. In December of 2000, the U.S. Department of Education sent a packet of religious-liberty guidelines to every public school principal in the nation. These guidelines focussed on religious-liberty rights of students, the relationship between public schools and religious communities, and the role of religion in the curriculum.[1]

  3. Change in textbook treatment of the role of religion. As a result, textbooks have begun to include more about the story of religious liberty and the role of religion in American history and society.

III. The new challenges of exploding pluralism.

The confusion and ignorance surrounding the Religious Liberty clauses of the Constitution leave Americans in a weak position to meet the challenges of exploding religious pluralism in the United States. The violent religious divisions throughout the world serve as a dramatic reminder of how vital it is for Americans to understand and affirm the principles of religious liberty in a nation of some 3,000 religious groups.

A. Pluralism as meaning all faiths or none. Religious pluralism in the United States has expanded beyond the Protestant, Catholic, and Jewish pluralism of the 1950s.

  1. Expanding pluralism. Pluralism now includes a growing number of people from all the world's religions, especially Islam and Buddhism. Pluralism must also

---

[1] These publications included *A Teacher's Guide to Religion in Public Schools, Religious Expression in Public Schools: A Statement of Principles,* and *A Parent's Guide to Religion in the Public Schools* found in chapters 6, 10, and 12 of this guide.

take into account the nearly 12 percent of Americans who express no religious preference at all. This expansion will only continue.

2. *The burdens of exploding pluralism.* The challenges of this diversity can be seen throughout American society. This pluralism is particularly evident in public schools. For example, dozens of different native languages are often found among the students of large urban schools. Similarly, many different religions are represented.

B. **The First Amendment as providing ground rules for living together.** As the United States begins its third century of constitutional government, the nation raises certain important questions.

1. *Living together without religious consensus.* Two urgent questions are how Americans of so many faiths will continue to live together as citizens of one nation and, since there is not (and cannot be) a religious consensus, what the civic values are that Americans of all faiths or none hold in common.

2. *Adherence to the principles of religious liberty.* To answer these questions, American citizens must return to the democratic first principles articulated in the Religious Liberty clauses of the First Amendment. Religious liberty, or freedom of conscience, is at the heart of what it means to be an American citizen. Only in these principles can Americans find the ground rules that allow all citizens to live together with deep religious differences.

C. **The Williamsburg Charter.**
One effort to return to first principles is the Williamsburg Charter. Drafted by members of America's leading faiths and revised over the course of two years in close consultation with political, academic, educational, and religious leaders, the Charter was signed in 1988 by former Presidents Gerald Ford and Jimmy Carter, the two living chief justices of the United States, and by nearly 200 leaders of

national life. With their signatures, these individuals strongly reaffirmed the principles of religious liberty as essential for developing a common vision for the common good. The Williamsburg Charter states in part:

> We affirm that a right for one is a right for another and a responsibility for all. A right for a Protestant is a right for an Eastern Orthodox is a right for a Catholic is a right for a Jew is a right for a Humanist is a right for a Mormon is a right for a Muslim is a right for a Buddhist—and for the followers of any other faith within the wide bounds of the republic.

> That rights are universal and responsibilities mutual is both the premise and the promise of democratic pluralism. The First Amendment in this sense, is the epitome of public justice and serves as the golden rule for civic life. Rights are best guarded and responsibilities best exercised when each person and group guards for all others those rights they wish guarded for themselves.

Written by Charles C. Haynes for Civitas: A Framework for Civic Education. *Copyright 1991, Council for the Advancement of Citizenship and the Center for Civic Education. Updated for this publication and reprinted by permission.*

CHAPTER 4

The Supreme Court, Religious Liberty, and Public Education

If there is any fixed star in our constitutional
constellation, it is that no official, high or petty, can
prescribe what shall be orthodox in politics,
nationalism, religion, or other matters of opinion or
force citizens to confess by word or act their faith
therein. If there are any circumstances which permit
an exception, they do not now occur to us.

—*West Virginia Board of Education v. Barnette*
Justice Robert H. Jackson
1943

The Supreme Court and the lower courts are the final arbiters of the Constitution. They tell us what the Constitution and, more specifically, the First Amendment mean. Their interpretation of the First Amendment's Religious Liberty clauses is critical to our understanding of the role of religion in public education.

For the first 150 years of our nation's history, there were very few occasions for the courts to interpret the religion clauses. This was due primarily to the fact that the First Amendment had not yet been applied to the states. As written, the First Amendment applied only to Congress and the federal government. In the wake of the Civil War, however, the 14th Amendment was passed. It reads in part that "no state shall ... deprive any person of life, liberty or property without due process of law ...." In the 1940 case of *Cantwell v. Connecticut*, the Supreme Court held that the free exercise of religion is one of the "liberties" protected by the due-process clause. Seven years later, the Court added the Establishment clause to the list. Together, these twin protections — free exercise and non-establishment — guarantee American religious liberty.

THE ESTABLISHMENT CLAUSE

The first of the two religion clauses reads: "Congress shall make no law respecting an establishment of religion ...." Note that the clause is absolute. It allows *no* law. It is also noteworthy that the clause forbids more than the establishment of religion by the government. It forbids even laws *respecting* an establishment of religion.

The Establishment clause sets up a line of demarcation between the functions and operations of the institutions of religion and government in our society. It does so because the framers of the First Amendment recognized that when the roles of the government and religion are intertwined, the result too often has been bloodshed or oppression.

There is much debate about the meaning of the term "establishment of religion." Although judges rely on history, the writing of the framers and prior judicial precedent, they

4
The Supreme Court,
Religious Liberty, and
Public Education

sometimes disagree. Some, including Chief Justice William Rehnquist, argue that the term was intended to prohibit only the establishment of a single national church or the preference of one religious sect over another. Others, including a majority of the justices of the current Supreme Court, believe the term prohibits the government from promoting religion in general as well as the preference of one religion over another. In the words of the Court's decision in *Everson v. Board of Education* (1947):

> The establishment of religion clause means at least this: Neither a state nor the federal government may set up a church. Neither can pass laws that aid one religion, aid all religions, or prefer one religion over another. Neither can force a person to go to or to remain away from church against his will or force him to profess a belief or disbelief in any religion ... Neither a state or the federal government may, openly or secretly, participate in the affairs of any religious organizations or groups and vice versa. In the words of Jefferson, the clause against establishment of religion by law was intended to erect "a wall of separation between church and state.[1]

To help interpret the Establishment clause, the Court developed a three-part test sometimes referred to as the "*Lemon* test." The test derives its name from the 1971 decision *Lemon v. Kurtzman*, in which the Court struck down a state program providing aid to religious elementary and secondary schools. Although the test has come under fire from several Supreme Court justices, many lower courts continue to use *Lemon* as a yardstick for deciding Establishment clause cases.

Let's look briefly at each prong of the test:

Does the law, or other government action, have a bona fide secular or civic purpose? As a general rule, the purpose of activities in the public schools should be educational. If, for example, a teacher is planning an activity associated with a religious holiday such as Christmas, she should ask herself, "What educational purpose am I trying to accomplish?" If the only purpose for the activity is to celebrate the religious holiday, it probably violates the first prong of the *Lemon* test.

[1] *Everson v. Board of Education*, 330 U.S. 1 (1947).

Accommodating a student's free exercise of religion is generally considered a legitimate civic purpose and, therefore, permissible under *Lemon* — assuming, of course, that the school is not promoting the student's faith. For example, a teacher could allow an art student to paint a picture with a religious theme. In fact, to prohibit such art would probably violate the free-speech and free-exercise rights of the student. On the other hand, a teacher should not make assignments requiring such religious art.

Returning to the issue of accommodation, the framers of the Constitution did not intend that the two religion clauses cancel each other out. Any interpretation of the Establishment clause must take into account the Free Exercise clause and vice versa. In the words of Justice O'Connor:

> Government pursues free exercise values when it lifts a government-imposed burden on the free exercise of religion ... When the manifest objective of a statute is to facilitate the free exercise of religion by lifting a government-imposed burden ... the religious purpose of such a statute is legitimated by the free exercise clause.[2]

Two years later in *Bishop v. Amos*, a unanimous Supreme Court echoed Justice O'Connor's sentiments: "Under *Lemon*, it is a permissible legislative purpose to alleviate significant governmental interference with the ability of religious organizations to define and carry out their missions."

This does not mean the government can lift all burdens on religion. To the contrary, the justices struck down a Texas law that provided a sales-tax exemption for

LEGAL INFO

The *Lemon* Test

The *Lemon* test asks three questions about the particular government action that is being challenged. (Remember, the Constitution limits the power of government, not of private citizens.) Each question must be answered in the affirmative if the government action is to be allowed under the Establishment clause. A negative answer to any of the questions means the act is unconstitutional. The questions are:

1. Does the law, or other government action, have a bona fide secular or civic purpose?

2. Does the primary effect neither advance nor inhibit religion? In other words, is it neutral?

3. Does the law avoid excessive governmental entanglement with religion?

If the answer to all three is "yes," the law passes the *Lemon* test.

[2] *Wallace v. Jaffree*, 472 U.S. 38, 83 (1985) (O'Connor, J., concurring).

religious periodicals only.[3] The Court did not believe that having citizens pay a modest sales tax when purchasing a magazine constituted any significant burden on religious exercise. On the other hand, the justices have been willing to give religion some breathing room under the Establishment clause, if the government burden is significant. For example, there is little doubt the courts would uphold the exemptions many states give students who object for religious reasons to attending sex-education classes.

Does the primary effect neither advance nor inhibit religion? In other words, is it neutral? Looking at the second prong of the *Lemon* test, a law is not unconstitutional simply because it allows individuals or churches and synagogues to advance religion, which is their very purpose. For a law to have effects that are forbidden under *Lemon*, the government itself must have advanced religion through its own actions. Allowing students to be released from school to receive religious instruction at a nearby church, for example, does not violate the Establishment clause.[4] It would violate the Establishment clause for the school to begin promoting, as opposed to merely announcing, such a meeting.

Not every government action that advances or inhibits religion is unconstitutional. Only government acts whose *primary* effect advances or inhibits religion are forbidden. Allowing a religious group to use a public school building after school hours would have an incidental or indirect effect of advancing religion. However, such a use would not violate the *Lemon* test. In fact, the Supreme Court in 1993 ruled unanimously that a public school is required to permit churches to use its facilities on the same basis as other community groups.[5]

Does the law avoid excessive governmental entanglement with religion?
The final prong of the *Lemon* test prohibits "excessive governmental entanglement with religion." Rarely at issue in cases involving public education, the entanglement prong is most often associated with cases involving aid to religious schools.

[3] *Bullock v. Texas Monthly*, 489 U.S. 1 (1989).
[4] *Zorach v. Clausen*, 343 U.S. 306 (1952).
[5] *Lamb's Chapel v. Center Moriches School District*, 508 U.S. 385 (1993).

Entanglement problems could arise if a public school was involving itself in religious matters, such as evaluating the content of student prayers or monitoring students' religious activities. Most often the legality of a public school's policies will be determined by their purpose and primary effect.

Alternatives to the *Lemon* Test

As noted, the *Lemon* test has come under sharp criticism from some scholars and from a majority of the justices of the Supreme Court. Several justices have proposed alternative tests. The most popular thus far was proposed by Justice Sandra Day O'Connor. This test asks whether a particular governmental action amounts to an *endorsement* of religion. According to Justice O'Connor, a government action is invalid if it creates a perception in the mind of a reasonable observer that the government is either endorsing or disapproving of religion. In short, she believes the Establishment clause is designed to separate one's standing in the civil society from one's standing in a church. Her fundamental concern is whether the particular government action conveys "a message to non-adherents that they are outsiders, not full members of the political community, and an accompanying message to adherents that they are insiders, favored members of the political community."[6]

Justice O'Connor's "endorsement test" has, on occasion, been subsumed into the *Lemon* test. The justices have simply incorporated it into the first two prongs of *Lemon* by asking if the challenged government act has the purpose or effect of advancing or endorsing religion. Still, Justice O'Connor has reiterated her dissatisfaction with *Lemon*, suggesting that the slide away from the test "is well under way."[7]

Other Supreme Court justices have proposed tests that allow more government support for religion than either the *Lemon* or endorsement tests. These justices support the adoption of a test developed by Justice Anthony Kennedy and known as the "coercion test." Under this test the government does not violate the Establishment clause unless it (1) provides direct aid to religion in a way that would tend to establish a state church, or (2) coerces people to support or participate in religion against their will.[8] Under such a test, the government would be permitted to erect such religious symbols as a Nativity scene standing alone in a public school or other public building at Christmas.[9] But even the coercion test is subject to varying interpretations, as illustrated by the Rhode Island graduation prayer decision in which Justice Kennedy and Scalia, applying the same test, reached different results.[10]

In one of the Court's more recent Establishment clause cases, the justices again reverted to *Lemon*, albeit in a somewhat modified form. The Court identified three primary criteria

[6] *Lynch v. Donnelly*, 465 U.S. 668, 688 (1984).
[7] *Board of Education of Kiryas Joel Village School Dist. v. Grumet*, 512 U.S. 687 (1994).
[8] *County of Allegheny v. A.C.L.U.*, 492 U.S. 573 (1989) (Kennedy, J., dissenting).
[9] *County of Allegheny v. ACLU*, 492 U.S. 573 (1989).
[10] See *Lee v. Weisman*, 505 U.S. 577 (1992).

for determining whether government action has a primary effect of advancing religion: 1) no government indoctrination, 2) no defining the recipients of government benefits based on religion, and 3) no excessive entanglement between government and religion.[11]

Although the Supreme Court is divided about which test to use in interpreting the Establishment clause, "neutrality" is a principle applied consistently in cases involving public schools. A majority of the Court agrees that school officials must be neutral among religions and between religion and non-religion. This means that under the First Amendment school officials may neither inculcate nor inhibit religion; they must protect the religious-liberty rights of students of all faiths or none.*

THE FREE EXERCISE CLAUSE

The second of the Religious Liberty clauses of the First Amendment states that the government shall make no law prohibiting the free exercise of religion. Although the text is absolute, the courts have had to place some limits on the exercise of religion. To take an easy example, courts would not hold that the First Amendment protects human sacrifice even if some religion required it. While the freedom to believe is absolute, the freedom to act on those beliefs is not.

As with the Establishment clause, the Supreme Court developed a test to help judges interpret the Free Exercise clause. First used in the 1963 case of *Sherbert v. Verner*, this test is sometimes referred to as the *Sherbert* test. While the test's application was curtailed in the 1990 decision of *Employment Division v. Smith*, many state courts and legislatures continue to look to *Sherbert* when addressing free-exercise issues. The test has four parts: two that apply to any person who claims his free-exercise rights have been violated and two that apply to the government agency accused of violating those rights.

In order to claim the protections of the Free Exercise clause, a person (in this case a student) must show that his actions (1) are motivated by a sincere religious belief, and (2) have been substantially burdened by the government.

Sincere Religious Belief

Notice that the religious beliefs need not be logical, rational or even sensible. Certainly, they need not be popular. They need only be sincere. Thus, the fact that a student's objection to something in the curriculum may seem unreasonable to the teacher is irrelevant. If the objection is sincere, it *may* be protected under the Free Exercise clause. Also, the fact that a person does not believe in God or a divine being does not mean his beliefs fall outside the protection of the Free Exercise clause. Many religions, such as Buddhism or Taoism, may be non-theistic. Courts tend to take a *functional* as opposed to *creedal* approach to religion.

[11] *Agostini v. Felton*, 521 U.S. 203 (1997).

* Although there is some consistency in how the Supreme Court applies "neutrality" in the public schools, the Court's 2002 decision in the Cleveland voucher case (*Zelman v. Simmons Harris*, 122 S.Ct. 2460), illustrates that the Justices remain divided over how to apply the Establishment clause to questions of school funding. Five Justices viewed the Cleveland voucher program as a neutral program involving parental choice while four justices saw the program as providing government aid to religion.

If the belief system functions like a religion in the life of the individual, it is likely to be protected for First Amendment purposes.

Substantial Burden

Sincere beliefs alone, however, do not make a free-exercise claim. In order to claim the protections of the Free Exercise clause, a student must also show that his religion has been substantially burdened by the government. Remote or incidental burdens will not suffice. Usually, coercion — direct or indirect — is required. If, for example, a school prohibited a

student from handing out religious tracts to her classmates, this would probably be a "substantial" burden on her religious exercise. Requiring her to conduct her proselytizing at a reasonable time and place during the school day would not. Although some experts criticize its decision, at least one federal appeals court has ruled that merely exposing students to ideas that may offend their religion does not amount to a substantial burden on their religious exercise.[12]

As noted, a burden on religious exercise need not be direct in order to be protected by the Constitution. Indirect burdens that penalize one for exercising his faith may also be illegal. For example, in the *Sherbert* case, the plaintiff was denied unemployment-compensation benefits because she refused to accept work on her Sabbath. The Supreme Court reversed, holding that Mrs. Sherbert could not be put to the "cruel choice" of having to give up either her government benefits or her religious convictions.[13]

Compelling State Interest

Even if a person has shown that her actions are motivated by a sincere religious belief and have been substantially burdened by the government, the inquiry is not over. Under the *Sherbert* test, the government will still prevail if it can show that (1) it is acting in furtherance of a "compelling state interest," and (2) it has pursued that interest in the manner least restrictive, or least burdensome, to religion.

A "compelling state interest" has been described as "an interest of the highest order"[14] and must involve such paramount concerns as public health and safety. Although public

---

[12] *Mozert v. Hawkins County Board of Education,* 827 F.2d. 1058 (6th Cir. 1987).
[13] *Sherbert v. Verner,* 374 U.S. 398 (1963).
[14] *Wisconsin v. Yoder,* 406 U.S. 205 (1971).

schools clearly have a compelling interest in the education and welfare of children, a school must demonstrate that it has a compelling interest in applying a particular policy to a particular child. For example, the courts have recognized a compelling interest in compulsory-attendance laws, but in *Wisconsin v. Yoder*, the Supreme Court held that the state did not have a compelling reason to force Amish families to send their children to school beyond the eighth grade. The Court has also ruled that students may not be forced to salute the flag or recite the Pledge of Allegiance.[15] Similarly, a school may have a compelling interest in teaching children how to prevent the spread of AIDS through sex-education classes, but the school may not have a compelling reason to teach this to a child whose parents object on religious grounds. As a result, many states provide exemptions from their sex-education programs.

Least Restrictive Means

Even if the school has a compelling interest, it may have to pursue that interest in the manner least restrictive of a complaining student's religion. In other words, the school should choose a course of action that does not violate the student's religion if such a course of action is available and feasible for the school.

If, for example, a student objects to a particular reading assignment on religious grounds, the school may be required to assign an alternate selection. If requests for exemption become too frequent or too burdensome for the school, a court might find the school's refusal to offer additional alternatives to be justified. For students in such a situation, the only reasonable alternative may be home schooling or a private religious school.

While courts may occasionally be willing to order alternative assignments for individual students, as a general rule they will not alter the curriculum for the entire class unless the assigned material amounts to an establishment of religion.[16] The courts have also held that the mere fact that assigned material coincides with the doctrines of a particular religion — be it Catholicism or secular humanism — does not mean that the school has violated the Establishment clause. In fact, it is unconstitutional to allow a person's religion to determine the curriculum for all others.[17]

As noted, the application of the *Sherbert* test was sharply curtailed by the 1990 Supreme Court decision, *Employment Division v. Smith*. In *Smith*, a slim majority of the justices ruled that burdens on religious exercise no longer had to be justified if they were the unintended result of laws of general application. After *Smith*, only laws that (1) were intended to prohibit the free exercise of religion, or (2) violated other constitutional rights such as

---

[15] *Barnette v. West Virginia State Board of Education,* 319 U.S. 624 (1943).
[16] *Mozert v Hawkins County Board of Education,* 827 F.2d. 1058 (6th Cir. 1986); *Smith v. Board of Commissioners,* 827 F.2d. 684 (11th Cir.1987).
[17] *Epperson v. Arkansas,* 393 U.S. 97 (1968); See also *Edwards v. Aguillard* 482 U.S. 578 (1987).

freedom of speech were subject to the compelling-interest test. Thus, a state could not pass a law stating that Native Americans are prohibited from using peyote, but it could accomplish the same result by prohibiting the use of peyote by everyone. In each case, the central religious ritual for some American Indians would be illegal.

In the three years following *Smith*, more than 50 reported cases were decided against religious groups and individuals. As a result, more than 60 religious and civil-liberties groups, including the American Civil Liberties Union, Concerned Women for America, People for the American Way and the National Association of Evangelicals, joined to draft

and support the passage of the Religious Freedom Restoration Act. The Act, which was signed by President Clinton on November 17, 1993, restored the compelling-interest test and ensured its application in all cases where religious exercise is substantially burdened.[18]

Although the Religious Freedom Restoration Act was applied to public schools, its tenure was short-lived.[19] On June 25, 1997, the Supreme Court, by a vote of 6-3, struck the Act down as applied to state and local government. The case *City of Boerne v. Flores* holds that Congress overstepped its bounds by forcing states to provide more protection for religious liberty than the First Amendment, as interpreted by the Supreme Court in *Employment Division v. Smith,* requires.

[18] Public Law 103-141 codified at 42 USC sections 2000bb through 2000bb-4 (1993).
[19] *Cheema v. Thompson*, 67 F. 3d 883 (9th Cir. 1995).

Some states – such as Texas, Rhode Island and Connecticut – have passed their own Religious Freedom Restoration Acts which do apply to the public schools. In other states – such as Minnesota, Massachusetts, and Wisconsin – the courts have held that the compelling-interest test is applicable to religion claims by virtue of the state's own constitution. In many states, however, we are uncertain about the level of protection that applies to free exercise claims.

Some argue that in virtually every case involving a public school, the religion claim can be linked with the parents' constitutional right to control the upbringing of their children, thereby triggering the compelling interest test even under *Smith*. Others maintain that parents and students no longer can force schools to accommodate their religious concerns. Regardless of how this legal dispute is finally resolved, schools fulfill the *spirit* of the First Amendment when they accommodate the religious claims of students and parents where feasible.

CONCLUSION

The Establishment and Free Exercise clauses protect the liberty of conscience of every citizen by providing the legal basis for religious freedom in the United States. Though frequently criticized, the three-part *Lemon* test remains the principal yardstick for deciding cases under the Establishment clause. This test and its likely replacements require the government to be neutral among religions as well as between religion and non-religion. The standard for free-exercise claims is less certain, but schools are encouraged to accommodate religion when they can. Taken together, the two clauses are intended to ensure fairness and neutrality in the schools with respect to religion. Schools must at times accommodate students' religious rights, but teachers and other school personnel may neither advance nor inhibit religious faith.

The Religious Liberty clauses should not be thought of as at odds with one another — one favoring freedom of religion and the other opposed to an establishment of it. The framers wrote the provision forbidding establishment in order to safeguard the principle of religious liberty. Both clauses secure the rights of believers and nonbelievers alike to be free from government involvement in matters of conscience. Together, they secure religious freedom. In the words of the Williamsburg Charter, the two Religious Liberty clauses are "mutually reinforcing provisions [that] act as a double guarantee of religious liberty." It declared that the two clauses were:

> [E]ssentially one provision for preserving religious liberty. Both parts, No Establishment and Free Exercise, are to be comprehensively understood as being in the service of religious liberty as a positive good. At the heart of the Establishment clause is the prohibition of state sponsorship of religion and at the heart of Free Exercise clause is the prohibition of state interference with religious liberty.

HOW DOES THIS LEGAL FRAMEWORK APPLY TO THE SCHOOLS?

Is it legal to pray in public schools?

It depends. What it depends on is the kind of prayer we are talking about, and more importantly, who is doing the praying. Because people who ask this question are usually referring to organized classroom prayer, often led by a teacher, we will begin our discussion there.

The Supreme Court has made clear that prayers organized or sponsored by a public school violate the First Amendment, whether in the classroom, over the public-address system, at a graduation exercise or even at a high school football game.[20] The same rule applies whether the activity is prayer or devotional Bible reading.

What about moments of silence?

Even moments of silence, if used to promote prayer, will be struck down by the courts.[21] A "neutral" moment of silence that does not encourage prayer over any other quiet, contemplative activity will not be struck down, even though many students choose to use the time for prayer.[22]

Why is the Court so strict in its application of the First Amendment to public schools?

The Court has emphasized that it is none of the business of government to promote or sponsor religious exercises — especially among impressionable young students who are at school as a result of compulsory-attendance laws. This combination of children and a captive audience distinguishes the school prayer cases from other situations such as legislative sessions or college graduations, where courts may be more lax in applying the Establishment Clause.

As the caretaker for all the children in the community, a public school has the responsibility to protect the conscience of every student. This will include children of various religious faiths, as well as those of no religious faith. Only by maintaining a posture of neutrality can the school be fair to all.

---

[20] *Engel v. Vitale,* 370 U.S. 421 (1962); *School District of Abington Township v. Schempp,* 374 U.S. 203 (1963); *Lee v. Weisman,* 505 U.S. 577 (1992); *Doe v. Santa Fe,* 530 U.S. 290 (2000).
[21] *Wallace v. Jaffree,* 472 U.S. 38 (1985).
[22] See *Bown v. Gwinnett County School District* 112 F.3d 1464 (11th Cir., 1997).

Does this mean that students shed their religious liberty rights when they enter the public schools?

No school should be disrespectful of the important role religion plays for many students. To the contrary, the courts have made clear that students retain the right to exercise their religion, subject to some limitations, even in a public school.

What sorts of religious rights do the students have?

Generally, individual students are free to pray, read their Bibles, express religious viewpoints and even invite others to join their particular religious group as long as they are not disruptive of the school or disrespectful of the rights of other students. A student should not be allowed to pressure or coerce others in a public school setting, but within these broad parameters a student has wide latitude to exercise his faith. For example, a student may wish to pray before meals, read her Bible during study hall, create an art project with a religious theme or invite other students to attend church. All of these activities would appear permissible. In fact, the school might be guilty of violating the student's free-speech and free-exercise rights if it tried to prohibit such nondisruptive religious activities. Under most circumstances, however, students may not use the captive audience of the classroom or other school-sponsored events to deliver a proselytizing sermon.[23]

Do the religious rights of students extend to group activities?

Yes. Students have the right to gather with their fellow students for prayer and other religious activities within the limits described above. For example, students are permitted to gather around the flagpole for prayer before school begins, as many evangelical students do annually, as long as the event is not sponsored or endorsed by the school and other students are not pressured to attend. A school is not required, however, to allow adults to come on campus to lead such an event. It is the rights of students, not outside adults, that are protected.

May teachers participate in such activities?

Teachers, like outside adults, generally have no right to pray with students in a public school.[24] As representatives of the state, teachers are under an obligation to protect the rights of all students, including non-believers. A teacher who abuses this position of trust may be terminated. On the other hand, teachers are not subject to the Establishment clause when they are on their own time outside the school setting. Whether teachers can participate in religious activities outside the contract day may depend on a variety of factors, including where the activities occur. If the activities occur on or near campus, such as at the flagpole, they must be sufficiently removed in time from the school day to prevent a reasonable

---

[23] *DeNooyer v. Livonia Public Schools*, 799 F.Supp. 744 (E.D. Mich. 1992); *Guidry v. Broussard*, 897 F.2d 181 (M.D. La. 1989); *Cole v. Oroville Union High School*, 228 F. 3d 1092 (9th Cir., 2000).
[24] *Roberts v. Madigan*, 921 F.2d. 1047 (10th Cir. 1991); *Webster v. New Lenox School District*, 917 F.2d. 1009 (7th Cir. 1990).

observer (such as a parent dropping off her child) from concluding that the teacher or school is endorsing religion. Teachers may not use their position either to promote or to discourage such religious activities.

What about student clubs?

Students in secondary schools may also form religious clubs pursuant to the federal Equal Access Act. If a school permits extracurricular student groups to meet during noninstructional time, this Act requires that religious groups be given equal treatment. Again, the Act does not allow teachers or other adults to lead such meetings.[25] The Act applies only to secondary schools as defined by state law. (See Chapter 9 on Student Religious Clubs).

Do students have the right to form religious clubs below the secondary level?

Probably not. Although the Equal Access Act does not apply, some argue that the free-speech clause protects the right of middle-school students to form religious clubs on an equal footing with secular clubs. Congress declined to apply equal access to the primary grades due to the difficulty younger students may have distinguishing between government speech endorsing religion and student speech endorsing religion. School officials confronted with such requests should consult their school-board attorney.

May community groups, including religious organizations, use public school facilities during non-school hours?

A unanimous Supreme Court has ruled schools may not discriminate on the basis of religious viewpoint when making their facilities available to community groups.[26] Schools are not required to open their facilities to any community group, but once the facilities are opened, all groups should be treated the same. Schools may, of course, impose reasonable, content-neutral restrictions on the use of their facilities. For example, schools may decide when meetings may be held, how long they may last, whether they may continue during weeks or months when school is not in session, what sort of maintenance fee must be paid and what sort of insurance might be required. Some content-based restrictions may also be allowed. For example, schools may probably exclude for-profit, commercial businesses even though community nonprofits are allowed to use school facilities after hours. They may also limit the use of the facilities to such things as "educational purposes," but such distinctions may prove difficult to administer, as many groups may claim to meet the stipulated purpose.

Content-based restrictions can raise difficult constitutional questions. For example, the Supreme Court has held in *Good News v. Milford*, that in the case of the Good News Club a

---

[25] 20 U.S.C. Section 4071 et seq.
[26] *Lamb's Chapel v. Center Moriches Union Free School District*, 508 U.S. 384 (1993); *Good News Club v. Milford*, 533 U.S. 98 (2001).

content-based restriction excluding religious worship and instruction amounted to impermissible viewpoint discrimination. School districts should be especially mindful to consult with local counsel when drafting content-based restrictions.

May religious communities and public schools enter into cooperative agreements to help students with such things as tutoring and after school care?

Yes, but only if appropriate constitutional safeguards are in place. Remember, public schools must remain *neutral*, neither favoring nor disfavoring religious faith. For that reason, religious groups must refrain from proselytizing students when they are taking part in joint ventures with public schools. Participation by a student in such cooperative programs should not affect the student's academic ranking or ability to participate in other school activities. In addition, cooperative programs may not be limited to religious groups, but must be open to all responsible community groups. For more information, see the guidelines *Public Schools & Religious Communities: A First Amendment Guide,* (Pub. No. 99-F02 (b), available from the First Amendment Center at 1-800-830-3733).

What about graduation prayer?

One of the most confusing and controversial areas of the current school-prayer debate involves graduation prayer. While the courts have not clarified all of the issues, some are clear.

For instance, the Supreme Court ruled in the 1992 case of *Lee v. Weisman* that inviting outside adults to pray at graduation ceremonies was unconstitutional. The case involved prayers delivered by clergy at middle-school commencement exercises in Providence, Rhode Island.[27] The school designed the program, provided for the invocation, selected the clergy and even supplied guidelines for the prayer. The Supreme Court held that the practice violated the First Amendment's prohibition against laws "respecting an establishment of religion." The majority based their decision on the fact that (1) it is not the business of schools to sponsor or organize religious activities, and (2) students who might have objected to the prayer were subtly coerced to participate. This coercion was not mitigated by the fact that attendance at

[27] *Lee v. Weisman*, 505 U.S. 577 (1992).

the graduation was "voluntary." In the Court's view, few students would want to miss the culminating event of their academic career.

A murkier issue is student-initiated, student-led prayer at school-sponsored events. On one side of the debate are those who believe that student religious speech at graduation ceremonies or other school-sponsored events violates the Establishment clause. They are bolstered by the 2000 Supreme Court case of *Santa Fe v. Doe*.[28] The *Santa Fe* case involved the traditional practice of student-led prayers over the public-address system before high school football games. Students would vote each year on whether they would have prayers at home football games and then select a student who would deliver the prayers. The school district required these prayers to be "non-sectarian, non-proselytizing."

For a number of reasons, a 6-3 majority of the Supreme Court found the Santa Fe policy to be unconstitutional. The majority opinion first points out that constitutional rights are not subject to a vote. To the contrary, the purpose of the Bill of Rights was to place some rights beyond the reach of political majorities. Thus, the Constitution protects a person's right to freedom of speech, press or religion even if no one else agrees with the ideas he or she professes. Therefore, the students could not vote to suspend the Establishment clause and have organized prayer at a school-sponsored event.

Having a student, as opposed to an adult, lead the prayer also failed to solve the constitutional dilemma. A graduation exercise is still a school-sponsored event, and the students are still being coerced, however subtly, to participate in a religious exercise.

Finally, the requirement that the prayer be "nonsectarian" and "non-proselytizing" not only fails to solve the problems addressed in *Weisman*, it may aggravate them. While some might like the idea of an inclusive, nonsectarian "civil" religion, many do not. To some Americans the idea of nonsectarian prayer is offensive. Many Americans, for example, feel compelled to pray "in Jesus' name." Moreover the Supreme Court made clear in *Weisman* that even nondenominational prayers may not be established by government in the public schools. There is also the thorny problem of determining whether a particular prayer tends to proselytize. Such entanglement of school officials in religious matters could itself be unconstitutional. In fact, one Texas school district was sued for discriminating against those who wished to offer more sectarian prayers at graduation exercises.

On the other side of this debate are those who contend that not allowing students to express themselves religiously at school events violates the students' free exercise of religion and free-speech rights. Case law indicates that this may be true only in instances involving strictly student speech and not where a student is conveying a message controlled or endorsed by the school. As the 11th Circuit case of *Adler v. Duval County* suggests, it may be possible for a school to provide a forum for student speech within a graduation

[28] *Santa Fe v. Doe*, 530 U.S. 290 (2000).

ceremony, during which time prayer or religious speech might occur. For example, a school might allow the valedictorian or class president an opportunity to speak during the ceremony. If such a student chose to express a religious viewpoint, it seems unlikely it would be found unconstitutional unless the school had suggested or otherwise encouraged the religious speech.[29] In effect, the school must create a genuine forum for student speech in the graduation program, thus distancing itself from the students remarks.

Again, there is a risk to such an approach. By creating a forum for student speech, the school may be stuck with most anything the student wishes to say. While the school would not be required to allow speech that was profane, sexually explicit, defamatory or disruptive, the speech could include political or religious views offensive to many, as well as speech critical of school officials.

A far better approach to the graduation-prayer dilemma would seem to be a privately sponsored, voluntarily attended baccalaureate service held after school hours, perhaps at a local church. The school could announce the event and even allow it to be held on campus if other community groups were given similar privileges. In fact, schools are prohibited from discriminating against religious groups in the after-hours use of their facilities.[30] Schools may not, however, sponsor such religious exercises.

If school officials still see the need to accommodate religion at the graduation exercise, a neutral moment of silence might be considered.

Is there a key principle that might help school officials when confronted with questions about religious expression?

Yes. Although the school-prayer debate has caused much confusion for teachers, administrators and board members, most questions are easily resolved if the school will keep in mind the distinction between government (in this case "school") speech endorsing religion — which the Establishment clause prohibits — and private (in this case "student") speech endorsing religion, which the free speech and Free Exercise clauses protect.[31]

May students distribute religious literature in a public school?

Court decisions on the issue generally fall into two categories. A minority of decisions hold that schools can prohibit the distribution of any publication that is not sponsored by the school. Of course, the ban must be applied even-handedly to all student publications. A school could not, for example, allow the distribution of political literature while barring religious publications. This is particularly evident in light of the Supreme Court's decision in *Westside Community School Board v. Mergens*, upholding the federal Equal Access Act.

[29] See *Doe v. Madison School District*, 177 F.3d 789 (9th Cir., 1998); *Adler v. Duval County*, 206 F.3d 1070 (11th Cir., 2000).
[30] *Lamb's Chapel v. Center Moriches Union Free School District*, 508 U.S. 384 (1993); *Good News Club v. Milford*, 533 U.S. 98 (2001).
[31] See *Board of Education v. Mergens*, 496 U.S. 226 (1990).

Under this minority view, however, a blanket prohibition on all student publications would be permissible.

The majority of courts take a different view. These courts hold that while schools may place some restrictions on the distribution of student publications, they may not ban it altogether. The courts base their decisions on the landmark case of *Tinker v. Des Moines School District*, which upheld the right of students to wear black armbands protesting the Vietnam War, even in a public school. Included in this right of free speech is not only the right to speak for oneself but also to distribute the writings (i.e., speech) of others. Thus, courts have generally upheld the rights of students to distribute non-school publications, subject to the school's right to suppress such publications if they create substantial disruption, harm the rights of other students or infringe upon other compelling interests of the school. Again, the *Mergens* decision makes clear that the fear of a First Amendment violation is not sufficient justification to suppress a student publication that happens to be religious. Some states, such as California, have incorporated the majority view into their own state education codes.[32]

Do schools that permit the distribution of student religious literature give up all control over how it is done?

No. Just because schools may not prohibit the distribution of all student materials does not mean that schools have no control over what may be distributed on school premises. On the contrary, courts have repeatedly held that schools may place reasonable "time, place and manner" restrictions on all student materials distributed on campus. Thus, schools may specify when the distribution can occur (e.g., lunch hour or before or after classes begin), where it can occur (e.g., outside the school office) and how it can occur (e.g., from fixed locations as opposed to roving distribution). One recent decision upheld a policy confining the distribution of student literature to a table placed in a location designated by the principal and to the sidewalks adjacent to school property. Of course, any such restriction must be reasonable.

It is also likely that schools may insist on screening all student materials prior to distribution to ensure their appropriateness for a public school. Any such screening policy should provide for a speedy decision, a statement of reasons for rejecting the literature and a prompt appeals process. Because the speech rights of students are not coextensive with those of adults, schools may prohibit the distribution of some types of student literature altogether. Included in this category would be:

1. Materials that would be likely to cause substantial disruption of the operation of the school. Literature that uses fighting words or other inflammatory language about students or groups of students would be an example of this type of material.

[32] See e.g., West's Ann.Cal.Educ.Code § 48907.

2. Material that violates the rights of others. Included in this category would be literature that is libelous, invades the privacy of others or infringes on a copyright.

3. Materials that are obscene, lewd or sexually explicit.

4. Commercial materials that advertise products unsuitable for minors.

5. Materials that students would reasonably believe to be sponsored or endorsed by the school. One recent example of this category of speech was a religious newspaper that was formatted to look like the school newspaper.

While schools have considerable latitude in prohibiting the distribution of materials that conflict with their educational mission, schools generally may not ban materials based solely on content. Similarly, schools should not allow a heckler's veto by prohibiting the distribution only of those materials that are unpopular or controversial. If Christian students are allowed to distribute their newsletters, Buddhists, Muslims and even Wiccans must be given the same privilege.

What about the right of outside groups to distribute material on campus?

Adults and teachers from outside the school, on the other hand, have no right to distribute materials to students in a public school. Moreover, schools generally may not give the Gideons and other religious groups access to distribute their materials on campus. At least one state attorney general has suggested outside religious groups could distribute materials on campus if the distribution were "passive"(i.e. materials were left for students to browse through and take if they wished), a wide variety of other outside community groups were given similar privileges and school personnel did not promote the materials. One federal appeals court has ruled that such passive distribution of religious materials would not be appropriate in an elementary school.[33]

[33] *Peck v. Upshur County,* 155 F.3d 274 (4th Cir., 1998)

What about the power of schools to control speech in the classroom?

Schools have great latitude to control the speech that occurs in a classroom and, in that setting, can probably prohibit the distribution of student publications altogether. Similarly, schools may impose any reasonable constraint on student speech in a school-sponsored publication such as the school newspaper.

How do schools resolve the tension between freedom of speech and the need for discipline and control?

Preserving the speech rights of students and maintaining the integrity of public education are not mutually exclusive. Schools should model First Amendment principles by encouraging and supporting the rights of students to express their ideas in writing. On the other hand, students should not expect to have unfettered access to their classmates and should be prepared to abide by reasonable time, place and manner restrictions.

Schools must continue to maintain order, discipline and the educational mission of the school as they seek to accommodate the rights of students.

Are released-time programs legal?

Many states have laws authorizing students to be released periodically for off-campus religious instruction during the school day. Such off-campus released-time programs have been ruled constitutional by the United States Supreme Court. In an opinion by staunch separationist William O. Douglas, the court stated: "When the state encourages religious instruction or cooperates with religious authorities by adjusting the schedule of public events to accommodate sectarian needs, it follows the best of our traditions."

What about on-campus released time?

Earlier, the justices had been asked to rule on a released-time program that provided for on-campus religious instruction. In this program, students were released from classes once a week to receive religious training in the public school. There were separate classes for Protestants, Catholics and Jews, and all religious instructors were under the supervision of the superintendent of schools. Students who did not wish to receive religious instruction were required to leave their classrooms and go elsewhere in the school for additional nonreligious studies. The Supreme Court held that the use of public schools and compulsory-attendance laws for religious training violated the First Amendment's ban against laws respecting an establishment of religion.[34] In the words of Justice Hugo Black: "Here not only are the State's tax-supported public school buildings used for the dissemination of religious doctrines. The State also affords sectarian groups an invaluable aid in that it helps to provide pupils for their religious classes through use of the state's compulsory public school machinery. This is not separation of Church and State."

[34] *McCollum v. Board of Education,* 333 U.S. 203 (1948).

4

The Supreme Court,
Religious Liberty, and
Public Education

Must schools provide for off-campus released time?

No. While released-time programs were upheld by the Supreme Court, schools are under no obligation to create such programs. The Court's decision simply permits them. States are free to allow released-time programs when they are requested by students and their parents, but most states leave this decision up to individual school districts. If a released-time program is created, schools may not discriminate among religious groups. That is to say, the program must be administered in a fair and even-handed manner so that all religious groups are treated the same.

May schools promote off-campus religious instruction?

It should be noted that schools are not permitted to endorse or promote religious instruction, even when it is held off campus. Solicitation of students to attend religious classes may not be done at the expense of the school,[35] and only those students whose parents have signed permission slips should be allowed to attend. Students who do not wish to attend may not be penalized. Of course, schools may not rent their facilities to religious groups for religious instruction during the school day.[36]

May schools give academic credit for released-time programs?

The question has arisen whether schools may give academic credit for released-time courses. Although the answer remains unclear, it is likely such a program would be unconstitutional, especially if credit is not given for other nonschool courses. There is very little to distinguish many of these religious courses from a religious education class, a nonacademic exercise for which schools could almost certainly not give credit.[37]

[35] *Doe v. Shenandoah County School Board*, 737 F.Supp. 913 (W.D., 1990); *Smith v. Smith*, 523 F.2d. 121 (4th Cir. 1975); *Perry v. School District*, 344 P.2d. 1036 (9th Cir., 1959).
[36] *Arizona O.A.G.* 86-078 (1986); Iowa O.A.G. 292 (1965).
[37] See *Lanner v. Wimmer* 463 F.Supp. 867 (D.Utah 1978), aff'd in relevant part, 662 F.2d 1349 (10th Cir. 1981); *State ex rel Dearle v. Frazier*, 173 P. 35 (9th Cir., 1918).

CHAPTER 5

Strategies for Finding Common Ground

FIRST AMENDMENT TO THE
UNITED STATES CONSTITUTION

No free government or the blessings of liberty
can be preserved by any people but by a firm
adherence to justice, moderation, temperance,
frugality and virtue and by frequent recurrence
to fundamental principles.

—Virginia Declaration of Rights
George Mason
1776

Court decisions provide important legal guidance for school districts, but case law alone will not enable us to live with our deepest differences. Too often (and too quickly) in disputes about religion and public education, lawyers are called and lawsuits filed. Communities are further divided, and support for public education continues to erode.

We need to remind ourselves that First Amendment Religious Liberty clauses do not belong only to lawyers and judges; they belong to all of us. The principles of rights, responsibility and respect that flow from the First Amendment are obligations of citizenship for *every* American. When properly understood and applied, these principles allow communities to go beyond conflict and achieve consensus on the role of religion in the public schools. The strategies outlined below indicate some ways in which the civic framework provided by the First Amendment has worked in school districts to build common ground.

STRATEGIES FOR FINDING COMMON GROUND

1. Agree on the ground rules.

No religious consensus is possible in the United States, and to impose one would be both unconstitutional and unjust. A civic consensus, however, is not only possible, but necessary if we are to continue as one nation of many peoples and faiths. In any public-policy debate, all sides need to recall that, as citizens, each of us has already agreed to the democratic first principles that govern our common life. These principles are the "ground rules" within which we negotiate our differences in the public square of America.

What are the ground rules that flow from the First Amendment? Part of the answer is found in Supreme Court decisions as discussed in Chapter 4. Court cases, however, are not the best starting point for establishing guidelines and ground rules in a school district.

We suggest that communities begin with the *Statement of Principles* from Chapter 2. In so doing, all sides are asked to go behind the court cases and to give fresh consideration to the guiding principles of our nation's charter. At the heart of these principles are the "three Rs" of religious liberty:

Rights: Religious liberty, or freedom of conscience, is a precious, fundamental and inalienable right for all. Every effort should be made in public schools to protect the conscience of all students and parents.

Responsibilities: Central to the notion of the common good, and of greater importance each day because of the increase of pluralism, is the recognition that religious liberty is a universal right joined to a universal duty to respect that right for others. Rights are best guarded and responsibilities best exercised when each person and group guards for all others those rights they wish guarded for themselves. The Williamsburg Charter calls this "the Golden Rule for civic life."

Respect: Conflict and debate are vital to democracy. Yet if controversies about religion and schools are to reflect the highest wisdom of the First Amendment and advance the best interest of the disputants and the nation, then *how* we debate, and not only *what* we debate, is critical.[1]

If these or similar civic ground rules are in place, then all sides come to the table prepared to take responsibility to protect the rights of others and to debate differences with civility and respect. Within this framework, concern for fairness and for protection of conscience shapes the discussion and all agreements that may follow.

2. Include all of the stakeholders.

If agreements and policies are to inspire broad support in the community, all stakeholders must be fully represented in the discussion. On the school level or district-wide, the committee members appointed to make recommendations should represent a broad range of perspectives, making sure that those who are concerned about violations of conscience in the schools are given significant representation.

Religion-and-school policies — no matter how wise or clear — that are developed without strong community participation risk doing more damage than good. Policies shaped by a broad cross-section of the community are widely supported and successful. (See Chapter 15 for examples of policies created by a few school districts.)

[1] These definitions of the principles of rights, responsibilities, and respect that flow from the First Amendment are drawn from the Williamsburg Charter, a document that has greatly influenced our conception of a civil public school. The full text of the Charter may be found in Appendix B. *Articles of Faith, Articles of Peace: The Religious Liberty Clauses and the American Public Philosophy,* edited by James Davison Hunter and Os Guinness (1990), contains essays that provide a context for understanding the significance of the Williamsburg Charter.

Using the Three Rs to Find Common Ground

"Rights, Responsibilities, and Respect"

Using the principles of rights, responsibilities and respect that flow from the First Amendment, a number of initiatives around the nation are discovering new ways to resolve conflict.

Once in place, a civic framework of rights, responsibilities and respect can help schools and communities to find common ground on educational philosophy, school reform and the role of religion and values in public schools.

Statewide Programs

The most extensive 3Rs programs are the California and Utah 3Rs Projects. The California 3Rs project is sponsored jointly by the First Amendment Center and the California County Superintendents Educational Services Association, while the Utah Project is sponsored jointly by the First Amendment Center and Utah Office of Education.

Using First Amendment principles, many California and Utah educators, parents and community leaders have been able to agree on policies and practices that protect the religious liberty rights of students of all faiths or none. These projects work to prepare teachers to teach about religions and cultures in ways that are constitutionally permissible and educationally sound.

Begun in 1991, the California project is underway in all 11 educational regions of the state. Regional leaders for the 3Rs project have been appointed by the California County Superintendents Educational Services Association to assist school districts and communities. For more information about the California 3Rs Project, contact:

Dr. Bruce Grelle
Department of Religious Studies
California State University - Chico
Chico, CA 95929-0740
Phone: (530) 898-4739
Email: bgrelle@csuchico.edu

The Utah project began in 1996 and already there is a broad network of supporters throughout the state. For more information about the Utah 3Rs project, contact:

Martha Ball
Utah 3Rs Project Director
Utah State Office of Education
250 East 500 South
Instructional Materials, 26A
Salt Lake City, UT 84111
Phone: (801) 538-7503   Fax: (801) 538-7588

Other States

A number of other school districts in Texas, Pennsylvania, Oklahoma and other states have adopted a "3Rs" approach to religious liberty issues. For more information about these efforts contact Charles Haynes at the First Amendment Center. Email address: chaynes@freedomforum.org.

When school boards or administrators reach out to critics of the schools, particularly religious conservatives, they must look beyond media stereotypes and identify those representatives most interested in dialogue and consensus. If school leaders are unsure who might best represent a particular point of view, they might contact national organizations such as those listed in the Appendix for suggestions about strong leadership in the local community.

Because we are a democracy, there will be "winners" and "losers" on policy issues and curriculum decisions. But if the different perspectives have been given full and fair hearing and if every effort has been made to protect the conscience of all parents and students, then even those who may "lose" on a particular policy will most likely remain supporters of the public schools.

3. Listen to all sides.

Given the opportunity, the vast majority of parents, teachers, administrators and school board members will commit to a principled dialogue and will work for fair, open public schools. While it is true that a small number of people on all sides of these issues resist efforts to reach common ground, most Americans, when given an opportunity, want to find a way forward that best serves the schools and the community. We have found this to be true in every region of the country and across all religious and political lines.

Establishing a climate where people listen to one another requires that we go beyond labels and rebuild trust. Public-school educators must keep in mind that, as leaders of institutions established by the people through the government, they are required to represent the Constitution and the Bill of Rights. Public schools are first and foremost models of the nation's charter. All else, including educational philosophy and proposals for change, should be decided by the people of each community working with school boards, administrators and teachers.

If we are to rebuild trust and to truly listen to one another, public-education leaders must acknowledge what is valid about criticisms of the way religion has been treated in many public schools and in the curriculum. At the same time, critics of the schools must recognize that the vast majority of public-school administrators and teachers do not intend to be hostile to religion, and want only to be fair in their treatment of parents and students. Putting aside labels and stereotypes and taking seriously the position of the "other side" are the starting points for genuine dialogue.

4. Work for comprehensive policies.

School districts would be well advised to address a broad range of religion-and-schools issues in a "religion-and-schools" policy. By doing so, schools are able to say "yes" to a role for religion, even as they must say "no" to state-sponsored religious practices. No, public schools may not promote religion (or hostility to religion), nor may schools sponsor religious practices. But yes, there is a place for teaching about religions, and there are ways to accommodate the needs and requirements of religious students. Policies can be developed on student speech, distribution of literature, equal access, and other areas that signal strong support for protection of conscience and expression.

Once the commitment is made to establish a comprehensive policy, begin the search for common ground with the areas where agreement is most likely to be achieved. Many communities have found it useful to begin with the role of religion in the curriculum (especially in light of the national agreement reprinted in Chapter 7). It is not difficult to reach consensus about the importance of study about religion as a part of a complete education in the social studies, literature, art, music, and other subjects. (More difficult is the question of *how* it will be done.) Once the first agreement is reached, a foundation is created for consideration of more divisive questions.

An important key throughout the process is to go beyond asking "What is legal?" and to begin asking "What is the right thing to do for my community?" and "What best protects the conscience of every student and parent?"

5. Be pro-active.

Some school leaders avoid addressing religion and school issues, convinced that to raise these questions may cause controversy where there is currently none. While it may be true that a pro-active approach to religious liberty questions is a risky and delicate undertaking, it could be argued that the greater risk is to do nothing. Districts unprepared for controversy fare poorly when a conflict arises (and it will). Where there are no policies (or policies not known or supported by parents), there is a much greater likelihood of lawsuits, shouting matches at school board meetings and polarization in the community.

Students, parents, teachers and administrators all need to know how the school or school district advises where and how religion be discussed in the classroom, how requests by students to form a religious club or to distribute religious literature will be handled, how holidays will be treated and how any number of other questions concerning religion and values will be addressed. A pro-active approach takes seriously the importance of articulating the proper role for religion and religious perspectives in the public schools. The resulting policies and practices create a climate of trust in the community, and demonstrate the public schools' active commitment to the guiding principles of our democracy.

6. Civil Debate.

Remember throughout the process to commit to civil debate. Conflict and debate are a vital part of a democratic system. Yet, if Americans are going to negotiate deep differences, then how we debate — not only what we debate — is critical. Personal attacks, name-calling, and similar tactics destroy the fabric of our society and undermine the educational mission of schools. All parties should agree to treat one another with civility and respect and should strive to be accurate and fair.

7. Follow-Through

Be sure that the entire community is informed of all policies concerning religion, values and religious liberty. If an effort has been made to keep the broader community involved through participation in the committee and through periodic public meetings, there will be people available to help explain the policy to the various constituents of the school.

Once disseminated and explained, policies raise expectations about school performance. That is why it is vitally important for schools to follow up policy statements with staff development for administrators and teachers. A commitment to teach about religion, for example, means nothing unless teachers are given support for such teaching. A policy that permits student-initiated religious clubs may do more harm than good unless accompanied by a clear understanding by administrators of how the Equal Access Act is to be applied (see Chapter 9). Adoption of these or other policies concerning religion and public education should be immediately followed by forums for parents, workshops for teachers and administrators, and distribution of resources for classroom use.

Remember

First Amendment religious-liberty principles do work — when tried. Without asking anyone to compromise their deepest convictions, schools and communities can find areas of agreement on questions that have long divided Americans. "A common vision for the common good" is still possible in public education.

Schoolbook Protests: Advice for Both Sides
Stephen Bates*

Conflicts over the public-school curriculum are commonplace, clamorous and unproductive. The two sides talk (more frequently, shout) past each other. Protesters often suggest that anyone who disagrees must be un-Christian, immoral, racist or sexist. And as journalist Joseph Nocera has observed, school people often treat anyone who questions their judgment as "a potential enemy who must be bludgeoned into submission with a First Amendment tire-iron."

Tips for Parents

1. **Examine and comment on textbooks before they're adopted.** If your state or district doesn't make books available for pre-adoption inspection, lobby for such a policy.

2. **Choose your battles.** Administrators will be more receptive on your first visit than on your tenth.

3. **Read the book before you complain about it.** Don't rely on others' critiques.

4. **Think before banning.** Think long and hard before trying to have a book removed from the curriculum or the library. You're in a stronger position if you seek an alternative assignment for your child.

5. **In seeking an alternative, consider the magnitude of what you're asking.** You're in a stronger position if you try to excuse your child from a brief assignment — a story or two in a reader, a supplemental novel, a film — rather than an entire textbook. Don't ask for more special treatment (and more work on the part of the teacher) than you absolutely need.

6. **Start with the teacher.** If necessary, work your way up the chain of command.

7. **Recognize, and show that you recognize, that teachers and administrators may not view the assignment as you do.** When seeking an alternative, say that there's no need for one of you to convince the other, but you hope your family's views will be respected. When seeking to remove a book, say that you believe it conflicts with community values, even though it may reflect the values of school officials. In both cases, the issue isn't who's right, it's who decides.

8. **Recognize, and show that you recognize, that teachers and administrators want what they believe to be best for the children.**

9. **Resist the temptation to engage in name-calling.** Don't suggest, even indirectly, that school officials are less devout, less moral or less sensitive to minorities or women than you are.

Tips for Teachers and Administrators

1. **To preempt some protests, solicit community input before books are chosen.** Make books publicly available before they are adopted. When dealing with a particularly controversial topic, consider forming an advisory committee reflecting a wide range of community views. *CONTINUED*

* Stephen Bates, a former senior fellow at the Annenberg Washington Program, is author of *Battleground: One Mother's Crusade, the Religious Right, and the Struggle for Control of Our Classrooms.*

5 Strategies for Finding Common Ground

2. Put in place a written procedure for dealing with complaints. Make clear what is required to initiate reconsideration of materials, who will act on the complaint, how quickly a decision will be made and how a dissatisfied party can appeal the decision to a higher authority.

3. **When a protest does arise, focus on how the public participated in the book selection.** Look at what's in the book and how it's used in the classroom. Don't imply that the adoption process was the only opportunity for public participation and that subsequent complaints are somehow illegitimate. Don't expect protesters to be swayed by the book's pedigree — its awards, reviews, or status as a classic — or by your expertise.

4. **Keep in mind both sides of the public-schooling paradox: The curriculum must reflect the will of the community.** Truth is never a matter of majority rule, but, to a considerable extent, the public school curriculum is (within the bounds of the Constitution and federal and state law). Consequently, it's important to acknowledge the protesters' right to complain about what's going on in their tax-funded schools. Don't simply call them "censors"; respond to their arguments on the merits.

5. **Recognize that context doesn't erase all offenses.** For instance, some parents simply won't allow their children to read racial epithets or profanity, even as a minuscule part of an assignment and even in a classic book.

6. **Remember the civic obligation to respect freedoms of belief, speech and religion, even for people with whom you disagree.** Try to put yourself in the protesters' shoes. How would you feel, and how would you want to be treated, if your child were being taught something contrary to your deepest beliefs? Remember, too, that students learn important lessons about American liberties by seeing how school officials deal with dissent.

7. **Church-state separation is an issue with sectarian material too, if the protesters want sectarian material in the classroom, if they want teachers to make religious judgments on their behalf or if they want to remove material solely because it conflicts with their religious beliefs.** It's not an issue if they want to remove material because it conflicts with their moral beliefs. To be sure, the distinction isn't always clear. Both faith and morality condemn stealing, for example. And it's not an issue if they want an alternative assignment, no matter what their motivation.

8. **When parents are seeking an alternative assignment, don't accuse them of misconstruing the assignment or its impact on students.** Don't enlist psychologists or pastors to rebut their views. Rather, focus on whether an alternative is administratively and pedagogically feasible.

9. **When parents request an alternative assignment, the school system should respond privately.** When protesters seek to remove a book from the curriculum or the school library, however, administrators should ordinarily respond publicly, especially before removing a book. Decisions that affect an entire classroom or an entire school affect the community; in most circumstances, the community should be fully informed.

10. **Recognize, and show that you recognize, that the protesters want what they believe to be best for the children.**

11. **Resist the temptation to engage in name-calling.** Don't suggest, even indirectly, that protesters are extremists, zealots or kooks.

12. **Remember: Obnoxious people have rights too.**

CHAPTER 6

A Teacher's Guide to Religion in the Public Schools

FIRST AMENDMENT TO THE
UNITED STATES CONSTITUTION

A Teacher's Guide to Religion and Public Schools has been endorsed by the following organizations:

American Association of School Administrators

American Federation of Teachers

American Jewish Committee

American Jewish Congress

Anti-Defamation League

Association for Supervision and Curriculum Development

Baptist Joint Committee on Public Affairs

Catholic League for Religious and Civil Rights

Christian Educators Association International

Christian Legal Society

Council on Islamic Education

First Amendment Center

National Association of Elementary School Principals

National Association of Evangelicals

National Association of Secondary School Principals

National Council of Churches of Christ in the U.S.A.

National Council for the Social Studies

National Education Association

National PTA

National School Boards Association

Union of American Hebrew Congregations

Union of Orthodox Jewish Congregations of America

Each day millions of parents from diverse religious backgrounds entrust the education of their children to the teachers in our nation's public schools. For this reason, teachers need to be fully informed about the constitutional and educational principles for understanding the role of religion in public education.

This teacher's guide is intended to move beyond the confusion and conflict that has surrounded religion in public schools since the early days of the common school movement. For most of our history, extremes have shaped much of the debate. On one end of the spectrum are those who advocate promotion of religion (usually their own) in school practices and policies. On the other end are those who view public schools as religion-free zones. Neither of these approaches is consistent with the guiding principles of the Religion Clauses of the First Amendment.

Fortunately, however, there is another alternative that is consistent with the First Amendment and broadly supported by many educational and religious groups. The core of this alternative has been best articulated in "Religious Liberty, Public Education, and the Future of American Democracy," a statement of principles issued by 24 national organizations. Principle IV states:

> Public schools may not inculcate nor inhibit religion. They must be places where religion and religious conviction are treated with fairness and respect. Public schools uphold the First Amendment when they protect the religious liberty rights of students of all faiths or none. Schools demonstrate fairness when they ensure that the curriculum includes study *about* religion, where appropriate, as an important part of a complete education.[1]

[1] This shared vision of religious liberty in public education is remarkable both for who says it and for what it says. The National Education Association, the American Federation of Teachers, the National School Boards Association, the Association for Supervision and Curriculum Development, the National PTA and the American Association of School Administrators join with the Christian Legal Society, the American Center for Law and Justice, and Citizens for Excellence in Education in asserting these principles. People for the American Way, the Anti-Defamation League and the Union of American Hebrew Congregations are on the list, as are the Council on Islamic Education and the Christian Educators Association International, and the Christian Coalition. A full text of the Statement of Principles may be found in chapter 2.

The questions and answers that follow build on this shared vision of religious liberty in public education to provide teachers with a basic understanding of the issues concerning religion in their classrooms. The advice offered is based on First Amendment principles as currently interpreted by the courts and agreed to by a wide range of religious and educational organizations. This guide is not intended to render legal advice on specific legal questions; it is designed to provide general information on the subject of religion and public schools.

Keep in mind, however, that the law alone cannot answer every question. Teachers and administrators, working with parents and others in the community, must work to apply the First Amendment fairly and justly for all students in our public schools.

A TEACHER'S GUIDE TO RELIGION IN THE PUBLIC SCHOOLS

"Congress shall make no law respecting an establishment of religion, or prohibiting the free exercise thereof …"

—Religion Clauses of the First Amendment to the U.S. Constitution

1. Is it constitutional to teach about religion?

Yes. In the 1960s school prayer cases (that prompted rulings against state-sponsored school prayer and Bible reading), the U.S. Supreme Court indicated that public school education may include teaching about religion. In *Abington v. Schempp,* Associate Justice Tom Clark wrote for the Court:

> [I]t might well be said that one's education is not complete without a study of comparative religion or the history of religion and its relationship to the advancement of civilization. It certainly may be said that the Bible is worthy of study for its literary and historic qualities. Nothing we have said here indicates that such study of the Bible or of religion, when presented objectively as part of a secular program of education, may not be effected consistently with the First Amendment.

2. Why should study about religion be included in the curriculum?

Growing numbers of educators throughout the United States recognize that study about religion in social studies, literature, art, and music is an important part of a well-rounded education. "Religion in the Public School Curriculum: Questions and Answers," issued by a coalition of 17 major religious and educational organizations—including the Christian Legal Society, the American Jewish Congress, the National Education Association, the American Federation of Teachers, the American Association of School Administrators, the Islamic Society of North America, the National Council for the Social Studies, the Association for Supervision and Curriculum Development, the Baptist Joint Committee on Public Affairs, the National Association of Evangelicals, and the National School Boards Association—describes the importance of religion in the curriculum thus:

> Because religion plays a significant role in history and society, study about religion is essential to understanding both the nation and the world. Omission of facts about religion can give students the false impression that the religious life of humankind is insignificant or unimportant. Failure to understand even the basic symbols, practices, and concepts of the various religions makes much of history, literature, art, and contemporary life unintelligible.

> Study about religion is also important if students are to value religious liberty, the first freedom guaranteed in the Bill of Rights. Moreover, knowledge of the roles of religion in the past and present promotes cross-cultural understanding essential to democracy and world peace.

A number of leading educational groups have issued their own statements decrying the lack of discussion about religion in the curriculum and calling for inclusion of such information in curricular materials and in teacher education.

Three major principles form the foundation of this consensus on teaching about religion in public schools:

1. As the Supreme Court has made clear, study about religion in public schools is constitutional.

2. Inclusion of study about religion is important in order for students to be properly educated about history and cultures.

3. Religion must be taught objectively and neutrally. The purpose of public schools is to educate students about a variety of religious traditions, not to indoctrinate them into any tradition.

6

A Teacher's Guide
to Religion in the
Public Schools

3. Is study about religion included in textbooks and standards?

"Knowledge about religions is not only characteristic of an educated person, but is also absolutely necessary for understanding and living in a world of diversity."
—National Council for the Social Studies

Agreement on the importance of teaching about religion has begun to influence the treatment of religion in textbooks widely used in public schools, as well as state frameworks and standards for the social studies. The current generation of history textbooks mention religion more often than their predecessors, and, in world history, sometimes offer substantive discussions of religious ideas and events.

State frameworks and standards are also beginning to treat religion more seriously. Most state standards in the social studies require or recommend teaching about religion through specific content references and general mandates, and many also include such references in fine arts and literature standards. In California, for example, the History-Social Science Framework and the new History-Social Science Content Standards require considerable study of religion. Students studying U.S. History in California are expected to learn about the role of religion in the American story, from the influence of religious groups on social reform movements to the religious revivals, from the rise of Christian fundamentalism to the expanding religious pluralism of the 20th century.

Teaching about religion is also encouraged in the *National Standards for History,* published by the National Center for History in the Schools. The elaborated standards in world history are particularly rich in religious references, examining the basic beliefs and practices of the major religions as well as how these faiths influenced the development of civilization in successive historical periods. While the U.S. history standards include religion less frequently, many historical developments and contributions that were influenced by religion are nevertheless represented.

Geography for Life: The National Geography Standards, published by the Geography Standards Project, and the *National Standards for Civics and Government,* published by the Center for Civic Education, include many references to teaching about religious belief and practice as historical and contemporary phenomena. Study of religion in the social studies would be expanded considerably if curriculum developers and textbooks writers were guided by these standards.

4. How should I teach about religion?

Encouraged by the new consensus, public schools are now beginning to include more teaching about religion in the curriculum. In the social studies especially, the question is no longer "Should I teach about religion?" but rather "How should I do it?"

The answer to the "how" question begins with a clear understanding of the crucial difference between the teaching of religion (religious education or indoctrination) and teaching about religion. "Religion in the Public School Curriculum," the guidelines issued by 17 religious and educational organizations, summarizes the distinction this way:

- The school's approach to religion is *academic*, not *devotional*.

- The school strives for student *awareness* of religions, but does not press for student *acceptance* of any religion.

- The school sponsors study *about* religion, not the *practice* of religion.

- The school may *expose* students to a diversity of religious views, but may not *impose* any particular view.

• The school *educates* about all religions; it does not *promote* or *denigrate* religion.

• The school *informs* students about various beliefs; it does not seek to *conform* students to any particular belief.[2]

Classroom discussions concerning religion must be conducted in an environment that is free of advocacy on the part of the teacher. Students may, of course, express their own religious views, as long as such expression is germane to the discussion. But public-school teachers are required by the First Amendment to teach about religion fairly and objectively, neither promoting nor denigrating religion in general or specific religious groups in particular. When discussing religion, many teachers guard against injecting personal religious beliefs by teaching through attribution (e.g., by using such phrases as "most Buddhists believe ..." or "according to the Hebrew scriptures ...").

5. Which religions should be taught and how much should be said?

Decisions about which religions to include and how much to discuss about religion are determined by the grade level of the students and the academic requirements of the course being taught.

In the elementary grades, the study of family, community, various cultures, the nation, and other themes and topics may involve some discussion of religion. Elementary students are introduced to the basic ideas and practices of the world's major religions by focusing on the generally agreed-upon meanings of religious faiths—the core beliefs and symbols as well as important figures and events. Stories drawn from various faiths may be included among the wide variety of stories read by students, but the material selected must always be presented in the context of learning about religion.

On the secondary level, the social studies, literature, and the arts offer opportunities for the inclusion of study about religions—their ideas and practices. The academic needs of the course determine which religions are studied. In a U.S. history curriculum, for example, some faith communities may be given more time than others but only because of their predominant influence on the development of the American nation.

[2] Based on guidelines originally published by the Public Education Religion Studies Center at Wright State University.

In world history, a variety of faiths are studied in each region of the world in order to understand the various civilizations and cultures that have shaped history and society. The overall curriculum should include all of the major voices and some of the minor ones in an effort to provide the best possible education.

Fair and balanced study about religion on the secondary level includes critical thinking about historical events involving religious traditions. Religious beliefs have been at the heart of some of the best and some of the worst developments in human history. The full historical record (and various interpretations of it) should be available for analysis and discussion. Using primary sources whenever possible allows students to work directly with the historical record.

Of course, fairness and balance in U.S. or world history and literature is difficult to achieve, given the brief treatment of religious ideas and events in most textbooks and the limited time available in the course syllabus. Teachers will need scholarly supplemental resources that enable them to cover the required material within the allotted time, while simultaneously enriching the discussion with study of religion. Some schools now offer electives in religious studies in order to provide additional opportunities for students to study about the major faith communities in greater depth.

6. May I invite guest speakers to help with study about religion?

When teaching about religions in history, some teachers may find it helpful to invite a guest speaker for a more comprehensive presentation of the religious tradition under study. Teachers should consult their school district policy concerning guest speakers in the classroom.

If a guest speaker is invited, care should be taken to find someone with the academic background necessary for an objective and scholarly discussion of the historical period and the religion being considered. Faculty from local colleges and universities often make excellent guest speakers or can make recommendations of others who might be appropriate for working with students in a public-school setting. Religious leaders in the community may also be a resource. Remember, however, that they have commitments to their own faith. Be certain that any guest speaker understands the First Amendment guidelines for teaching about religion in public education and is clear about the academic nature of the assignment.

7. How should I treat religious holidays in the classroom?

Teachers must be alert to the distinction between teaching about religious holidays, which is permissible, and celebrating religious holidays, which is not. Recognition of and information about holidays may focus on how and when they are celebrated, their origins, histories and generally agreed-upon meanings. If the approach is objective and sensitive, neither promoting nor inhibiting religion, this study can foster understanding and mutual respect for differences in belief. Teachers may not use the study of religious holidays as an opportunity to proselytize or otherwise inject personal religious beliefs into the discussion.

The use of religious symbols, provided they are used only as examples of cultural or religious heritage, is permissible as a teaching aid or resource. Religious symbols may be displayed only on a temporary basis as part of the academic lesson being studied. Students may choose to create artwork with religious symbols, but teachers should not assign or suggest such creations.

The use of art, drama, music or literature with religious themes is permissible if it serves a sound educational goal in the curriculum. Such themes should be included on the basis of their academic or aesthetic value, not as a vehicle for promoting religious belief. For example, sacred music may be sung or played as part of the academic study of music. School concerts that present a variety of selections may include religious music. Concerts should avoid programs dominated by religious music, especially when these coincide with a particular religious holiday.

This advice about religious holidays in public schools is based on consensus guidelines adopted by 18 educational and religious organizations.[3]

8. Are there opportunities for teacher education in study about religion?

Teacher preparation and good academic resources are needed in order for study about religion in public schools to be constitutionally permissible and educationally sound.

The First Amendment Center supports initiatives in several regions of the country designed to prepare public-school teachers to teach about religion. The most extensive of these programs is the California 3Rs Project (Rights, Responsibilities, and Respect). Co-sponsored by the California County Superintendents Educational Services Association, the project has created a network of resource leaders and scholars throughout the state providing support for classroom teachers. Teachers trained by the project give workshops for their colleagues on the constitutional and educational

---

[3] "Religious Holidays and Public Schools: Questions and Answers" may be found in chapter 8.

A Teacher's Guide to Religion in the Public Schools

guidelines for teaching about religion. Religious studies scholars from local colleges and universities are linked with school districts to provide ongoing expertise and periodic seminars on the religious traditions that teachers are discussing in the curriculum.

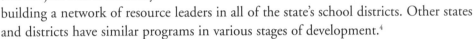

The Utah State Office of Education co-sponsors a Utah 3Rs Project that is currently building a network of resource leaders in all of the state's school districts. Other states and districts have similar programs in various stages of development.[4]

Harvard University and the University of Pennsylvania offer master's level programs that are excellent opportunities for both current and prospective public- and private-school teachers interested in learning more about the study of religion and religious-liberty issues in American public life.[5]

Other colleges and universities offer assistance to teachers, including in-service programs focused on teaching about religion. A notable example is the Religion and Public Education Resource Center at California State University – Chico. This center provides resources, including curriculum guides and sample lessons in several subject areas.[6] Other organizations, such as the Council on Islamic Education, offer academic resources and workshops on teaching about specific religious traditions.[7]

9. What are good classroom resources for teaching about religion?*

Teaching about religion in the public schools requires that sound academic resources be made readily available to classroom teachers. Fortunately, good classroom resources, especially in the social studies, are now available for helping teachers integrate appropriate study about religion.

---

[4] For details about the "Rights, Responsibilities and Respect" programs, contact Charles Haynes at (703) 284-2809.

[5] For more information about the Program in Religion and Secondary Education at Harvard University, contact The Divinity School, 45 Francis Ave., Cambridge, MA 02138. Attention: Diane Moore, Ph.D., Director. Inquiries about the Religion in Public Life Certificate Program at the University of Pennsylvania should be addressed to Janet Theophano, Associate Director, Master of Liberal Arts Program, College of General Studies, University of Pennsylvania, 3440 Market St., Suite 100, Philadelphia, PA 19104-3335.

[6] Contact the Religion and Public Education Resource Center by writing to Dr. Bruce Grelle, Dept. of Religious Studies, California State University – Chico, Chico, CA 95929.

[7] The Council on Islamic Education may be reached by calling (714) 839-2929.

* Additional resources are listed at the end of Chapter 7.

Two recent publications are examples of what is now available for study about religion in a secondary school classroom:

Religion in American Life is a 17-volume series written by leading scholars for young readers. Published by Oxford University Press, the series includes three chronological volumes on the religious history of the U.S., nine volumes covering significant religious groups (Protestants, Catholics, Jews, Orthodox Christians, Mormons, Muslims, Hindus, Buddhists, Native Americans and others), and four volumes addressing specific topics of special importance for understanding the role of religion in American life (women and religion, church-state issues, African American religion, and immigration).[8]

Columbia University Press has published a CD-ROM entitled *On Common Ground: World Religions in America.* This multimedia resource uses text, primary sources, photographs, music, film, and the spoken word to bring alive the extraordinary religious diversity in the United States. Fifteen different religions in various regions of America are represented, from the long-established Christian, Jewish, and Native American traditions to the more recent arrivals such as Hinduism and Buddhism.[9]

10. What is the relationship between religion and character education?

As discussed above, the First Amendment prohibits public-school teachers from either inculcating or inhibiting religion. Teachers must remain neutral concerning religion, neutral among religions and neutral between religion and non-religion. But this does not mean that teachers should be neutral concerning civic virtue or moral character.

Teachers should teach the personal and civic virtues widely held in our society, such as honesty, caring, fairness, and integrity. They must do so without either invoking religious authority or denigrating the religious or philosophical commitments of students and parents.

When school districts develop a plan for comprehensive character education, they should keep in mind that the moral life of a great many Americans is shaped by deep religious conviction. Both the approach to character education and the classroom materials used should be selected in close consultation with parents and other community members representing a broad range of perspectives. When care is taken to

---

[8] For more information about the Oxford University Press series, Religion in American Life, call (800) 451-7556.
[9] For more information about the CD-ROM On Common Ground: World Religions in America, call (800) 944-8648.

find consensus, communities are able to agree on the core character traits they wish taught in the schools and how they wish character education to be done.

For guidance on how to develop and implement a quality character education program, contact the Character Education Partnership in Washington, D.C.[10]

The Personal Beliefs of Teachers

11. May I pray or otherwise practice my faith while at school?

As employees of the government, public-school teachers are subject to the Establishment Clause of the First Amendment and thus required to be neutral concerning religion while carrying out their duties as teachers. That means, for example, that teachers do not have the right to pray with or in the presence of students during the school day.

[10] The Character Education Partnership is located at 1025 Connecticut Ave. NW, Suite 1011, Washington, DC 20036. Call (800) 988-8081. Web site: www.character.org.

Outside of their school responsibilities, public-school teachers are free like other citizens to teach or otherwise participate in their local religious community. But teachers must refrain from using their position in the public school to promote their outside religious activities.

Teachers, of course, bring their faith with them through the schoolhouse door each morning. Because of the First Amendment, however, teachers who wish to pray or engage in other religious activities—unless they are silent— should do so outside the presence of students. If a group of teachers wishes to meet for prayer or scriptural study in the faculty lounge during their free time in the school day, we see no constitutional reason why they may not be permitted to do so as long as the activity is outside the presence of students and does not interfere with their duties or the rights of other teachers.

Teachers are permitted to wear non-obtrusive jewelry, such as a cross or Star of David. But teachers should not wear clothing with a proselytizing message (e.g., a "Jesus Saves" T-shirt).

12. How do I respond if students ask about my religious beliefs?

Some teachers prefer not to answer the question, stating that it is inappropriate for a teacher to inject personal beliefs into the discussion. Other teachers may choose to answer the question straightforwardly and succinctly in the interest of an open and honest classroom environment.

Before answering the question, however, teachers should consider the age of the students. Middle and high school students may be able to distinguish between a personal view and the official position of the school; very young children may not. In any case, the teacher may answer at most with a brief statement of personal belief—but may not turn the question into an opportunity to proselytize for or against religion. Teachers may neither reward nor punish students because they agree or disagree with the religious views of the teacher.

Religious Expression of Students

13. May students express religious views in public schools?

In "Religion in the Public Schools: A Joint Statement of Current Law," 35 religious and civil liberties organizations give the following summary of the rights of students to express their faith in a public school:

> Students have the right to pray individually or in groups or to discuss their religious views with their peers so long as they are not disruptive. Because the Establishment Clause does not apply to purely private speech, students enjoy the right to read their Bibles or other scriptures, say grace before meals, pray before tests, and discuss religion with other willing student listeners. In the classroom, students have the right to pray quietly except when required to be actively engaged in school activities (e.g., students may not decide to pray just as a teacher calls on them). In informal settings, such as the cafeteria or in the halls, students may pray either audibly or silently, subject to the same rules of order as apply to other speech in these locations. However, the right to engage in voluntary prayer does not include, for example, the right to have a captive audience listen or to compel other students to participate.[11]

14. May students express religious views in their assignments?

"Religious Expression in Public Schools," guidelines published by the U.S. Department of Education, offers the following guidance about religious expression in student assignments:

> Students may express their beliefs about religion in the form of homework, artwork, and other written and oral assignments free of discrimination based on the religious content of their submissions. Such home and classroom work should be judged by ordinary academic standards of substance and relevance, and against other legitimate pedagogical concerns identified by the school.[12]

---

[11] "Religion in the Public Schools: A Joint Statement of Current Law" may be obtained by writing: "Religion in the Public Schools," 15 East 84th St., Suite 501, New York, NY 10028.

[12] The U.S. Department of Education guidelines may be found in chapter 10.

15. How should public schools respond to excusal requests from parents?

In "A Parent's Guide to Religion in the Public Schools," the National PTA and the First Amendment Center give the following advice concerning excusal requests:

> Whenever possible, school officials should try to accommodate the requests of parents and students for excusal from classroom discussions or activities for religious reasons. If focused on a specific discussion, assignment, or activity, such requests should be routinely granted in order to strike a balance between the student's religious freedom and the school's interest in providing a well-rounded education.
>
> If it is proved that particular lessons substantially burden a student's free exercise of religion and if the school cannot prove a compelling interest in requiring attendance, some courts may require the school to excuse the students.[13]

16. May public schools accommodate students with special religious needs?

Public schools are sometimes asked to accommodate students with special religious needs or practices. Sensitive and thoughtful school officials may easily grant many of these requests without raising constitutional questions. Muslim students, for example, may need a quiet place at lunch or during breaks to fulfill their prayer obligation during the school day. Jehovah's Witnesses ask for their children to be excused from birthday celebrations. As long as honoring these requests is feasible, school officials should do so in the spirit of the First Amendment.

Administrators and teachers should not, however, be placed in the position of monitoring a child's compliance with a particular religious requirement. Enforcing religious obligations such as prayer, dietary restrictions, or wearing a head covering is the responsibility of parents, not teachers.[14]

---

[13] "A Parent's Guide to Religion and the Public Schools," may be found in chapter 12.

[14] A good resource for understanding the religious needs and practices of students is *America's Religions: An Educator's Guide to Beliefs and Practices* by Benjamin J. Hubbard, John T. Hatfield, and James A Santucci. It is available from Teacher Ideas Press by calling (800) 237-6124.

17. May students form extracurricular religious clubs?

The Equal Access Act passed by Congress in 1984 ensures that students in secondary public schools may form religious clubs, including Bible clubs, if the school allows other "noncurriculum-related groups." The Act is intended to protect student-initiated and student-led meetings in secondary schools. According to the Act, outsiders may not "direct, conduct, control, or regularly attend" student religious clubs, and teachers acting as monitors may be present at religious meetings in a nonparticipatory capacity only.[15]

The U.S. Department of Education in "Religious Expression in Public Schools" gives the following guidance for interpreting the Equal Access Act:

The Equal Access Act is designed to ensure that, consistent with the First Amendment, student religious activities are accorded the same access to public school facilities as are student secular activities. Based on decisions of the Federal courts, as well as its interpretations of the Act, the Department of Justice has advised that the Act should be interpreted as providing, among other things, that:

- Student religious groups at public secondary schools have the same right of access to school facilities as is enjoyed by other comparable student groups. Under the Equal Access Act, a school receiving Federal funds that allows one or more student noncurriculum-related clubs to meet on its premises during noninstructional time may not refuse access to student religious groups.

- A meeting, as defined and protected by the Equal Access Act, may include a prayer service, Bible reading, or other worship exercise.

- A school receiving Federal funds must allow student groups meeting under the Act to use the school media—including the public address system, the school newspaper, and the school bulletin board—to announce their meetings on the same terms as other noncurriculum-related student groups are allowed to use the school media. Any policy concerning the use of school media must be applied to all noncurriculum-related student groups in a nondiscriminatory manner. Schools, however, may inform students that certain groups are not school-sponsored.

- A school creates a limited open forum under the Equal Access Act, triggering equal access rights for religious groups, when it allows students to meet during their lunch periods or other noninstructional time during the school day, as well as when it allows students to meet before and after the school day.

---

[15] The requirements of the Equal Access Act are described in detail in "Equal Access and the Public Schools: Questions and Answers," a pamphlet sponsored by 21 religious and educational groups. The full text is contained in Chapter 9.

18. May students distribute religious literature in school?

An increasing number of students are requesting permission to distribute religious literature on public-school campuses. According to the guidelines issued by the U.S. Department of Education:

Students have a right to distribute religious literature to their schoolmates on the same terms as they are permitted to distribute other literature that is unrelated to school curriculum or activities. Schools may impose the same reasonable time, place, and manner or other constitutional restrictions on distribution of religious literature as they do on nonschool literature generally, but they may not single out religious literature for special regulation.

HOT TIP

May teachers use role playing or simulations to teach about religion?

Recreating religious practices or ceremonies through role-playing activities should not take place in a public school classroom for three reasons:

1. Such reenactments run the risk of blurring the distinction between teaching about religion (which is constitutional) and school-sponsored practice of religion (which is unconstitutional).

2. Role-playing religious practices or rituals may violate the religious liberty, or freedom of conscience, of the students in the classroom. Even if the students are all volunteers, many parents don't want their children participating in a religious activity of a faith not their own. The fact that the exercise is "acting" doesn't prevent potential problems.

3. Simulations or role-playing, no matter how carefully planned or well-intentioned, risk trivializing, caricaturing or oversimplifying the religious tradition that is being studied. Teachers should use audiovisual resources and primary sources to introduce students to the ceremonies and rituals of the world's religions.

The Authors

CHAPTER 7

Religion in the Public School Curriculum

Religion in the Public School Curriculum:
Questions and Answers is sponsored jointly by:

American Academy of Religion

American Association of School Administrators

American Federation of Teachers

American Jewish Congress

Americans United Research Foundation

Association for Supervision and Curriculum Development

Baptist Joint Committee on Public Affairs

Christian Legal Society

The Church of Jesus Christ of Latter-day Saints

First Amendment Center

The Islamic Society of North America

National Association of Evangelicals

National Conference of Community and Justice

National Council of Churches of Christ in the USA

National Council for the Social Studies

National Education Association

National School Boards Association

Growing numbers of people in the United States think it is important to teach *about* religion in the public schools.[1]

But what is the appropriate place of religion in the public- school curriculum? How does one approach such issues as textbook content, values education, creation science and religious holidays?

QUESTIONS *and* ANSWERS:
RELIGION IN THE PUBLIC SCHOOL CURRICULUM

The following questions and answers are designed to assist school boards as they make decisions about the curriculum and educators as they teach about religion in ways that are constitutionally permissible, educationally sound, and sensitive to the beliefs of students and parents.

Is it constitutional to teach about religion in public schools?

Yes. In the 1960s school-prayer cases (that prompted rulings against state-sponsored school prayer and Bible reading), the U.S. Supreme Court indicated that public school education may include teaching about religion. In *Abington v. Schempp*, Associate Justice Tom Clark wrote for the Court:

> [I]t might well be said that one's education is not complete without a study of comparative religion or the history of religion and its relationship to the advancement of civilization. It certainly may be said that the Bible is worthy of study for its literary and historic qualities. Nothing we have said here indicates that such study of the Bible or of religion, when presented objectively as part of a secular program of education, may not be effected consistently with the First Amendment.

[1] "Teaching about religion" includes consideration of the beliefs and practices of religions; the role of religion in history and contemporary society; and religious themes in music, art and literature.

What is meant by "teaching about religion" in the public schools?

The following statements distinguish between teaching about religion in public schools and religious indoctrination:

1. The school's approach to religion is *academic*, not *devotional*.

2. The school may strive for student *awareness* of religions, but should not press for student *acceptance* of any one religion.

3. The school may sponsor *study* about religion, but may not sponsor the *practice* of religion.

4. The school may *expose* students to a diversity of religious views, but may not *impose* any particular view.

5. The school may *educate* about all religions, but may not *promote* or *denigrate* any religion.

6. The school may *inform* the student about various beliefs, but should not seek to *conform* him or her to any particular belief.[2]

Why should study about religion be included in the public school curriculum?

Because religion plays a significant role in history and society, study about religion is essential to understanding both the nation and the world. Omission of facts about religion can give students the false impression that the religious life of humankind is insignificant or unimportant. Failure to understand even the basic symbols, practices and concepts of the various religions makes much of history, literature, art and contemporary life unintelligible.

Study about religion is also important if students are to value religious liberty, the first freedom guaranteed in the Bill of Rights. Moreover, knowledge of the roles of religion in the past and present promotes cross-cultural understanding essential to democracy and world peace.

[2] This answer is based on guidelines originally published by the Public Education Religion Studies Center at Wright State University.

Religion in the Public School Curriculum

Where does study about religion belong in the curriculum?

Wherever it naturally arises. On the secondary level, the social studies, literature and the arts offer many opportunities for the inclusion of information about religions — their ideas and themes. On the elementary level, natural opportunities arise in discussions of the family and community life and in instruction about festivals and different cultures. Many educators believe that integrating study about religion into existing courses is an educationally sound way to acquaint students with the role of religion in history and society.

Religion also may be taught about in special courses or units. Some secondary schools, for example, offer such courses as world religions, the Bible as literature, and the religious literature of the West and of the East.

Do current textbooks teach about religion?

Rarely. Recent textbook studies conclude that most widely used textbooks largely ignore the role of religion in history and society. For example, readers of high school U.S. history texts learn little or nothing about the great colonial revivals, the struggles of minority faiths, the religious motivations of immigrants, the contributions of religious groups to many social movements, major episodes of religious intolerance, and many other significant events of history. Education without appropriate attention to major religious influences and themes is incomplete education.

How does teaching about religion relate to the teaching of values?

Teaching about religion is not the same as teaching values. The former is objective, academic study; the latter involves the teaching of particular ethical viewpoints or standards of behavior.

There are basic moral values that are recognized by the population at large (e.g., honesty, integrity, justice, compassion). These values can be taught in classes through discussion, by example and by carrying out school policies. However, teachers may not invoke religious authority.

Public schools may teach about the various religious and nonreligious perspectives concerning the many complex moral issues confronting society, but such perspectives must be presented without adopting, sponsoring or denigrating one view against another.

Is it constitutional to teach the biblical account of creation in the public schools?

Some states have passed laws requiring that creationist theory based on the biblical account be taught in the science classroom. The courts have found these laws to be unconstitutional on the ground that they promote a particular religious view. The Supreme Court has

acknowledged, however, that a variety of scientific theories about origins can be appropriately taught in the science classroom. In *Edwards v. Aguillard*, the Court stated:

> [T]eaching a variety of scientific theories about the origins of humankind to schoolchildren might be validly done with the clear secular intent of enhancing the effectiveness of science instruction.

7 Religion in the Public School Curriculum

Though science instruction may not endorse or promote religious doctrine, the account of creation found in various scriptures may be discussed in a religious studies class or in any course that considers religious explanations for the origin of life.

How should religious holidays be treated in the classroom?

Carefully. Religious holidays offer excellent opportunities to teach about religion in the elementary and secondary schools. Recognition of and information about such holidays should focus on the origin, history and generally agreed-upon meaning of the observances. If the approach is objective, neither advancing nor inhibiting religion, it can foster among students understanding and mutual respect within and beyond the local community.

Resources

The following resources offer excellent background material for understanding not only how religion has influenced the past, but also how it continues to influence society today. Additional assistance can often be found through local colleges and universities, which may provide both workshops and speakers.

Taking religion seriously in the curriculum will require a commitment by schools of education to give teachers more exposure to the study of religious influences and appropriate resources for teaching about these influences in the public school setting.

Religion in American Life - Oxford University Press

At long last, a series of scholarly works on religion written for young readers is available. Edited by Yale University professors Jon Butler and Harry Stout and published by Oxford University Press, *Religion in American Life* is a 17-volume series authored by some of the nation's leading scholars in the field of religious studies.

The series is an invaluable resource for teachers of junior and senior high school students. Teachers of U.S. history will find all of the volumes most useful, but world history, government and literature teachers will also be able to use many of the volumes in a variety of ways. Three chronological volumes give the religious history of the United States from the colonial period to the present. Nine volumes cover significant religious groups in America, including Protestants, Catholics, Jews, Muslims, Native Americans and Eastern faiths. Four volumes address specific topics — women, church-state issues, African American religion, and immigration — that are of special importance in understanding the role of religion in American life.

With the addition of these books to school and classroom libraries, students and teachers will have access to scholarly works that fill the gaps left by inadequate textbook treatment of religion. In fact, the chronological volumes would themselves be excellent textbooks for an elective course on religion in America or religion in U.S. history. A teacher's guide, prepared by the First Amendment Center, suggests ways to use the volumes for supplemental reading and research projects in history and other courses.

For more information, visit Oxford University press at www.oup-usa.org.

CONTINUED

RESOURCE

On Common Ground (CD-ROM)

Another groundbreaking resource for students and teachers is *On Common Ground: World Religions in America,* a CD-ROM published in 1997 by Columbia University Press. This multimedia resource uses text, primary sources, photographs, music, film and the spoken word to bring alive the extraordinary religious diversity in the United States. Prepared by Harvard Divinity School professor Diana Eck, the CD-ROM draws on the Pluralism Project, a Harvard-based study that has documented America's religious landscape.

Using the CD-ROM, students can find out about the beliefs and practices of America's many faith traditions. They are able to explore the religious diversity of eighteen cities and regions of the United States. Fifteen different religions are represented, from the long-established Native American, Christian and Jewish traditions to more recent arrivals such as Hinduism and Buddhism.

What is especially impressive about this resource is its use of documents, photographs, film, and music to enable practitioners of each faith to provide students with some experience of the religion from the inside. It is also noteworthy that differences within various traditions are discussed (e.g., Orthodox and Reform Judaism). Even issues debated within various traditions — the role of women in Islam, for example — are included. In short, this is an essential resource for every secondary social studies and literature classroom.

For more information, visit the web site at www.columbia.edu/cu/cup/catalog/electronic/idx_cd.html.

Orders can be placed at: 1-800-944-8648 (phone); 1-800-944-1844 (fax); or Columbia University Press Order Department, 136 South Broadway, Irvington, NY 10533.

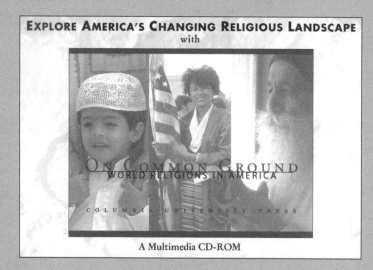

EXPLORE AMERICA'S CHANGING RELIGIOUS LANDSCAPE
with
ON COMMON GROUND
WORLD RELIGIONS IN AMERICA
COLUMBIA UNIVERSITY PRESS

A Multimedia CD-ROM

CONTINUED

7 Religion in the Public School Curriculum

RESOURCE

Taking Religion Seriously Across the Curriculum

In *Taking Religion Seriously Across the Curriculum*, Warren A. Nord and Charles C. Haynes chart a middle course in our culture wars over religion and public education – one that builds on a developing national consensus among educational and religious leaders. In Part One, Nord and Haynes explain why schools should take religion seriously, and they outline the civic, constitutional and educational frameworks that should shape the treatment of religion in the curriculum and classroom. In Part Two, they explore the major issues relating to religion in different domains of the curriculum – in elementary education and in middle- and high-school courses in history, civics, economics, literature and the sciences. They also discuss Bible courses and world religions courses, and they explore the relationship of religion to moral education and sex education. The result is a book that is unique in the scope of its consideration of the relevance of religion *across the curriculum*.

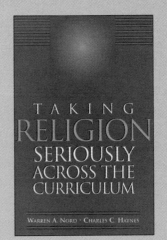

This book is available from: Association for Supervision and Curriculum Development, www.ascd.org.

The Bible & Public Schools: A First Amendment Guide

The First Amendment Center and the Bible Literacy Project jointly published these First Amendment guidelines for teachers on the appropriate role of the Bible in the public school curriculum. This guide is endorsed by a wide array of organizations, ranging from the People for the American Way Foundation and the American Jewish Congress to the Christian Legal Society and the National Association of Evangelicals. The guide is based on a question-and-answer format addressing such issues as whether the Bible can be taught in public schools, methods and approaches that are constitutional, and what the courts have said about the subject.

This guide is available online at www.freedomforum.org, or by calling 1-800-830-3733 and requesting publication No. 99-F03.

www.biblecurriculum.org

CONTINUED

RESOURCE

America's Religions: An Educator's Guide to Beliefs and Practices

Teacher Ideas Press presents a guide by Benjamin Hubbard, John Hatfield, and James Santucci to the beliefs and practices of a number of the world's religions. Designed specifically for teachers, the guide examines each religious group in terms of its origins, beliefs, sacred scriptures, practices, main subgroups, common misunderstandings and stereotypes, and classroom concerns.

This book is available from Teacher Ideas Press, Dept. B40, P.O. Box 6633, Englewood, CO 80155-6633; by phone at 1-800-237-6124, ext.1; or on the web at www.lu.com/tip.

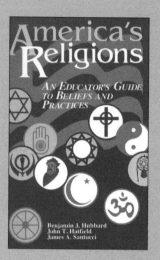

Religion in the Public School Curriculum

Organizations That Provide Classroom Resources

Council on Islamic Education

P.O. Box 20186
Fountain Valley
CA 92728-0186
(714) 839-2929
www.cie.org
email: CIE@Islam.org.

The Council on Islamic Education (CIE) is a national, non-profit resource organization dedicated to providing information on Islam and Muslim history to K-12 textbook publishers, education officials, curriculum developers, teachers, and other education professionals. CIE is comprised of scholars and academicians associated with major universities and institutions throughout the United States. CIE produces resource materials, conducts workshops, attends education conferences, and convenes events in its efforts towards accurate, balanced, and sensitive coverage of Islam in the context of a global approach to world history.

Religion and Public Education Resource Center

Director: Dr. Bruce Grelle
Department of Religious Studies
California State University — Chico
Chico, CA 95929-0740
(530) 898-4739
e-mail: bgrelle@csuchico.edu

The Religion and Public Education Resource Center (RPERC) provides resources for teaching about religions in public schools in ways that are constitutionally permissible and academically sound. The Center serves both as a depository of existing materials and as a catalyst for the development and distribution of new materials relating to pedagogical and legal issues that arise in connection with teaching about religion in public schools. RPERC offers curriculum guides and sample lessons in several subject areas for classroom teachers.

CONTINUED

Council for Spiritual and Ethical Education

Executive Director: Peter W. Cobb
1465 Northside Drive, Suite 220
Atlanta, GA 30318-4225
(800) 298-4599
fax: (404) 355-4435
e-mail: info@csee.org
www.csee.org

The Council for Spiritual and Ethical Education is a membership organization that serves as a national resource for schools to encourage the moral, ethical, and spiritual development of young people. CSEE promotes community service, provides resources and a network for schools' involvement in community service and service learning. CSEE also supports instruction in world religions and ethics as essential components of a complete education.

Religious Studies in Secondary Schools

7735 SW 87th Avenue
Portland, OR 97223
info@rsiss.org
www.rsiss.org

RSISS is a growing coalition of public and private secondary school teachers committed to the idea that education is not complete without the academic study of the world's religious traditions and the ethical values, literatures, and cultures so inextricably linked to them. There are no membership dues, just people in the field willing to help.

Religion and Education

Mike Waggoner, Editor
University of Northern Iowa
508 Schindler Education Center
Cedar Falls, IA 50614-0604
(319) 273-2605

email: jrae@uni.edu
www.uni.edu/jrae

Religion and Education is a journal devoted to news, reviews of books and curricular materials, and essays relating to interactions of religion and education. *Religion and Education's* mission is to facilitate informed, constitutionally appropriate teaching about religions in history and culture that enables students to participate in a pluralistic and religiously diverse world.

Internet Resources

The Internet has become a valuable tool for exploring religious liberty issues in education and the role of religion in the curriculum. In response to this growth, we have prepared a list of resources relating to various religious information sites that can be found on the Internet. Some of these sites target the academic community, and as such are more useful to the teacher who is trying to better understand a variety of faith traditions. A word of caution is due here. As the Internet is an ever-changing entity, the content of the sites mentioned is also changing. Whenever students are using the Internet, they should be closely monitored. In fact, we encourage teachers to preview these sites before students are allowed to access them. While we have attempted to choose sites that are well established, their addresses and locations can change frequently. Also, please remember that these sites are not endorsed by the First Amendment Center but are merely areas that might provide valuable information for the classroom.

APS Guide to Resources in Theology
www.utoronto.ca/stmikes/theobook.htm

This University of Toronto site is actually a list of links to other sites, primarily those dealing with Christian resources. It is of interest because it links to sites that provide primary materials (papyri, manuscripts, etc.) Most of the linked sites are fairly sophisticated and would be most useful as resources for teachers seeking a deeper understanding of some of the various Christian denominations and early source materials in Christian studies.

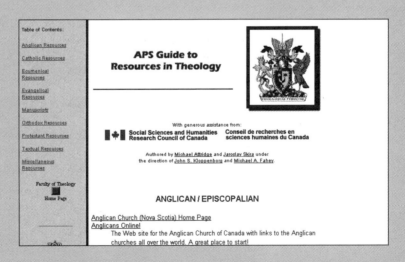

CONTINUED

Interfaith Calendar by Mall Area Religious Council
www.interfaithcalendar.org

This site is a listing of the religious holidays observed by various religious groups. It is a useful resource for teachers who are interested in these holidays.

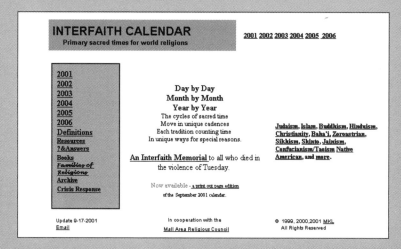

Religion in the Public School Curriculum

Teaching About Religion In Public Schools: Worldview Education
www.teachingaboutreligion.org

"This web site is designed to assist teachers of middle grades and secondary level history and social science programs in their handling of religion as curricular subject matter." It contains resource material, guidelines, and lesson plans, including the "Different Drummer" curriculum.

CONTINUED

Academic Information on Religion
www.academicinfo.net/religindex.html

This site lists various religions according to their presence in various geographic locations. This site is valuable in that it also links to the art and literature of the various belief systems, a useful feature for teachers seeking visual aids. This site links to college- and graduate-level sites and is too complex for younger children.

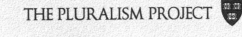

Home / Keyword Search / Subject Index / Reference Desk / Student Center

Academic Info : Religion Gateway

Humanities > Religion

Religious Studies

- Indexes & Directories
- Reference Desk
- Digital Library
- Libraries & Archives
- Academic Departments
- Societies & Associations
- Religious Tolerance

Alternative Spirituality

American Frontier History – Religion

Ancient History – Religion

Hinduism

Holocaust Studies

Islamic Studies

Jewish Studies

Law & Religion

Mythology

Native American Religions

Pagan

Rastafarianism

Pluralism Project
www.fas.harvard.edu/~pluralsm/

The Pluralism Project web site at Harvard University is filled with such resources as pictures of various U.S. worship centers, links to other sites with content related to various faiths, syllabi from college courses on the topic of religious pluralism, and archives of news articles reporting on recent faith traditions in the United States.

THE PLURALISM PROJECT

ABOUT
Mission • History • People • Contact

CURRENT RESEARCH
Affiliates • Articles • Research Template
Center Profiles • Guidelines • Grant Application

EVENTS
Working Group • Women's Networks
NEH Seminar • Past Symposia

PUBLICATIONS
A New Religious America • World Religions in Boston
On Common Ground • Becoming the Buddha in L.A.

RESOURCES
Calendar • Bibliographies • Links • Audio/Video
Directory • Images • Statistics • Syllabi • More...

NEW & NOTEWORTHY
What's New • FAQ • Site Map • Search
Feature of the Month • In the News

COMMITTEE ON THE STUDY OF RELIGION • HARVARD UNIVERSITY

CONTINUED

National Humanities Center
http://www.nhc.rtp.nc.us/tserve/tserve.htm

The National Humanities Center TeacherServ web site is designed to provide practical planning helps for teaching topics in the liberal arts. Instructional guides and resource materials are provided to assist teachers with secondary-school humanities topics, particularly as related to teaching about religion. The current guide, *Divining America*, is an invaluable resource for teachers attempting to achieve a deeper understanding of religion's place in American history.

Education for Freedom
http://www.freedomforum.org/templates/document.asp?documentID=13588

Education for Freedom is offered by The Freedom Forum's First Amendment Center. These lessons (beginning and advanced levels) address constitutional principles and contemporary issues involving the First Amendment. They will draw young people into an exploration of how their freedoms began and how they operate in today's world. Students will discuss just how far individual rights extend, examining rights in the school environment and public places. The lessons may be used in history and government, language arts and journalism, art and debate classes. They may be used in sections or in their entirety.

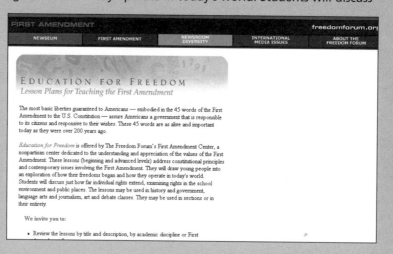

Religion in the Public
School Curriculum

CHAPTER 8

Religious Holidays in the Public Schools

Congress shall make
no law respecting an
establishment of religion,
or prohibiting the free
exercise thereof; or
abridging the freedom
of speech, or of the press,
or the right of the people
peaceably to assemble,
and to petition the
Government for a redress
of grievances.

FIRST AMENDMENT TO THE
UNITED STATES CONSTITUTION

Religious Holidays in the Public Schools:
Questions and Answers is sponsored jointly by:

American Academy of Religion

American Association of School Administrators

American Federation of Teachers

American Jewish Committee

American Jewish Congress

Americans United Research Foundation

Association for Supervision and Curriculum Development

Baptist Joint Committee on Public Affairs

Christian Legal Society

First Amendment Center

The Islamic Society of North America

National Association of Evangelicals

National Conference of Community and Justice

National Council of Churches of Christ in the USA

National Council for the Social Studies

National Education Association

National School Boards Association

Since 1776 the United States has grown from a nation of relatively few religious differences to one of countless religious groups. This expanding pluralism challenges the public schools to deal creatively and sensitively with students professing many religions and none.

The following questions and answers concern religious holidays and public education, a subject often marked by confusion and conflict. Teachers and school officials, as well as parents and students, should approach this discussion as an opportunity to work cooperatively for the sake of good education rather than at cross purposes.

School districts developing guidelines about religious holidays will want to base their policies in the shared commitment of respect for individual religious beliefs expressed in the constitutional guarantee of religious liberty. This means that public schools may neither promote nor inhibit religious belief or nonbelief. Drafters of such guidelines also will want to take account of the role of religion in history and culture.

The question-and-answers section is followed by a brief legal analysis of the issues. While awareness of legal issues is essential in considering religion and public education, the law does not supply answers to every question. Within the current legal framework, schools— their boards, administrators, teachers, parents and students—must make many practical decisions regarding religious holidays. This work can be done only by showing sensitivity to the needs of every student and indicating a willingness to steer between avoidance of all references to religion on the one hand and promotion of religion on the other.

QUESTIONS *and* ANSWERS:
RELIGIOUS HOLIDAYS IN THE PUBLIC SCHOOLS.

What do the courts say?

The Supreme Court has ruled that public schools may not sponsor religious practices (*Engel v. Vitale,* 1962; *Abington v. Schempp,* 1963) but may teach about religion. While it has made no definitive ruling on religious holidays in the schools, the Supreme Court has let stand a lower federal court decision stating that recognition of holidays may be constitutional if the purpose is to provide secular instruction about religious traditions rather than to promote the particular religion involved (*Florey v. Sioux Falls School District,* 8th Cir., 1980).

Do religious holidays belong in the curriculum?

The study of religious holidays may be included in elementary and secondary curricula as opportunities for teaching about religions. Such study serves the academic goals of educating students about history and cultures as well as about the traditions of particular religions in a pluralistic society.

When should teaching about religious holidays take place?

On the elementary level, natural opportunities arise for discussion of religious holidays while studying different cultures and communities. In the secondary curriculum, students of world history or literature have opportunities to consider the holy days of religious traditions. Teachers find it helpful when they are provided with an inclusive calendar noting major religious and secular holidays with brief descriptions of their significance.

How should religious holidays be treated in the classroom?

Teachers must be alert to the distinction between teaching about religious holidays, which is permissible, and celebrating religious holidays, which is not. Recognition of and information about holidays may focus on how and when they are celebrated, their origins, histories and generally agreed-upon meanings. If the approach is objective and sensitive, neither promoting nor inhibiting religion, this study can foster understanding and mutual respect for differences in belief. Teachers will want to avoid asking students to explain their beliefs and customs. An offer to do so should be treated with courtesy and accepted or rejected depending on the educational relevancy. Teachers may not use the study of religious holidays as an opportunity to proselytize or to inject personal religious beliefs into the discussion. Teachers should avoid this by teaching through attribution, i.e. by reporting that "some Buddhists believe …."

May religious symbols be used in public school classes?

Provided they are used only as examples of cultural or religious heritage, religious symbols are permissible to use as teaching aids or resources. Religious symbols may be displayed only on a temporary basis as part of the academic program. Students may choose to create artwork with religious symbols, but teachers should not assign or suggest such creations.

May religious music be used in public schools?

Sacred music may be sung or played as part of the academic study of music. School concerts that present a variety of selections may include religious music. Concerts dominated by religious music, especially when they coincide with a particular religious holiday, should be

Resources for Classroom Teachers

Elementary-school teachers may wish to use some of the many books of children's literature containing stories about the religious holidays and traditions of the world's faiths. A list of books often recommended by teachers can be obtained by contacting Euraine Brooks at the First Amendment Center (703) 284-2809.

Calendars of religious and ethnic holidays can be obtained from the following organizations:

National Conference for Community and Justice
71 5th Avenue
New York, NY 10003
(212) 206-0006

Educational Extension Systems
P.O. Box 259
Clarks Summit, PA 18411
(800) 447-8561

avoided. The use of art, drama or literature with religious themes also is permissible if it serves a sound educational goal in the curriculum, but not if used as a vehicle for promoting religious belief.

What about Christmas?

Decisions about what to do in December should begin with the understanding that public schools may not sponsor religious devotions or celebrations; study about religious holidays does not extend to religious worship or practice. Does this mean that all seasonal activities must be banned from the schools? Probably not, and in any event, such an effort would be unrealistic. The resolution would seem to lie in devising holiday programs that serve an educational purpose for all students—programs that do not make students feel excluded or identified with a religion not their own. Holiday concerts in December may appropriately include music related to Christmas and Hanukkah, but religious music should not dominate. Any dramatic productions should emphasize the cultural aspects of the holidays. Nativity pageants or plays portraying the Hanukkah miracle are not appropriate in the public school setting. In short, while they may recognize the holiday season, none of December's school activities should have the purpose, or effect, of promoting or inhibiting religion.

What about religious objections to some holidays?

Students from certain religious traditions may ask to be excused from classroom discussions or activities related to particular holidays. Some holidays considered by many people to be secular (for example, Halloween and Valentine's Day) are viewed by others as having

Tips for Planning Religious Holidays in Public Schools

Before planning a religious holiday activity in a public school, ask the following questions:

1. Is this activity designed in any way to either promote or inhibit religion?

2. How does this activity serve the academic goals of the course, or the educational mission of the school?

3. Will any student or parent be made to feel like an outsider, not a full member of the community, by this activity?

4. If in December: Do we plan activities to teach about religious holidays at various times of the year or only in December?

5. Are we prepared to teach about the religious meaning of this holiday in a way that enriches students' understanding of history and cultures?

religious overtones. Excusal requests may be especially common in the elementary grades, where holidays often are marked by parties and similar non-academic activities. Such requests are routinely granted. In addition, some parents and students may make requests for excusals from discussions of certain holidays, even when these holidays are treated from an academic perspective. If focused on limited, specific discussions, such requests may be granted in order to strike a balance between the student's religious freedom and the school's interest in providing a well-rounded education. Administrators and teachers should understand that a policy or practice of excusing students from specific activities or discussions cannot be used as a rationale for school sponsorship of religious celebration or worship for the remaining students.

May students be absent for religious holidays?

Sensitive school policy on absences will take account of the religious needs and requirements of students. Students should be allowed a reasonable number of excused absences, without penalties, to observe religious holidays within their traditions. Students may be asked to complete makeup assignments or examinations in conjunction with such absences.

What steps should school districts take?

In a pluralistic society, public schools are places for persons of all faiths and none. Schools may neither promote nor denigrate any religion. In order to respect religious liberty and advance education, we recommend that each school district take the following steps:

1. Develop policies about the treatment of religious holidays in the curricula and inform parents of those policies.

2. Offer pre-service and in-service workshops to assist teachers and administrators in understanding the appropriate place of religious holidays in the schools.

3. Become familiar with the nature and needs of the religious groups in the school community.

4. Provide resources for teaching about religions and religious holidays in ways that are constitutionally permissible and educationally sound.

Religious Holidays and Public Schools: A Brief Legal Analysis

Although many controversies have arisen over religious holidays in public schools, the case law is scant. Because the Supreme Court has not ruled on the issue, there are no final or definitive answers.

The high court has ruled, however, that the government may not erect an explicitly religious symbol (such as a creche or menorah) unless it is part of a larger "secular" holiday display.[1] Many have criticized the Court's ruling, describing it as the "plastic reindeer test" — referring to the nonreligious symbols that must accompany the display. Interestingly, a majority of the justices has stated that Christmas trees, unlike creches and menorahs, have attained a secular status in our society and can be displayed standing alone. This does not mean that schools should erect Christmas trees during the holiday season, but only that they probably can. Many Americans continue to view Christmas trees as religious symbols, and for this reason schools may wish to be more sensitive than the law requires. The Court also has acknowledged approvingly that Christmas carols are frequently sung in public schools.

One federal appeals court has addressed the recognition of religious holidays by public schools. The decision, *Florey v. Sioux Falls School District*, upheld the school district's policy and was allowed to stand by the U.S. Supreme Court. It is frequently cited as the controlling case on this controversial issue.[2] The relevant portions of the policy were as follows:

It is accepted that no religious belief or nonbelief should be promoted by the school district or its employees, and none should be disparaged. Instead, the school district should encourage all students and staff members to appreciate and be tolerant of each other's religious views .... In that spirit of tolerance, students and staff members should be excused from participating in practices which are contrary to their religious beliefs unless there are clear issues of overriding concern that would prevent it.

The Sioux Falls School District recognizes that one of its educational goals is to advance the students' knowledge and appreciation of the role that our religious heritage has played in the social, cultural and historical development of civilization...

The practice of the District shall be as follows:

1. The several holidays throughout the year which have a religious and a secular basis may be observed in the public schools.

2. The historical and contemporary values and the origin of religious holidays may be explained in an unbiased and objective manner without sectarian indoctrination.

3. Music, art, literature and drama having religious themes or bases are permitted as part of the curriculum for school-sponsored activities and programs if presented in a prudent and objective manner and as a traditional part of the cultural and religious heritage of the particular holiday. *CONTINUED*

8 Religious Holidays in the Public Schools

4. The use of religious symbols such as a cross, menorah, crescent, Star of David, creche, symbols of Native American religions or other symbols that are a part of a religious holiday is permitted as a teaching aid or resource, provided such symbols are temporary in nature. Among these holidays are included Christmas, Easter, Passover, Hanukkah, St. Valentine's Day, St. Patrick's Day, Thanksgiving and Halloween.

5. The school district's calendar should be prepared so as to minimize conflicts with religious holidays of all faiths.[3]

It is important to note that the Sioux Falls policy was permissible, not required. A better policy might have included more non-Christian holidays such as Rosh Hashana, Ramadan and Yom Kippur. Moreover, particular practices and activities under such a policy, such as Nativity pageants and reenactments of the Hanukkah miracle, might still be unconstitutional.

Any teacher or administrator should ask herself the following questions as she plans holiday activities:

1. Do I have a distinct educational purpose in mind? If so, what is it? It should not be the purpose of public schools to celebrate or observe religious holidays.

2. If I use holidays as an opportunity to teach about religion, am I balanced and fair in my approach? If I teach about Christmas and Easter, for example, do I also teach about non-Christian holidays?

3. Does the planned activity have the primary effect of advancing or inhibiting religion? Does it, for example, promote one faith over another or even religion in general? Remember that the school's approach should be academic, not devotional. It is never appropriate for public schools to proselytize.

A common misconception is that it is permissible to promote Christianity at Christmas, provided that other religions receive similar treatment at other times. For example, some teachers may try to justify celebrating Christmas by celebrating Hanukkah. This approach is wrong. First, Hanukkah is not a major Jewish holiday and should not be equated with Christmas, one of the two most important holidays in the Christian year. Second, one violation of the First Amendment does not justify another. If it is wrong to promote religion in the public schools at Christmas, it is wrong every other day of the year. Instead of "balancing" Christmas with Hanukkah, teachers should work to ensure that all holiday activities focus on objective study about religion, not indoctrination.

We have discussed what schools should and shouldn't do regarding religious holidays, but what about the school's duty to accommodate students and teachers who wish to observe religious holidays on their own time? What obligation do schools have to accommodate these concerns?

CONTINUED

LEGAL ANALYSIS

Schools are not required to close on a particular religious holiday but may choose to do so as a matter of administrative convenience as, for example, when large numbers of students are likely to be absent. When schools choose not to close on particular holidays, conflicts may arise. Most states have laws permitting a certain number of excused absences for religious holidays. Where no statutory exemption exists, the First Amendment's Free Exercise clause would seem to require a reasonable number of excused absences for such religious observance.[4] In no event should a student be penalized for being absent from school to observe religious holidays.

A slightly different rule applies to teachers who wish to be absent to observe religious holidays. Title VII of the Civil Rights Act of 1964 requires school boards to make "reasonable accommodation" of their employees' religious needs. School boards may offer any accommodation that is reasonable, however, and are not required to accept the accommodation proposed by the employee.[5] Moreover, schools are not required to accommodate an employee's religious needs if doing so would cause "undue hardship" on the employer, such as disturbing the board's collective-bargaining agreement with the teachers' union or imposing more than *de minimis* costs on the employer.[6] Courts have split over whether schools may provide teachers with extra days off with pay in order to observe religious holidays. Schools that provide employees with paid "personal" days, however, should not be allowed to deny their use for religious observances.

The Authors

Endnotes

[1] *Lynch v. Donnelly,* 465 U.S. 688 (1984); *County of Allegheny v. American Civil Liberties Union,* 492 U.S. 573 (1989).

[2] See e.g. *Johnson v. Shiverman,* 658 S.W. 2d. 910 (Mo.App. 1983).

[3] 619 F.2d. 1311 (8th Cir.1980).

[4] See e.g. *Church of God v. Amarillo Independent School District,* 511 F.Supp. 613 (N.D. Tex. 1981), aff'd 670 F.2d. 46 (5th Cir. 1982).

[5] *Ansonia Board of Education v. Philbrook,* 479 U.S. 60 (1986).

[6] *T.W.A. v. Hardison,* 432 U.S. 63 (1977); *Estate of Thornton v. Caldor,* 472 U.S. 702 (1985).

8 Religious Holidays in the Public Schools

CHAPTER 9

Student Religious Clubs

FIRST AMENDMENT TO THE
UNITED STATES CONSTITUTION

The Equal Access Act: Questions and Answers is jointly sponsored by:

American Academy of Religion

American Association of School Administrators

American Federation of Teachers

American Jewish Committee

American Jewish Congress

Americans United Research Foundation

Association for Supervision and Curriculum Development

Baptist Joint Committee on Public Affairs

Christian Legal Society

Department of Education of the U.S. Conference of Catholic Bishops

First Amendment Center

General Conference of Seventh-day Adventists

National Association of Secondary School Principals

National Association of Evangelicals

National Conference for Community and Justice

National Council of Churches of Christ in the USA

National Council for the Social Studies

National Education Association

National PTA

National School Boards Association

The Equal Access Act became law on August 11, 1984, passing the Senate 88-11 and the House 337-77. Congress's primary purpose in passing the Act, according to the Supreme Court, was to end "perceived widespread discrimination" against religious speech in public schools. While Congress recognized the constitutional prohibition against government promotion of religion, it believed that non-school-sponsored student speech, including religious speech, should not be excised from the school environment.

The Supreme Court, by a vote of 8-1, held in *Westside Community Schools v. Mergens* (1990) that the Equal Access Act is constitutional. This chapter is designed to help school board members, administrators, teachers, parents, religious leaders and students understand and conform to the Act.

The title—*the Equal Access Act*—explains the essential thrust of the Act. There are three basic concepts.

The first is *nondiscrimination*. If a public secondary school permits student groups to meet for student-initiated activities not directly related to the school curriculum, it is required to treat all such student groups equally. This means the school cannot discriminate against any students conducting such meetings "on the basis of the religious, political, philosophical, or other content of the speech at such meetings." This language was used to make clear that religious speech was to receive equal treatment, not preferred treatment.

The second basic concept is protection of *student-initiated and student-led meetings*. The Supreme Court has held unconstitutional state-initiated and state-endorsed religious activities in the public schools. (This Act leaves the "school prayer" decisions undisturbed.) However, in upholding the constitutionality of the Act, the Court noted the "crucial difference between government speech endorsing religion, which the Establishment clause forbids, and private speech endorsing religion, which the Free Speech and Free Exercise clauses protect."

The third basic concept is *local control*. The Act does not limit the authority of the school to maintain order and discipline or to protect the well-being of students and faculty.

While the Act does not cover every specific situation, an understanding of the three basic concepts—as fleshed out by the questions and answers below—should be a sufficient guide for addressing most situations.

Many of the sponsors of these guidelines were actively involved in the debate over equal access. Some supported the Act, others remained neutral, and some opposed it. All of the sponsors, however, agree that the provisions of the Act need to be understood clearly as public secondary schools develop policies concerning student groups.

LEGAL INFO

9 — Student Religious Clubs

The Equal Access Act (20 U.S.C. 4071-74)

Denial of Equal Access Prohibited Sec. 4071.

(a) It shall be unlawful for any public secondary school which receives Federal financial assistance and which has a limited open forum to deny equal access or a fair opportunity to, or discriminate against, any students who wish to conduct a meeting within that limited open forum on the basis of the religious, political, philosophical, or other content of the speech at such meetings.

(b) A public secondary school has a limited open forum whenever such school grants an offering to or opportunity for one or more noncurriculum-related student groups to meet on school premises during noninstructional time.

(c) Schools shall be deemed to offer a fair opportunity to students who wish to conduct a meeting within its limited open forum if such school uniformly provides that—

    (1) the meeting is voluntary and student-initiated;

    (2) there is no sponsorship of the meeting by the school, the government, or its agents or employees;

    (3) employees or agents of the school or government are present at religious meetings only in a nonparticipatory capacity;

    (4) the meeting does not materially and substantially interfere with the orderly conduct of educational activities within the school; and

    (5) nonschool persons may not direct, conduct, control, or regularly attend activities of student groups.

(d) Nothing in this subchapter shall be construed to authorize the United States or any State or political subdivision thereof—

    (1) to influence the form or content of any prayer or other religious activity;

    (2) to require any person to participate in prayer or other religious activity;

CONTINUED

(3) to expend public funds beyond the incidental cost of providing the space for student-initiated meetings;

(4) to compel any school agent or employee to attend a school meeting if the content of the speech at the meeting is contrary to the beliefs of the agent or employee;

(5) to sanction meetings that are otherwise unlawful;

(6) to limit the rights of groups of students which are not of a specified numerical size; or

(7) to abridge the constitutional rights of any person.

(e) Notwithstanding the availability of any other remedy under the Constitution or the laws of the United States, nothing in this subchapter shall be construed to authorize the United States to deny or withhold Federal financial assistance to any school.

(f) Nothing in this subchapter shall be construed to limit the authority of the school, its agents or employees, to maintain order and discipline on school premises, to protect the well-being of students and faculty, and to assure that attendance of students at meetings is voluntary.

Definitions Sec. 4072. As used in this subchapter—

(1) The term "secondary school" means a public school which provides secondary education as determined by State law.

(2) The term "sponsorship" includes the act of promoting, leading, or participating in a meeting. The assignment of a teacher, administrator, or other school employee to a meeting for custodial purposes does not constitute sponsorship of the meeting.

(3) The term "meeting" includes those activities of student groups which are permitted under a school's limited open forum and are not directly related to the school curriculum.

(4) The term "noninstructional time" means time set aside by the school before actual classroom instruction begins or after actual classroom instruction ends.

Severabililty Sec. 4073.

If any provision of this subchapter or the application thereof to any person or circumstances is judicially determined to be invalid, the provisions of the remainder of the subchapter and the application to other persons or circumstances shall not be affected thereby.

Construction Sec. 4074.

The provisions of this subchapter shall supersede all other provisions of Federal law that are inconsistent with the provisions of this subchapter.

QUESTIONS *and* ANSWERS:
EQUAL ACCESS AND
THE PUBLIC SCHOOLS

The following questions and answers indicate how the act is to work:

What triggers the Equal Access Act?

The creation of a "limited open forum." A limited open forum is created whenever a public secondary school provides an opportunity for one or more "noncurriculum-related student groups" to meet on school premises during noninstructional time. The forum created is said to be "limited" because it is only the school's own students who can take advantage of the open forum. Outsiders are not granted an independent right of access by the Act.

Must a school board create a limited open forum for students?

No. The local school board has exclusive authority to determine whether it will create or maintain a limited open forum. However, if a school has a "limited open forum," it may not discriminate against a student group because of the content of the group's speech.

What is a "noncurriculum-related student group"?

In *Mergens*, the Supreme Court interpreted a noncurriculum-related student group to mean "any student group [or club] that does not directly relate to the body of courses offered by the school." According to the Court, a student group directly relates to a school's curriculum only if (1) the subject matter of the group is actually taught, or will soon be taught, in a regularly offered course; (2) the subject matter of the group concerns the body of courses as a whole; or (3) participation in the group is required for a particular course or results in academic credit.

Schools may not substitute their own definition of "noncurriculum-related student group" for that of the Court.

Did the Supreme Court give any examples of "noncurriculum-related student groups"?

The Court noted that unless a school could show that groups such as a chess club, stamp-collecting club, or community service club fell within the definition of curriculum-related set forth by the Court, they would be considered noncurriculum-related for purposes of the Act.

In *Mergens*, the Court found at least three groups that were noncurriculum-related for that school: (1) a scuba club, (2) a chess club, and (3) a service club. Each of these clubs was found to be noncurriculum-related because it did not meet the Court's criteria set forth in the question above.

What examples did the Court give of curriculum-related student groups?

The Court noted that "a French club would directly relate to the curriculum if a school taught French in a regularly offered course or planned to teach the subject in the near future. A school's student government would generally relate directly to the curriculum to the extent that it addresses concerns, solicits opinions and formulates proposals pertaining to the body of courses offered by the school. If participation in a school's band or orchestra were required for the band or orchestra classes, or resulted in academic credit, then those groups would also directly relate to the curriculum."

Who determines which student groups are, in fact, curriculum-related?

Local school authorities, subject to review by the courts. However, the Supreme Court has made clear that a school cannot defeat the intent of the Act by defining "curriculum-related" in a way that arbitrarily results in only those student clubs approved by the school being allowed to meet.

When can noncurriculum-related student groups meet?

A limited open forum requiring equal access may be established during "noninstructional time," which is defined as time set aside by the school before actual classroom instruction begins or after it ends.

Can noncurriculum-related student groups meet during the day?

The Equal Access Act is not triggered by student club meetings that occur only during instructional time. The constitutionality of allowing or disallowing student religious clubs to meet during instructional time has not been expressly ruled upon by the Supreme Court.

To what schools does the Act apply?

The Act applies only to public secondary schools (as defined by state law) that receive federal financial assistance.

May a school establish regulations for meetings that take place in its limited open forum?

Yes. The Act does not take away a school's authority to establish reasonable time, place and manner regulations for its limited open forum. For example, a school may establish a reasonable time period on any one school day, a combination of days or all school days. It may assign the rooms in which student groups can meet. It may enforce order and discipline during the meetings. The key is that time, place and manner regulations must be uniform and nondiscriminatory.

May schools promote, and teachers participate in, some club meetings and not others in a limited open forum?

Some of the Act's language implies that schools may not sponsor any noncurriculum-related club. Other language suggests that schools can sponsor all noncurriculum clubs except religious ones. Subsequent to the *Mergens* decision, some schools have in fact promoted, or assigned teachers to teach, drama or debate clubs and the like, even though the school does not offer formal instruction in these subjects or give credit to those who participate in such clubs. There may be other clubs (such as political clubs) for which school sponsorship is inappropriate.

School sponsorship of some noncurriculum-related student clubs does not mean, however, that a limited open forum does not exist or that non-sponsored clubs may not meet.

May a school require a minimum number of students to form a noncurriculum-related club?

Not if it "limit[s] the rights of groups of students." Care must be exercised that the school not discriminate against numerically small student groups that wish to establish a club. If the number of clubs begins to tax the available space in a particular school, one teacher might be used to monitor several small student groups meeting in the same large room. The key is to be flexible in accommodating student groups that want to meet.

What does "student-initiated" mean?

It means that the students themselves are seeking permission to meet and that they will direct and control the meeting. Teachers and other school employees may not initiate or direct such meetings, nor may outsiders.

9 Student Religious Clubs

May outsiders attend a student meeting?

Yes, if invited by the students and if the school does not have a policy barring all "nonschool persons." However, the nonschool persons "may not direct, conduct, control, or regularly attend activities of student groups."

A school may decide not to permit any nonschool persons to attend any club meetings, or it may limit the number of times during an academic year a nonschool person may be invited to attend.

Obviously, no nonschool person should be permitted to proselytize students who are not voluntarily attending the meeting to which the nonschool person is invited.

May teachers be present during student meetings?

Yes, but there are important limitations. For insurance purposes or because of state law or local school policy, teachers or other school employees are commonly required to be present during student meetings. In order to avoid any appearance of state endorsement of religion, teachers or employees are to be present at student religious meetings only in a "nonparticipatory capacity." The Act also prohibits teachers or other school officials from influencing the form or content of any prayer or other religious activity.

May a teacher or other school employee be required to be present at a student meeting if that person does not share the beliefs of the students?

The Act provides that no school employee may be required to attend a meeting "if the content of the speech at the meeting is contrary to the beliefs" of that employee. If a school establishes a limited open forum, however, it is responsible for supplying a monitor for every student group meeting if a monitor is required.*

Editor's Note: Although the endorsers of this guide agreed on this answer, legal experts are divided about whether or not school officials are required to provide a monitor.

Does the assignment of a teacher to a meeting for custodial purposes constitute sponsorship of the meeting?

No.

Does the expenditure of public funds for the incidental cost of providing the space (including utilities) for student-initiated meetings constitute sponsorship?

No.

If a school pays a teacher for monitoring a student religious club, does this constitute sponsorship?

Congressional debate apparently took for granted that payment of a school-required monitor for any club was an "incidental cost of providing the space for student-initiated meetings."

Does the use of school media to announce meetings of noncurriculum-related student groups constitute sponsorship of those meetings?

No. The Supreme Court has interpreted the Act to require schools to allow student groups meeting under the Act to use the school media—including the public address system, school paper and school bulletin board—to announce their meetings if other noncurriculum-related student groups are allowed to use the school media. Any policy concerning the use of school media must be applied to all noncurriculum-related student groups in a nondiscriminatory manner. Schools, however, may inform students that certain groups are not school-sponsored.

Do school authorities retain disciplinary control?

Yes. The Act emphasizes the authority of the school "to maintain order and discipline on school premises, to protect the well-being of students and faculty, and to assure that attendance of students at meetings is voluntary." Furthermore, the school must provide that the meeting "does not materially and substantially interfere with the orderly conduct of educational activities within the school." These two provisions, however, do not appear to authorize a school to prohibit certain student groups from meeting because of administrative inconvenience or speculative harm. For example, a group cannot be barred at a particular school solely because a similar student group at another school has caused problems.

What about groups that wish to advocate or discuss changes in existing law?

Students who wish to discuss controversial social and legal issues such as abortion, drinking age, the draft and alternative lifestyles may not be barred on the basis of the content of their speech. The school is not required, however, to permit meetings in which unlawful conduct occurs.

What if some students object to other students meeting?

The right of a lawful, orderly student group to meet does not depend on the approval of other students. All students enjoy the constitutional guarantee of free speech. It is the school's responsibility to maintain discipline in order that all student groups are afforded an equal opportunity to meet peacefully without harassment. The school must not allow a "hecklers' veto."

May any groups be excluded?

Yes. Student groups that are unlawful or that materially and substantially interfere with the orderly conduct of educational activities may be excluded. However, a student group cannot be denied equal access simply because its ideas are unpopular. Freedom of speech includes ideas the majority may find repugnant.

Must noncurriculum-related student groups have an open admissions policy?

The Act does not address this issue. There are, however, several federal, as well as state and local, civil rights laws that may be interpreted to prohibit student groups from denying admission on the basis of race, national origin, gender or handicap.

What may a school do to make it clear that it is not promoting, endorsing, or otherwise sponsoring noncurriculum-related student groups?

A school may issue a disclaimer that plainly states that in affording such student groups an opportunity to meet, it is merely making its facilities available, nothing more.

What happens if a school violates The Equal Access Act?

The law contemplates a judicial remedy. An aggrieved person may bring suit in a U.S. district court to compel a school to observe the law. Violations of equal access will not result in the loss of federal funds for the school. However, a school district could be liable for damages and the attorney's fees of a student group that successfully challenges a denial by the school board of its right to meet under the Act.

Should a school formulate a written policy for the operation of a limited open forum?

If a school decides to create a limited open forum or if such a forum already exists, it is strongly recommended that a uniform set of regulations be drawn up and made available to administrators, teachers, students, and parents. The importance of having such a document will become clear if the school either denies a student group the opportunity to meet or is forced to withdraw that opportunity. When the rules are known in advance, general acceptance is much easier to obtain.

What about situations not addressed in these guidelines?

Additional questions may be directed to the organizations listed as sponsors of these guidelines.*

Student Religious Clubs

*See Appendix for contact information for these organizations (listed on page 114).

CHAPTER 10

Student Religious Expression in Public Schools: United States Department of Education Guidelines

It can hardly be argued that either students or teachers
shed their constitutional rights to freedom of speech or
expression at the schoolhouse gate. This has been the
unmistakable holding of this Court for almost 50 years.

—Justice Abe Fortas
Tinker v. Des Moines School District
1969

RELIGIOUS EXPRESSION IN PUBLIC SCHOOLS: A STATEMENT OF PRINCIPLES

Student prayer and religious discussion

The Establishment Clause of the First Amendment does not prohibit purely private religious speech by students. Students, therefore, have the same right to engage in individual or group prayer and religious discussion during the school day as they do to engage in other comparable activity. For example, students may read their Bibles or other scriptures, say grace before meals, and pray before tests to the same extent they may engage in comparable nondisruptive activities. Local school authorities possess substantial discretion to impose rules of order and other pedagogical restrictions on student activities, but they may not structure or administer such rules to discriminate against religious activity or speech.

Generally, students may pray in a nondisruptive manner when not engaged in school activities or instruction, and subject to the rules that normally pertain in the applicable setting. Specifically, students in informal settings, such as cafeterias and hallways, may pray and discuss their religious views with each other, subject to the same rules of order as apply to other student activities and speech. Students may also speak to, and attempt to persuade, their peers about religious topics just as they do with regard to political topics. School officials, however, should intercede to stop student speech that constitutes harassment aimed at a student or a group of students.

Students may also participate in before- or after-school events with religious content, such as "see you at the flag pole" gatherings, on the same terms as they may participate in other noncurriculum activities on school premises. School officials may neither discourage nor encourage participation in such an event.

The right to engage in voluntary prayer or religious discussion free from discrimination does not include the right to have a captive audience listen or to compel other students to participate. Teachers and school administrators should ensure that no student is in any way coerced to participate in religious activity.

Graduation prayer and baccalaureates

Under current Supreme Court decisions, school officials may not mandate or organize prayer at graduation nor organize religious baccalaureate ceremonies. If a school generally opens its facilities to private groups, it must make its facilities available on the same terms to organizers of privately sponsored religious baccalaureate services. A school may not extend preferential treatment to baccalaureate ceremonies and may in some instances be obliged to disclaim official endorsement of such ceremonies.

Official neutrality regarding religious activity

Teachers and school administrators, when acting in those capacities, are representatives of the state and are prohibited by the Establishment clause from soliciting or encouraging religious activity, and from participating in such activity with students. Teachers and administrators also are prohibited from discouraging activity because of its religious content and from soliciting or encouraging antireligious activity.

Teaching about religion

Public schools may not provide religious instruction, but they may teach *about* religion, including the Bible or other scripture; the history of religion, comparative religion, the Bible (or other scripture)-as-literature, and the role of religion in the history of the United States and other countries all are permissible public school subjects. Similarly, it is permissible to consider religious influences on art, music, literature and social studies. Although public schools may teach about religious holidays, including their religious aspects, and may celebrate the secular aspects of holidays, schools may not observe holidays as religious events or promote such observance by students.

Student assignments

Students may express their beliefs about religion in the form of homework, artwork and other written and oral assignments free of discrimination based on the religious content of their submissions. Such home and classroom work should be judged by ordinary academic standards of substance and relevance and against other legitimate pedagogical concerns identified by the school.

10 Student Religious Expression in Public Schools: United States Department of Education Guidelines

Religious literature

Students have a right to distribute religious literature to their schoolmates on the same terms as they are permitted to distribute other literature that is unrelated to school curriculum or activities. Schools may impose the same reasonable time, place and manner or other constitutional restrictions on distribution of religious literature as they do on nonschool literature generally, but they may not single out religious literature for special regulation.

Religious excusals

Subject to applicable state laws, schools enjoy substantial discretion to excuse individual students from lessons that are objectionable to the student or the students' parents on religious or other conscientious grounds. However, students generally do not have a federal right to be excused from lessons that may be inconsistent with their religious beliefs or practices. School officials may neither encourage nor discourage students from availing themselves of an excusal option.

Released time

Subject to applicable state laws, schools have the discretion to dismiss students to off-premises religious instruction, provided that schools do not encourage or discourage participation or penalize those who do not attend. Schools may not allow religious instruction by outsiders on school premises during the school day.

Teaching values

Though schools must be neutral with respect to religion, they may play an active role with respect to teaching civic values and virtue and the moral code that holds us together as a community. The fact that some of these values are held also by religions does not make it unlawful to teach them in school.

Student garb

Schools enjoy substantial discretion in adopting policies relating to student dress and school uniforms. Students generally have no federal right to be exempted from religiously neutral and generally applicable school dress rules based on their religious beliefs or practices; however, schools may not single out religious attire in general, or attire of a particular religion, for prohibition or regulation. Students may display religious messages on items of clothing to the same extent that they are permitted to display other comparable messages. Religious messages may not be singled out for suppression, but rather are subject to the same rules as generally apply to comparable messages.

THE EQUAL ACCESS ACT

The Equal Access Act is designed to ensure that, consistent with the First Amendment, student religious activities are accorded the same access to public school facilities as are student secular activities. Based on decisions of the federal courts as well as its interpretations of the Act, the Department of Justice has advised that the Act should be interpreted as providing, among other things, that:

General provisions

Student religious groups at public secondary schools have the same right of access to school facilities as is enjoyed by other comparable student groups. Under the Equal Access Act, a school receiving federal funds that allows one or more student noncurriculum-related clubs to meet on its premises during noninstructional time may not refuse access to student religious groups.

Prayer services and worship exercises covered

A meeting, as defined and protected by the Equal Access Act, may include a prayer service, Bible reading, or other worship exercise.

Equal access to means of publicizing meetings

A school receiving federal funds must allow student groups meeting under the Act to use the school media—including the public address system, the school newspaper and the school bulletin board—to announce their meetings on the same terms as other noncurriculum-related student groups are allowed to use the school media. Any policy concerning the use of school media must be applied to all noncurriculum-related student groups in a nondiscriminatory matter. Schools, however, may inform students that certain groups are not school-sponsored.

Lunch-time and recess covered

A school creates a limited open forum under the Equal Access Act, triggering equal access rights for religious groups, when it allows students to meet during their lunch periods or other noninstructional time during the school day, as well as when it allows students to meet before and after the school day.

Revised May 1998

Student Religious Expression in Public Schools: United States Department of Education Guidelines

LIST OF ORGANIZATIONS THAT CAN ANSWER QUESTIONS ON RELIGIOUS EXPRESSION IN PUBLIC SCHOOLS

Religious Action Center of Reform Judaism

Name: Rabbi David Saperstein
Address: 2027 Massachusetts Ave., NW, Washington, DC 20036
Phone: (202) 387-2800
Fax: (202) 667-9070
E-mail: rac@uahc.org
Web site: www.cdinet.com/RAC/

American Association of School Administrators

Name: Barbara Knisely
Address: 1801 N. Moore St., Arlington, VA 22209
Phone: (703) 528-0700
Fax: (703) 841-1543
E-mail: BKnisely@aasa.org
Web site: www.aasa.org

American Jewish Congress

Name: Marc Stern
Address: 15 East 84th Street, New York, NY 10028
Phone: (212) 360-1545
Fax: (212) 861-7056
E-mail: Marc_S_AJC@aol.com

National PTA

Name: Maribeth Oakes
Address: 1090 Vermont Ave., NW, Suite 1200, Washington, DC 20005
Phone: (202) 289-6790
Fax: (202) 289-6791
E-mail: m_oakes@pta.org
Web site: www.pta.org

Christian Legal Society

Name: Gregory Baylor
Address: 4208 Evergreen Lane, #222, Annandale, VA 22003
Phone: (703) 642-1070
Fax: (703) 642-1075
E-mail: clrf@mindspring.com
Web site: www.christianlegalsociety.org

National Association of Evangelicals

Name: Richard Cizik
Address: 1023 15th Street, NW #500, Washington, DC 20005
Phone: (202) 789-1011
Fax: (202) 842-0392
E-mail: oga@nae.net
Web site: www.nae.net

National School Boards Association

Name: Julie Underwood
Address: 1680 Duke Street, Alexandria, VA 22314
Phone: (703) 838-6710
Fax: (703) 548-5613
E-mail: junderwood@nsba.org
Web site: www.nsba.org

First Amendment Center

Name: Charles Haynes
Address: 1101 Wilson Blvd., Arlington, VA 22209
Phone: (703) 528-0800
Fax: (703) 284-2879
E-mail: chaynes@freedomforum.org
Web site: www.firstamendmentcenter.org

CHAPTER 11

Student Religious Practices

FIRST AMENDMENT TO THE
UNITED STATES CONSTITUTION

Our first challenge in America today is simply to open our eyes to these changes, to discover America anew, and to explore the many ways in which the new immigration has changed the religious landscape of our cities and towns, our neighborhoods and schools.

—Diana L. Eck
A New Religious America

Many school districts are making efforts to inform administrators and teachers about the religious practices of their students. Knowledge about students' religious needs and requirements promotes understanding between parents and school officials and prepares teachers for questions or concerns when they arise.

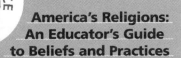

America's Religions: An Educator's Guide to Beliefs and Practices

Teacher Ideas Press presents Benjamin Hubbard, John Hatfield and James Santucci's guide to the beliefs and practices of a number of the world's religions. Designed specifically for teachers, the book examines each religious group in terms of its origins, beliefs, sacred scriptures, practices, main subgroups, common misunderstandings and stereotypes, and classroom concerns.

This book is available from Teacher Ideas Press, Dept. B40, P.O. Box 6633, Englewood, CO 80155-6633; by phone at 1-800-237-6124, ext. 1; or on the web at www.lu.com/tip.

Adherence to religious requirements such as special diet or dress is the responsibility of parents and students, not of the public school. In some cases, however, parents may request special accommodation (e.g., excusal from participation in certain school parties or events). Most of these requests may be easily granted without disrupting the educational work of the school.

In rare cases, requests for accommodation may be impossible to grant for practical or constitutional reasons. Even in these instances, some accommodation may be offered. For example, schools are unable to prepare special foods for some religious needs, but they can label foods and offer a variety of choices. When considering these requests, school officials should use the First Amendment framework discussed in Chapters 2 and 4 as a guide to treating the claims of religious conscience seriously and sensitively without putting the school in the position of endorsing or sponsoring religion.

The following information about student religious practices was compiled by the Religious Community Task Force in the Dallas Independent School District as part of a comprehensive policy on religion and schools issues. It is included here as an example of how a large, religiously diverse school district has acted to inform teachers and administrators about the religious practices of many students in the community. For the complete policy of the DISD and for more information about the task force that helped create the policy, contact Jane Didear, Communications Division, Dallas Independent School District, 3700 Ross Avenue, Dallas, TX 75204.

Religious Practices Within Dallas Public Schools

A NOTE FROM THE RELIGIOUS COMMUNITY TASK FORCE

The following information was collected from members of the Dallas Public Schools Religious Community Task Force . The items listed are general in nature. Some situations described are a blend of religious/ethnic/cultural practices which might have an impact on students during the school day. If you have questions or need more information about any of the items mentioned, inquiries are invited.

Most of the members of the Task Force represent large organizations, within which are many different levels of religious observation. Some students within each faith may follow all the dictates of the religion and others may observe only a few rituals. If the school can allow those things which do not disrupt normal classroom operations to occur, it avoids conflict for the student who feels under obligation to comply with family and religious mandates. If there must be an accommodation made for a practice to occur away from class, please arrange that through the principal.

Regarding the following material: Task force members have submitted the following information for easy reference, to cover areas which do not follow general cultural trends. The symbolic reference codes below indicate:

 Medical restrictions

 Special diet or foods

 Particular dress/clothing

 Observances or rituals during school hours

 Possible absences due to High Holy Days

Various Protestant Christian Traditions	The following Christian denominations on the task force: **Baptists, Disciples, Episcopalians, Evangelicals, Lutherans, Methodists** and **Presbyterians**, have students in Dallas Public Schools whose beliefs and practices are culturally predominant, and therefore do not require special accommodations during school time. For example, many families worship on Sunday mornings and/or on Sunday and Wednesday evenings, when school is not in session. There are no medical, dietary, clothing or holiday needs that require special attention. However, some denominations report that extracurricular school activities and parent conferences conflict with some evening worship.

Baha'i

 None.

 Students 15 years and older may refrain from eating or drinking during school hours between March 2-20.

 None.

 None.

 Eleven holy days throughout the year, during which students may be absent or not allowed to do ordinary work.

Buddhism

 Ethnic medical attitudes may differ.

 Students may prefer to be vegetarians; and some may abstain from dairy products and eggs.

 None.

 Beliefs do not include the existence of a creator. Terms such as idol-worshippers or heathens are offensive to these students. Students follow five moral Precepts & the Noble Eightfold Path which include respect for all animal and human life. Some students may object to participation in the dissection of animals and insects.

 Holy Days established on lunar calendar: Birth of the Buddha; Bodhi Day; the Cambodian, Laotian and Vietnamese New Year.

11 | Student Religious Practices

Christian Science

 Reliance on prayer for effective health care. Legal exemptions from innoculations, vaccinations and immunizations. Request exemption from disease study. No medications, no physical exams, no testing of vision, hearing or intelligence.

 No caffeine, tobacco or alcoholic beverages.

 None.

 None.

 None.

Church of Jesus Christ of the Latter Day Saints *(Mormon)*

 None.

 No coffee, tea, tobacco, alcoholic beverages.

 Modest clothing.

 None.

 Normal school holidays.

Religious Practices

Eastern Orthodox

(includes: Antiochan, Armenian, Ethiopian (Coptic), Greek, Kenyan, Korean, Lebanese, Mexican, Syrian, and 5 Slavonic peoples: Bulgarian, Romanian, Russian, Serbian and Ukrainian)

 None.

 Fasting (abstinence) is the refraining from eating identified foods and is not considered a special diet. Certain Feast Days are observed with a fast either prior to or on the feast day itself. If a student is fasting, he/she may: 1) fast every Wednesday and Friday except for designated fast-free periods, or 2) fast from at least meat or dairy products. Students who observe strict fasts may bring food from home. Lunchroom menus provide a varied selection for either fast.

 None required.

 None other than fasting, which occurs during lunch hour; no academic interruptions.

 Students may attend services on their nameday to celebrate the Saint whose name they bear; or the following: Elevation of the Cross, beginning of the 40 Day Fast of the Nativity; Nativity; Epiphany; Great Lent; Annunciation of the Virgin Mary; Holy Week; Pasca (Resurrection) and Ascension Thursday.

Hare Krishna

 No animal-derived medications.

 Lacto-vegetarians (do not eat meat, fish, fowl or eggs).

 Male students may have small tail of hair at back of head (Sikha).

 None. Students respectful of authority.

 Dates according to lunar calendar. Janmastami; Vyasa-Puja Day; Diwali; Govardhana-Puja; Srila Prabhupada's Disappearance Day; Nityananda's Appearance Day; Gaura Purnima; Ram Navami; Nirshringhadev's Appearance Day.

Hinduism

 None.

No animal-derived medications.

Students may be strict vegetarians.

An area at home or office is often designated as an altar.

Students may have paint-like mark on the forehead from morning worship, usually done with family at home.

 Dates according to Lunar calendar. Diwali; Govardhana-Puja, Ram Navami.

Islam

Males examined by male doctors; females examined by female doctors. No injections during Ramadan.

No alcohol. No pork and any blood. No animals unless they are slaughtered (with prayer). Fish, if caught alive, may be eaten.

Males must cover bodies from abdomen to knees; females must cover all except face, hands, feet.

 Worship prayers (Salah) five times: at dawn, noon, afternoon, sunset and night. Students need silent and convenient places to perform daily prayers. Weekly Friday noon prayers for males. Polytheistic or atheistic statements and negative words against any Holy Books may not show respect for students.

Ramadan Feast or Eidul-Fitr (end of fasting month); Eidul-Adha. Dates depend on actual sighting of the moon.

Jain Society Temple

None

No eating of root plants (for some members)

None

Fasting from 1-14 days.

Late August through early September.

Jehovah's Witnesses

Parents may request no blood transfusions.

No addictive or habit-forming drugs or tobacco.

None.

 The only celebration is the memorial of Christ's death (lunar calendar—the first full moon after spring, after sunset).

 Views on nationalism prohibit participation in flag saluting, the singing of national anthems or voting on elective offices. No participation in any religious celebrations or national holidays, such as Christmas, Easter, Thanksgiving, Halloween, Valentine's Day, etc. Areas that are a matter of conscience include extra-curricular activities such as sports, cheerleading, dating, attending parties or joining clubs. Alternative classroom materials and assignments could be directed to seasons versus holidays (such as "winter" rather than Christmas).

Judaism

 None.

 Some boys may wear a skull cap and/or a fringed undergarment under their shirts. Some girls may dress with arms and legs covered.

 Some students may ask to wash hands or pray before a meal. Some students may refrain from doing school projects that occur on Friday evenings and/or Saturdays before sundown. Some students will not be able to participate in musical experiences and on programs whose content affirms religious positions that differ from their own.

 Kosher food (marked with Kosher seal, "K", Ⓤ, etc.). Meat and chicken slaughtered by ritual law allowed. No shellfish or fish that do not have scales. No mixing of milk and meat products. No pork products. During Passover, a restricted diet allows no leavened food items such as bread; other holidays may require fasting.

 Holidays begin at sundown the day before. Sabbath begins at sundown each Friday night and is complete at sundown on Saturdays. *Rosh Hashanah*; Yom Kippur; *Sukkot* ; Shemini Atzeret; Simchat Torah; Chanukah; Purim; *Passover* (first two and last two days of eight); and *Shavuot*. (Holidays in italics may be observed for two days.)

Student Religious Practices 11

Religious Practices, *continued*

Native American Religions
(American Indians: 114 tribes)

 None.

 None.

 The Pueblo Indians of New Mexico, a few of whom attend Dallas Public schools, observe religious feast days throughout the year. Importance of attendance at religious or healing ceremonies in Texas, Oklahoma, New Mexico, South Dakota or Arizona is related to the tribe with which the student is affiliated; children are expected to accompany their parents. Some tribes have "days of mourning" or "mourning periods" for the deceased of immediate or extended-family members.

Longer hair length for some male students; some older high school students wear medicine bags which may be seen conspicuously. Beaded and silver-crafted bolo ties. Girls wear hair/braid tie and beaded hair combs.

Religious observances vary from tribe to tribe. Students' practices and self image are derived from the tribes in which they are enrolled. Dallas Schools observe American Indian Heritage Month in November. The Parents Advisory Committee of the American Indian Education Program plans various cultural enrichment activities for the month.

Roman Catholic

 No "contraceptive" teaching.

 No meat on Ash Wednesday or Fridays of Lent, for students 14 or older. There is a period of fasting during the 40 days between Ash Wednesday and Easter.

 Modest. Some wear religious medals. Ashes are placed on the foreheads of Catholics on Ash Wednesday as reminder of mortality.

Sign of the Cross before taking a test, before meals, as an act of thanksgiving or petition.

 Holy Days include: Assumption of Blessed Virgin Mary; All Saints' Day; All Souls' Day; Immaculate Conception of the Virgin Mary; Our Lady of Guadalupe (preceded by 9 days of special prayers and services); Advent, 4 weeks before Christmas, observed as a "waiting" period; The Posada, celebrated 9 days before Christmas, with visiting each evening to different homes and churches; Christmas Day; Mary, Mother of God; Lent, 40 days before Easter; Ascension Thursday; Pentecost. *Special note:* Many Hispanic families travel to their native countries for Holy Week celebrations at Easter time. Family ties are strengthened by summer visits to grandparents.

Seventh Day Adventists

 None.

 No pork or pork products. May prefer to be lacto-vegetarians. No habit forming drugs, alcohol or tobacco.

Modest dress.

None.

 Sabbath begins at sundown Friday and concludes at sundown on Saturday. Students may not be able to participate in school events on Friday nights.

Sikh

 None.

 No alcohol or tobacco.

 Baisakhi (Brotherhood), Birthday of Guru Nanak Dev.

None.

Boys wear headgear or turbans.

Unitarian/ Universalists

 None.

 None.

 None.

Families would like to have their children participate in public school activities without having them required to pray publicly. Students have the choice of whether or not to salute flags or pledge certain allegiances.

 During the spring, 13-14 year old students are often taken to U/U historic sites in other parts of the country.

Zoroastrian

 None.

 None.

 Muslin undershirts with wool cords at waist for boys and girls (may be taken off for sports).

None.

 New Year at Vernal Equinox, usually during March of each year.

Quick reference symbolic codes:

 Medical restrictions

 Special diet or foods

 Particular dress/clothing

Observances or rituals during school hours

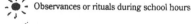 Possible absences due to High Holy Days

For more information from RCTF members, call Dallas Schools Communications Department, 989-8329

CHAPTER 12

A Parent's Guide to Religion in the Public Schools*

*A joint publication of the National PTA and the First Amendment Center

The Citizens of the United States of America have a right
to applaud themselves for having given to mankind
examples of an enlarged and liberal policy: a policy
worthy of imitation. All possess alike liberty of
conscience and immunities of citizenship. It is now no
more that toleration is spoken of, as if it was by the
indulgence of one class of people, that another enjoyed
the exercise of their inherent natural rights. For happily
the Government of the United States, which gives to
bigotry no sanction, to persecution no assistance,
requires only that they who live under its protection
should demean themselves as good citizens, in giving it
on all occasions their effectual support.

George Washington
Letter to the Hebrew Congregation in Newport
Rhode Island
1790

*Congress shall make
no law respecting an
establishment of religion
or prohibiting the free
exercise*

Parents are recognized as having the primary responsibility for the upbringing of their children, including education. For this reason, parents need to be fully informed about school policies and practices, including all issues concerning religion and religious liberty in public education.

The following questions and answers are intended to help parents understand the religious liberty rights of students and the appropriate role for religion in the public school curriculum. A number of recent documents represent a growing consensus among many religious and educational groups about the constitutional and educational role of religion in public schools.[1] This pamphlet is designed to build on these agreements, and to encourage communities to find common ground when they are divided.

The following questions and answers provide general information on the subject of religious expression and practices in schools. The answers are based on First Amendment religious liberty principles as currently interpreted by the courts and agreed to by a wide range of religious and educational organizations. If parents have specific legal questions, the services of a qualified attorney should be sought.

Keep in mind, however, that the law alone cannot answer every question. Parents in each community must work with school officials to do not only what is constitutional, but also what is right for all citizens. The religious liberty principles of the First Amendment provide the civic framework within which we are able to debate our differences, to understand one another and to forge school policies that serve the common good in public education.

A Parent's Guide
to Religion in the
Public Schools

12

[1] One of these documents is a presidential directive sent to school superintendents from the U.S. Department of Education (see Chapter 10). Another document, "Religion in the Public Schools: A Joint Statement of Current Law," has been endorsed by a broad range of religious organizations. It is available by writing: "Religion in the Public Schools" 15 East 84th St., Suite 501, New York, NY 10028.

FINDING COMMON GROUND

1. In our community we want to work together to address religion-in-schools issues. How do we go about finding common ground?

Parents and school officials in many local communities have had success finding common ground using the following strategies:

Include all of the stakeholders. Because public schools belong to all citizens, they must model the democratic process and constitutional principles in the development of policies and curricula. Policy decisions by officials or governing bodies should be made only after appropriate involvement of those affected by the decisions and with due consideration of those holding dissenting views.

Listen to all sides. If we are to build trust and to truly listen to one another, school officials must acknowledge what is valid about criticism of school policies and practices, particularly concerning the treatment of religion and religious perspectives. At the same time, parents with deep religious convictions need to acknowledge that the vast majority of public school administrators and teachers do not intend to be hostile to religion and want to be fair in their treatment of parents and students.

Work for comprehensive policies. Many school districts contribute to confusion and distrust by having no policies concerning many of the issues addressed in this publication. By working with parents to develop comprehensive policies, schools demonstrate the importance of taking religious liberty seriously.

Be pro-active. School districts unprepared for controversy fare poorly when a conflict arises. Where there are no policies (or policies are not known or supported by parents), there is a much greater likelihood of lawsuits, shouting matches at school-board meetings and polarization in the community. A pro-active approach takes seriously the importance of articulating the proper role for religion and religious perspectives in the public schools. The resulting policies and practices create a climate of trust in the community and demonstrate the public schools' active commitment to the guiding principles of our democracy.

Commit to civil debate. Conflict and debate are vital in a democracy. Yet, if we are going to live with our deepest differences, then *how* we debate, and not only *what* we debate, is critical. Personal attacks, name-calling, ridicule and similar tactics destroy the fabric of our society and undermine the educational mission of our schools. All parties should treat one another with civility and respect and should strive to be accurate and fair. Through constructive dialogue we have much to learn from one another.

RELIGIOUS LIBERTY AND PUBLIC SCHOOLS

2. Is there general agreement on how religious faith should be treated in public schools under the First Amendment?

Yes. In a recent statement of principles, a broad range of religious and educational groups agreed to the following description of religious liberty and public schools within the First Amendment framework:

> Public schools may not inculcate nor inhibit religion. They must be places where religion and religious conviction are treated with fairness and respect.

> Public schools uphold the First Amendment when they protect the religious liberty rights of students of all faiths or none. Schools demonstrate fairness when they ensure that the curriculum includes study about religion, where appropriate, as an important part of a complete education.[2]

[2] The full text of "Religious Liberty, Public Education, and the Future of American Democracy: A Statement of Principles," may be found in Chapter 2.

STUDENT RELIGIOUS EXPRESSION

3. Does this mean that students may express their faith while in school?

Yes. Schools should respect the right of students to engage in religious activity and discussion.

Generally, individual students are free to pray, read their scriptures, discuss their faith and invite others to join their particular religious group. Only if a student's behavior is disruptive or coercive should it be prohibited. No student should be allowed to harass or pressure others in a public school setting.

If it is relevant to the subject under consideration and meets the requirements of the assignment, students also have the right to express their religious views during a class discussion or as part of a written assignment or art activity.

STUDENT PRAYER

4. May students pray together in public schools?

Yes. Students are free to pray alone or in groups, as long as the activity is not disruptive and does not infringe upon the rights of others. These activities must be truly voluntary and student-initiated. For example, students are permitted to gather around the flagpole for prayer before school begins, as long as the event is not sponsored by the school and other students are not pressured to attend. Students do not have a right to force a captive audience to participate in religious exercises.

12

A Parent's Guide to Religion in the Public Schools

5. Didn't the Supreme Court rule against student prayer in public schools?

No. The Supreme Court has struck down state-sponsored or state-organized prayer in public schools. The Court has interpreted the First Amendment to mean that government must be neutral among religions and between religion and nonreligion. This means that school officials may not organize, mandate or participate in student religious activities, including prayer. A moment of silence, however, may be led by school officials, as long as it does not promote prayer over other types of quiet contemplation.

6. Does this mean that students may offer prayers at graduation ceremonies?

Not necessarily. Lower courts are divided about whether a student may offer prayers at graduation exercises. Parents should seek legal advice about what rules apply in their state.

Some schools create a "free-speech forum" at school-sponsored events, during which time students are free to express themselves religiously or otherwise. Such a forum, however, would have to be open to all kinds of speech, including speech critical of religion or the school.

BACCALAUREATE SERVICES

7. What about baccalaureate services?

Although public schools may not sponsor religious baccalaureate ceremonies, parents, faith groups and other community organizations are free to sponsor such services for students who wish to attend. The school may announce the baccalaureate in the same way it announces other community events. If the school allows community groups to rent or otherwise use its facilities after-hours, then a privately sponsored baccalaureate may be held on campus under the same terms offered to any private group.

TEACHING ABOUT RELIGION

8. Is it constitutional to teach about religion in public schools?

Yes. The Supreme Court has indicated many times that teaching about religion, as distinguished from religious indoctrination, is an important part of a complete education. The public school's approach to religion in the curriculum must be academic, not devotional.

Study about religion belongs in the curriculum wherever it naturally arises. On the secondary level, the social studies, literature and the arts offer many opportunities for the inclusion of information about religions—their ideas and practices. On the elementary level, natural opportunities arise in discussions of the family and community life and in instruction about festivals and different cultures.

Religion may also be studied in special courses. Some secondary schools, for example, offer electives in "World Religions," "Bible as/in Literature," and "Religion in America."

RELIGIOUS HOLIDAYS

9. How should religious holidays be treated in the schools?

Religious holidays offer opportunities to teach about religion in elementary and secondary schools. Teaching about religious holidays, which is permissible, is different from celebrating religious holidays, which is not. Study of holidays serves academic goals of educating students about history and cultures as well as about the traditions of particular religions.

The use of religious symbols as examples of religious or cultural heritage is permissible as a teaching aid or resource. Religious symbols should only be displayed on a temporary basis as part of the academic program.

Sacred music may be sung or played as part of the school's academic program. School concerts that present a variety of selections may include religious music. The use of music, art, drama or literature with religious themes is permissible if it serves a sound educational goal in the curriculum, but not if used as a vehicle for promoting religious belief.

EXCUSAL REQUESTS

10. May students be excused from parts of the curriculum for religious reasons?

Whenever possible, school officials should try to accommodate the requests of parents and students for excusal from classroom discussions or activities for religious reasons. If focused on a specific discussion, assignment, or activity, such requests should be routinely granted in order to strike a balance between the student's religious freedom and the school's interest in providing a well-rounded education.

If it is proved that particular lessons substantially burden a student's free exercise of religion and if the school cannot prove a compelling interest in requiring attendance, some courts may require schools to excuse the student.

STUDENT RELIGIOUS CLUBS

11. May students form religious clubs in public schools?

Under the federal Equal Access Act,[3] secondary public schools receiving federal funds must allow students to form religious clubs if the school allows other noncurriculum-related clubs to meet during noninstructional time. "Noncurriculum-related" means any club not directly related to the courses offered by the school. Student religious clubs may have access to school facilities and media on the same basis as other noncurriculum-related student clubs.

The Equal Access Act protects the rights of students to form religious clubs. Outside adults may not direct or regularly attend meetings of such clubs. Teachers may be present at religious club meetings as monitors, but they may not participate in club activities.

Public schools are free to prohibit any club activities that are illegal or that would cause substantial disruption of the school.[4]

STUDENT RELIGIOUS GARB

12. May students wear religious garb and display religious symbols in public schools?

Yes. Students who must wear religious garb such as head scarves or yarmulkes should be permitted to do so in school. Students may also display religious messages on clothing to the same extent that other messages are permitted.

DISTRIBUTION OF RELIGIOUS LITERATURE

13. May students distribute religious literature in the schools?

Generally, students have a right to distribute religious literature on public school campuses subject to reasonable time, place and manner restrictions imposed by the school. This means that the school may specify at what times the distribution may occur (e.g., lunch hour or before or after classes begin), where it may occur (e.g., outside the school office) and how it may occur (e.g., from fixed locations as opposed

[3] See 20 United States Code Section 4071 to 4074.
[4] For comprehensive guidelines on how to interpret the Equal Access Act, consult Chapter 9.

to roving distribution). These restrictions should be reasonable and must apply evenly to all non-school student literature.

Public schools may prohibit the distribution of some literature altogether. Some examples would be materials that are obscene, defamatory or disruptive of the educational environment.

RELEASED TIME

14. May students be released for off-campus religious instruction during the school day?

Yes. The Supreme Court has long recognized that public schools may choose to create off-campus released-time programs as a means of accommodating the needs of religious students and parents. The schools may not encourage or discourage participation or penalize students who do not attend.

CHARACTER EDUCATION

15. What is the relationship between religion and character education in public schools?

Parents are the first and most important moral educators of their children. Thus, public schools should develop character-education programs only in close partnership with parents and the community. Local communities need to work together to identify the core moral and civic virtues that they wish to be taught and modeled in all aspects of school life.[5]

In public schools, where teachers may neither promote nor denigrate religion, the core moral and civic values agreed to in the community may be taught if done so without religious indoctrination. At the same time, core values should not be taught in such a way as to suggest that religious authority is unnecessary or unimportant. Sound character- education programs affirm the value of religious and philosophical commitments and avoid any suggestion that morality is simply a matter of individual choice without reference to absolute truth.

A Parent's Guide to Religion in the Public Schools

[5] The Character Education Partnership provides complete information on how to start a character education program and a clearinghouse of character education resources. Contact the Character Education Partnership at 1025 Connecticut Ave. NW, Suite 1011, Washington, DC 20036 or call (800) 988-8081. Web site: www.character.org.

CHAPTER 13

Character Education*

*The contents of this chapter are from the Character Education Partnership and are used by permission.

FIRST AMENDMENT TO THE
UNITED STATES CONSTITUTION

We must remember that intelligence is not enough.

Intelligence plus character—that is the goal of true education.

—Martin Luther King Jr.,
Speech at Morehouse College
1948

Is there no virtue among us? If there be not, we are in a wretched situation. No theoretical checks - no form of government can render us secure. To suppose that any form of government will secure liberty or happiness without virtue in the people is a chimerical idea.

—James Madison

DEFINING AND UNDERSTANDING CHARACTER EDUCATION

What is character education?

Character education is a national movement creating schools that foster ethical, responsible and caring young people by modeling and teaching good character through emphasis on universal values that we all share. It is the intentional, proactive effort by schools, districts and states to instill in their students important core ethical values such as caring, honesty, fairness, responsibility and respect for self and others. Character education is not a "quick fix." It provides long-term solutions that address moral, ethical and academic issues of growing concern to our society and key to the safety of our schools.

- Character education not only cultivates minds, it nurtures hearts.
- Character education gets to the heart of the matter – literally.

Why do we need character education?

As Dr. Thomas Lickona, author of *Educating for Character*, stated, "Moral education is not a new idea. It is, in fact, as old as education itself. Down through history, in countries all over the world, education has had two great goals: to help young people become smart and to help them become good." Good character is not formed automatically; it is developed over time through a sustained process of teaching, example, learning and practice. It is developed through character education. The intentional teaching of good character is particularly important in today's society since our youth face many opportunities and dangers unknown to earlier generations. They are bombarded with many more negative influences through the media and other external sources prevalent in today's culture. At the same time, there are many more day-to-day pressures impinging on the time that parents and children have together. Studies show that children spend only 38.5 minutes a week (33.4 hours a year) in meaningful conversation with their parents, while they spend 1,500 hours watching television. (American Family Research Council, 1990 and *Harper's,* November 1999.) Since children spend about 900 hours a year in school, it is essential that schools resume a proactive role in assisting families and communities by developing caring, respectful environments where students learn core, ethical values. In order to create our schools as the caring and respectful communities we know they can be, we must look deeper. We must be intentional, proactive and comprehensive in our work to encourage the development of good character in young people.

How does character education work?

To be effective, character education must include the entire school community and must be infused throughout the entire school curriculum and culture. Character education promotes core values in all phases of school life and includes proactive strategies and practices that help children not only understand core ethical values, but to care about and act upon them. Based on research by the nation's leading character education experts, CEP's Eleven Principles of Effective Character Education,™ provide guidelines for the elements needed for **effective, comprehensive** character education.

1. Promotes core ethical values.
2. Teaches students to understand, care about, and act upon these core ethical values.
3. Encompasses all aspects of the school culture.
4. Fosters a caring school community.
5. Offers opportunities for moral action.
6. Supports academic achievement.
7. Develops intrinsic motivation.
8. Includes whole-staff involvement.
9. Requires positive leadership of staff and students.
10. Involves parents and community members.
11. Assesses results and strives to improve.

Schools: According to Lickona, when a comprehensive approach to character education is used, a positive moral culture is created in the school—a total school environment that supports the values taught in the classroom. This is accomplished through the leadership of the principal, schoolwide discipline, a sense of community, democratic student government, a moral community among adults and opportunities to address moral concerns. Schools recruit parents and the community as partners and foster caring beyond the classroom by using inspiring role models and opportunities for community service to help students learn to care by giving care.

13 Character Education

Teachers: Teachers act as caregivers, models and mentors, treating students with love and respect, setting a good example, supporting pro-social behavior and correcting hurtful actions. The teacher creates a moral community, helping students respect and care about each other and feel valued within the group, and a democratic classroom environment, where students are involved in decision-making. Teachers practice moral discipline, using the creation and application of rules as opportunities to foster moral reasoning, self-control and a respect for others, and teaching values through the curriculum by using academic subjects as vehicles for examining ethical values. They use cooperative learning to teach children to work together, and they help develop their students' academic responsibility and regard for the value of learning and work. They encourage moral reflection through reading, writing, discussion, decision-making exercises and debate, and they teach conflict resolution to help students learn to resolve conflicts in fair, non-violent ways.

What is the goal of character education?

To develop students socially, ethically and academically by infusing character development into every aspect of the school culture and curriculum. To help students develop good character, which includes knowing, caring about and acting upon core ethical values such as respect, responsibility, honesty, fairness and compassion.

What is a school of character like?

There is no one particular look or formula, but schools of character have one thing in common: a school-wide commitment to nurture the "whole child." They develop students socially, ethically and academically by infusing character development into every part of their curriculum and culture. Specifically, a school committed to character education explicitly names and publicly stands for specific core values and promulgates them to all members of the school community. They define the values in terms of behaviors that can be observed in the life of the school, and they model, study, discuss and use them as the basis for all human relations in the school. They uphold the values by making all school members accountable to consistent standards of conduct, and they celebrate their manifestation in the school and community. Character education works in nearly every school environment, from small to large and from urban to suburban to rural. It works in both public and private schools, and with unique school populations and structures, such as charter, magnet, faith-based, and at-risk. The key to success is that character educators are able to find what works in their particular school, district or community.

How does a school implement character education?

Formalized character education begins when members of a school, along with the broad involvement of community members, come together to determine the core ethical values that they share and that form the basis for good education in their particular school. These values then become the foundation for all that the school does—curriculum, teaching strategies, school culture, extracurricular activities, etc. Character education is thereby infused into the broader community.

Is character education as important as academics?

Absolutely. The social, ethical and emotional development of young people is just as important as their academic development. As Theodore Roosevelt stated: "To educate a man in mind and not in morals is to educate a menace to society." After all, we know that good workers, citizens, parents and neighbors all have their roots in good character. Therefore, it is critical to create schools that simultaneously foster character development and promote learning. In fact, character education promotes academic excellence because it lays a foundation for all learning that takes place in school. While research is in the early stages, it is clear that character education builds classrooms where students are ready to learn and where teachers are freer to teach.

Isn't character education just another "add-on" that contributes to teachers' workloads?

Character education is not an "add-on" but is instead a different way of teaching; it is a comprehensive approach that promotes core values in all phases of school life and permeates the entire school culture. It is not an imposition on already overburdened schools; rather, it helps educators fulfill their fundamental responsibility to prepare young children for the future by laying a foundation for learning through the creation of caring, respectful school environments. Teachers are reporting that their jobs become easier with the implementation of character education because there are fewer discipline and behavioral problems to detract from teaching time.

How much time each day/week is needed for character education?

Character education should take place throughout the entire school day as administrators, teachers and other staff are presented with opportunities to model and teach positive character traits. Character education should not be relegated to a "character education class" that is conducted periodically but should be infused throughout the structures and processes of the entire school curriculum and culture.

Can character education work at all grade levels?

Yes. Varying age-appropriate strategies and practices are being successfully applied to all grade levels, from teaching social and emotional skills in the earliest grades, to service learning and prejudice reduction in secondary schools. It is important to set a strong foundation during the earlier grades and to reinforce and build upon that foundation during the later grades. However, character education can be initiated at any grade level.

13 Character Education

Isn't character education just a new fad or buzzword?

No. Character education has always been an essential part of our schools' mission. In fact, since the founding of our nation's public schools, it was always intended that character education be an integral part of schooling along with academics. Today's character education movement is a re-emergence of that important mission.

Why is character education re-emerging now?

Although character education has always been of vital importance, schools strayed from proactive efforts to incorporate character development into their teaching in past decades. Ironically, this neglect came at a time when the need became greater due to increased challenges in raising ethical children. A number of factors, such as a weakening in guidance by some families and communities, brought on widespread reflection and introspection toward the end of the 20th century. The tragedy at Columbine and fatal shootings at a number of other schools punctuated these concerns across the country. Now, character education is becoming a priority in our nation's education reform as we are increasingly realizing that character development must be an intentional part of education rather than just a process that happens naturally.

Is religion a part of character education?

Parents are the primary and most important moral educators of their children. Thus public schools should develop character education programs in close partnership with parents and the community.

Character education focuses on the core civic virtues and moral values that are widely held in our society across our religious and other differences. Under the First Amendment, public-school teachers may neither inculcate nor denigrate religion. The moral values and civic virtues agreed to in the community may be taught in public schools if done so without religious indoctrination. At the same time, core values should not be taught in such a way as to suggest that religious authority is unnecessary or unimportant.

Sound character education programs affirm the value of religious and philosophical commitments. Faith formation is the province of families and religious communities. But public schools may teach about religion (as distinguished from religious indoctrination) as part of complete education. For example, the curriculum may include teaching about the role of religion in history and contemporary society, alerting students to the fact that moral convictions are often grounded in religious traditions.

PARTICIPATION IN CHARACTER EDUCATION

Shouldn't parents be the primary character educators?

Developing good character is first and foremost a parental responsibility, but the task must also be shared with schools and the broader community. As today's society provides more and tougher challenges to raising ethical, responsible children, increasingly parents and communities are looking to schools for assistance. And sadly, school may be the only place where some children are taught virtuous behavior because they live in homes where their families are not serving as positive role models and are not providing adequate character development.

Who decides what character education traits are emphasized?

It is very important that each school community reach consensus on what values should be taught in a school in order to create the sense of ownership that is needed to obtain "buy-in" for the program. To be effective, school-based character education programs need broad support from all stakeholders in the community—educators, parents, community leaders, youth service groups, businesses and faith and charitable groups.

Early in the planning process, schools should collaborate with parents and their communities to craft a shared vision and objectives. Collectively, they should identify the core values to be taught in their school as well as the particular approaches to teaching them.

13 Character Education

Effective character education schools across the country have shown that, despite deep differences, schools and communities can join together around a commitment to our common ethical inheritance. We know that there are some things that we all value for ourselves and for our children. We want our children to be honest. We want them to respect those different from themselves. We want them to make responsible decisions in their lives. We want them to care about their families, communities and themselves.

These things do not happen on their own. It takes all of us, with the support of our schools, to get us there.

Who teaches character education in a school?

Inherently, each and every adult in a school is a character educator by virtue of exposure to students. Regardless of whether a school has formalized character education, all adults serve as role models. Students constantly watch as all adults in the school – teachers, administrators, counselors, coaches, secretaries, cafeteria aides, bus drivers – serve as models for character, whether good or bad.

Beyond modeling, no matter what the academic subject or extracurricular activity, educators are afforded the opportunity to develop good character in their students on a daily basis by intentionally selecting character-based lessons and activities and by the way they educate their students.

Are schools qualified to teach character education?

Many teachers across the country are being trained in character education through staff development and in-services. Meanwhile, it appears that the nation's schools of education are doing very little to prepare future teachers to be character educators, according to a 1999 study conducted by CEP and the Center for the Advancement of Ethics and Character at Boston University.

The study found that, while character education is very strongly supported by the deans of education at the colleges and universities that are training new teachers, very few of the schools are addressing character education during teacher preparation. In order to implement effective initiatives, schools require access to resources and guidance in establishing, maintaining and assessing their programs.

PUBLIC SUPPORT FOR CHARACTER EDUCATION

What do Americans think about character education?

As Americans examine the moral standards of our society and the quality of our nation's education system, they are increasingly looking to schools and communities to help develop good character in our young people. Poll after poll shows that Americans place issues such as ethics and morality high on their list of concerns. For instance:

- Various studies show that more than 90 percent of the population believes schools should teach character traits to students.

- A 1998 Gallup poll found that Americans consider crime and violence; declines in ethics, morals and family values; and drug usage the issues of most concern in our society today.

- A 1998 poll (conducted by The Tarrance Group and Lake Snell Perry & Associates) of 1,000 likely voters showed that Americans want Congress to restore moral values and improve education more than anything else.

Should character education be mandated?

Legislation and policies should encourage character education in general, but not a particular approach or program. Character education works best when local schools and communities work together to identify the core values to be taught in their schools as well as the particular approaches to teaching those values.

States should encourage comprehensive approaches to character education that involve all aspects of school culture and curriculum. Since very few educators and administrators receive training on how to incorporate character education into their classrooms and schools during their initial preparation at teacher colleges and universities, providing funding for staff development is a critical role for states and districts.

Why should the business community support character education?

Since the American workforce ultimately comes from our schools, businesses have a vested interest in seeing that our youth develop into responsible, ethical people. The very qualities that today's work force needs are character traits and skills that form the building blocks of character education. In 1991, the U.S. Department of Labor issued a report "What Work Requires of Schools"—also known as the SCANS report—which cautioned that students must develop a new set of foundation skills and competencies such as interpersonal skills, individual responsibility, self-esteem, sociability, self-management and integrity.

13 Character Education

CHARACTER EDUCATION QUANTIFIED

How many schools/districts use character education?

While it is impossible to quantify the number of schools using character education, we do know that it is being implemented to varying degrees in schools all across the country. The combined number of states that are recipients of federal character education grants and states that either require or encourage character education through legislation is 40.

Do any states require character education?

Many state boards and departments of education and, currently, 19 states address character education through legislation. Nearly half a dozen others are currently pursuing legislation regarding character education.

- Eleven states *mandate* character education through legislation: Alabama, Arkansas, California, Florida, Georgia, Indiana, Louisiana, Nebraska, Tennessee, Utah and Virginia.

- Eight states *encourage* character education through legislation: Arizona, Maryland, Mississippi, North Carolina, Oklahoma, Oregon, Washington and West Virginia.

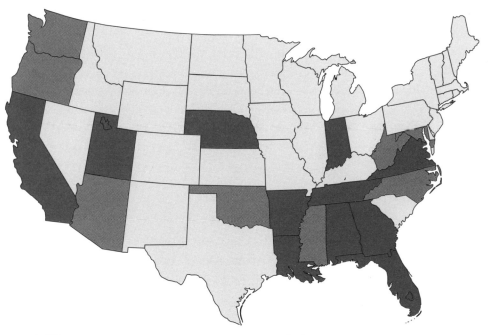

■ States **Mandating** Character Education (11)*
■ States **Encouraging** Character Education (8)*

As of October 2001

RESULTS OF CHARACTER EDUCATION

How do we know character education works?

Schools that are infusing character education into their curricula and cultures, such as CEP's National Schools of Character, are finding improved academic achievement, behavior, school culture, peer interaction and parental involvement. They are seeing dramatic transformations; pro-social behaviors such as cooperation, respect and compassion are replacing negative behaviors such as violence, disrespect, apathy and underachievement. When you walk into a character education school, you know it. You find an atmosphere of mutual caring and respect, where students value learning and care about their teachers, classmates, communities and themselves. Some specific examples of research conducted on character-based programs include:

- A 2000 evaluation of **South Carolina's four-year character education initiative,** which is a pilot program funded by the U.S. Department of Education, reports dramatic improvements among both students and adults. In surveys of South Carolina administrators, the study found that 91 percent reported improvement in student attitudes, 89 percent reported improvement in student behavior, 60 percent reported improvement in academic performance, and more than 65 percent reported improvement in teacher and staff attitudes since implementing character education. The independent study was conducted by the University of South Carolina's Center for Child and Family Studies.

- In three separate studies spanning almost 20 years, the Developmental Studies Center in Oakland, Calif., has documented numerous positive outcomes for students who have attended elementary schools implementing its **Child Development Project.** This research has consistently shown that students in CDP schools engage in more pro-social behavior (e.g., are helpful and cooperative), are more skilled at resolving interpersonal conflicts, are more concerned about others and are more committed to democratic values. Findings from the most recent study of CDP also showed significant reductions in use of alcohol and marijuana and in delinquent behaviors (outcome variables which were not examined in earlier studies). Preliminary findings from a follow-up study of students in middle school indicate that, relative to comparison students, former CDP students are more "connected" to school, work harder and are more engaged in their middle school classes and have higher course grades and achievement test scores. In addition, they engage in less misconduct at school and are more involved in positive youth activities (e.g., organized sports, community groups), and report that more of their friends are similarly positively involved in school and their communities than comparison students.

- Students trained in **Second Step,** a violence-prevention program, used less physical aggression and hostile, aggressive comments and engaged in more pro-social interactions than peers who were not exposed to the curriculum.

Character Education

13

• An independent evaluation of the **Resolving Conflict Creatively Program** found that, of those participating in the program, 64 percent of teachers reported less physical violence and 75 percent reported an increase in student cooperation. Additionally, 92 percent of students felt better about themselves, and more than 90 percent of parents reported an increase in their own communication and problem-solving skills.

• In a study of four schools using **Positive Action**, the average number of behavioral incidents (including violence and substance abuse) requiring discipline referral dropped by 74 percent after the program was implemented for one year and by an average of 80 percent during the next six years. Additionally, absenteeism decreased between 30 to 60 percent, and achievement scores improved from an average of the 43rd to an average of the 71st percentile range after the first year of implementation to an average of the 88th percentile after two to nine years.

• Longitudinal studies from the **Responsive Classroom** program, which emphasizes social skills and good character, have shown increased academic performance across several grade levels. Iowa Test of Basic Skills scores rose 22 percent for the Responsive Classroom students and only 3 percent for the control group. The Responsive Classroom has also resulted in above-average academic growth between grades four and eight, decreases in discipline referrals and increases in pro-social behaviors.

How can character education be assessed?

Through evaluation studies, the impact of character education can be seen through changes in school environment and student attitudes and behavior. For example, many character education schools are reporting reduced violence, discipline referrals and vandalism, and improved attendance and academic performance. While it is challenging for a district or school to assess its program, educators and administrators agree it is worth the effort. More assessment tools are needed, but some existing tools include school surveys, behavioral observations and statistics, and self-assessment questionnaires. CEP's assessment database provides the most comprehensive information available on assessment tools and instruments.

Can character education create safe schools?

Yes. While character education is not a panacea to ridding schools of violence, it is a long-term solution to creating environments where negative and anti-social behaviors are less likely to flourish or go unnoticed and unreported. Character education creates schools where children feel safe because they are in an atmosphere that values respect, responsibility and compassion—not because a guard or metal detector is posted at the door.

FUNDING FOR CHARACTER EDUCATION

How much funding is needed to implement character education?

Character education does not require vast funding. Primary expenses include initial staff training and periodic in-services.

What are possible funding sources for character education?

The U.S. Department of Education provides seed money for character education through its "Partnerships in Character Education Pilot Projects." Since 1995, a total of 36 states and the District of Columbia have received a combined total of approximately $27.5 million through the grants. State grant recipients include Alaska, California, Colorado, Connecticut, District of Columbia, Georgia, Hawaii, Idaho, Illinois, Indiana, Iowa, Kansas, Kentucky, Maine, Maryland, Massachusetts, Michigan, Minnesota, Missouri, Nebraska, New Hampshire, New Jersey, New Mexico, New York, North Carolina, North Dakota, Ohio, Oklahoma, Oregon, Rhode Island, Pennsylvania, Tennessee, South Carolina, Utah, Virginia, Washington and Wisconsin. Additionally, other federal programs that are tied to the goals of character education can be used to launch and support local initiatives. Some of the department's high-profile grant programs that can direct funds to character education include 21st Century Community Learning Centers, Safe and Drug-Free Schools, Teacher Quality Enhancement Grants to States and Partnerships, and America Reads.

HOT TIP

Character Education and Religion

When schools and communities adopt character education programs, they must keep in mind that the moral life of a great many Americans is shaped by deep religious conviction. Both the approach to character education and the classroom materials used should be selected in close consultation with parents representing a broad range of perspectives. When care is taken to find consensus, communities are able to agree on the core values they wish taught in the schools and how they wish it to be done.

The civic and moral values widely held in our society, such as honesty, caring, fairness and integrity, can be taught without invoking religious authority. In public schools, where teachers may neither promote nor denigrate religion, these values must be taught without religious indoctrination. At the same time, teaching core values may not be done in such a way as to suggest that religious authority is unnecessary or unimportant. Nothing in a school's approach to character education should undermine the religious conviction of parents and students.

Sound character education programs will acknowledge that many people look to religious authority and revelation for moral guidance. Such programs will affirm the value of religious and philosophical commitments and avoid any suggestion that values are simply a matter of individual choice without reference to absolute truth. Students will be encouraged to consult their parents and religious leaders for a fuller understanding of how their tradition addresses moral questions.

Character education can be hollow and misleading when taught within a curriculum that is silent about religion. When religion is largely ignored, students get the false and dangerous message that religious ideas and practices are insignificant for human experience. A complete education must of necessity include study about religion, where appropriate, throughout the curriculum. Religion and religious perspectives are taken seriously in the curriculum if students are exposed to the great ethical systems of world history and to America's rich and diverse religious heritage. Mentioning religion is not enough. Students need to explore the place of religion in history, literature, art and music if they are to understand the ultimate beliefs and world views that provide the deepest and strongest sources of human meaning for much of humanity.

The Authors

Character Education 13

CEP AND CHARACTER EDUCATION

What is the Character Education Partnership (CEP)?

CEP is a national advocate and leader for the character education movement. It is a Washington, D.C.-based nonprofit, nonpartisan, nonsectarian coalition of more than 1,200 organizations and individuals committed to fostering effective character education in our nation's K-12 schools. It is an umbrella organization for character education, serving as the leading resource for people and organizations that are integrating character education into their schools and communities. CEP focuses on defining and encouraging effective practices and approaches to quality character education and provides a forum for the exchange of ideas. CEP's membership includes the nation's leading education organizations, and its board of directors is made up of corporate leaders and leading experts in the field of character education.

What is CEP's mission?

CEP is dedicated to developing moral character and civic virtue in our young people as an essential way of promoting a more compassionate and responsible society.

How does CEP contribute to the character education movement?

CEP provides research and resources to policymakers, character educators, education leaders, the media and general public, while also setting high standards and recognizing quality initiatives nationwide.

CEP hosts the nation's largest and most comprehensive online Character Education Resource Center at www.character.org, connecting educators and communities with hundreds of organizations, curricula, videos, books, etc.

CEP has created the Eleven Principles of Effective Character Education,™ which provides quality standards and practical guidelines necessary to build comprehensive character education initiatives. The Eleven Principles will soon be brought to life through a new publication—the *Eleven Principles Sourcebook*—which will give educators the tools and support needed to implement effective character education.

The **National Schools of Character**™ **Awards** is CEP's flagship program which annually identifies and recognizes schools and districts nationwide that exemplify excellence in character education. The National Schools of Character Awards highlight character education's positive impact on school climate, academic excellence, and student success, and serve as exemplary models for schools and educators across the country. The winners' successful character education programs are promoted through a best practice publication, mentoring network and national media-outreach efforts.

Character Education

13

CEP's **National Forum** provides teachers, principals, counselors, professors, parents and business and community leaders with a chance to learn what works from the nation's leading character education experts and on-the-ground practitioners. Attendance continues to grow, with last year's numbers reaching approximately 700.

CEP's website includes an **online database of assessment tools**, including a hands-on primer in character education evaluation techniques

CEP is working to make character education an integral part of undergraduate and graduate training of educators. With support from the Center for the Advancement of Ethics and Character at Boston University, CEP released a 1999 landmark report, *Teachers as Educators of Character: Are the Nation's Schools of Education Coming Up Short?,* showing strong support for teaching character education in the nation's schools, although only 13 percent of deans are satisfied with their school's efforts to prepare our nation's future teachers.

For more information, contact Character Education Partnership, 1025 Connecticut Ave. NW, Suite 1011, Washington, DC 20036, or by phone at (800) 988-8081. CEP's web site is at www.character.org.

13 Character Education

CHAPTER 14

First Amendment Schools: Educating for Freedom and Responsibility

Congress shall make no law respecting an
establishment of religion, or prohibiting the free
exercise thereof; or abridging the freedom of speech,
or of the press; or the right of the people peaceably
to assemble, and to petition the Government for a
redress of grievances.

—First Amendment to the
United States Constitution

FIRST AMENDMENT SCHOOLS: EDUCATING FOR FREEDOM AND RESPONSIBILITY

What is the First Amendment Schools Project?

First Amendment Schools: Educating for Freedom and Responsibility, co-sponsored by the Association for Supervision and Curriculum Development (ASCD) and the First Amendment Center, is a nationwide initiative designed to help schools model and teach the rights and responsibilities that flow from the First Amendment to the U.S. Constitution. The project has four goals:

1. Provide guidelines for applying the First Amendment principles in schools.

2. Establish project schools in every region of the nation.

3. Promote curriculum reforms that deepen teaching about the First Amendment.

4. Educate school leaders, teachers, parents, students, community members and school board members about the meaning and significance of First Amendment principles and ideals.

The First Amendment Schools project serves as a national resource for all schools—K-12, public and private—interested in affirming First Amendment principles and putting them into action in their school communities.

The project offers schools the following resources:
- Grants to schools selected as project schools.
- Answers to frequently asked questions about First Amendment issues in schools.
- Lesson plans for teaching the First Amendment in classrooms.
- Model policies for creating schools that value First Amendment principles.
- News and commentaries on First Amendment issues.
- First Amendment publications.

To find out more about these and the other project resources, visit www.firstamendmentschools.org, or contact ASCD's Mike Wildasin (703-575-5475, mwildasi@ascd.org) or the First Amendment Center's Sam Chaltain (703-284-2808, schaltain@freedomforum.org).

VISION STATEMENT

THE CHALLENGE

First Amendment Schools are built on the conviction that the five freedoms protected by the First Amendment are a cornerstone of American democracy and essential for citizenship in a diverse society.

For more than 200 years, the First Amendment has been at the heart of history's boldest and most successful experiment in liberty. We readily acknowledge that the United States failed to live up to its founding principles in 1791, and that the nation still has a distance to go in the 21st century. But the history of our nation is the story of the ongoing struggle to extend the promise of freedom more fully and fairly to each and every citizen.

Today the need to sustain and expand our experiment in liberty is made more urgent by the challenge of living with our deepest differences in a diverse and complex society. The need to commit ourselves as a people to the rights and responsibilities that flow from the First Amendment has never been more vital—or more difficult. At a time in our history when we most need to reaffirm what we share as citizens across our differences, the ignorance and contention now surrounding the First Amendment threaten to divide the nation and undermine our freedom.

The key place to address this challenge is in our schools, the institutions most responsible for transmitting civic principles and virtues to each succeeding generation. Schools must not only teach the First Amendment; they must also find ways to model and apply the democratic first principles that they are charged with teaching. The rights and responsibilities of the First Amendment provide a much-needed civic framework for reaffirming and renewing the civic aims of education.

GUIDING PRINCIPLES

We envision First Amendment Schools as places where all members of the school community practice the civic habits of the heart necessary to sustain a free people that would remain free. Schools may carry out this mission in ways that vary greatly, depending on the age of the students, the size of the school, the needs of the local community and whether the school is public or private. What unites First Amendment Schools is not one view of democratic education or the First Amendment, but rather an abiding commitment to teach and model the rights and responsibilities that undergird the First Amendment.

We propose the following four principles as foundational for creating and sustaining a First Amendment School:

I. Create Laboratories of Democratic Freedom

The future of the American Republic depends upon instilling in young citizens an abiding commitment to the democratic first principles that sustain our experiment in liberty.

First Amendment Schools educate for freedom by providing students and all members of the school community with substantial opportunities to practice democracy. Knowledge of our framing documents and the structure and functions of government is important, but preparation for citizenship also requires virtues and skills acquired through participation in decision-making. By practicing democracy, students confront the challenges of self-government, including the difficult task of balancing a commitment to individual rights with a concern for the common good.

First Amendment Schools create organizational structures, allocate time and resources, and develop policies and curricula designed to support and promote democratic learning communities. Pedagogical decisions, including instructional and assessment practices, extend opportunities for authentic learning that inform a citizen's understanding of the world beyond the classroom.

First Amendment Schools 14

First Amendment Schools include administrators, teachers, staff, students, parents and community members when making decisions about organization, governance and curricula. When everyone is given a meaningful voice in shaping the life of the school, all have a real stake in creating and sustaining safe and caring learning communities. All members of the school community should have opportunities to exercise leadership, negotiate differences, propose solutions to shared problems, and practice other skills essential to thoughtful and effective participation in civic life.

II. Commit to Inalienable Rights and Civic Responsibility

Freedom of religion, speech, press, assembly, and petition are fundamental and inalienable rights. All Americans have a civic responsibility to guard these rights for every citizen.

First Amendment Schools are dedicated to educating for citizenship by teaching and modeling the democratic principles of the Constitution of the United States. Schools take this mission seriously by providing all members of the school community with daily opportunities to exercise their constitutional rights with responsibility.

First Amendment Schools uphold the principles of freedom and democracy when they protect religious liberty rights, encourage freedom of expression, promote academic freedom, ensure a free student press and support broad-based involvement in school governance. Acting responsibly, students, teachers, administrators, staff, parents and community members can do much to uphold the rights of every citizen.

14   First Amendment Schools

III. Include all Stakeholders

The First Amendment provides the civic framework of rights and responsibilities that enables Americans to work together for the common good in schools and communities.

First Amendment Schools affirm the importance of modeling the democratic process and upholding individual rights in the development of policies and curricula. Decisions are made after appropriate involvement of those affected by the decision and with due consideration for the rights of those holding dissenting views.

First Amendment Schools recognize that parents have the primary responsibility for the upbringing and education of their children. All Americans, however, share an important stake in educating students for responsible citizenship in a free society. Students and schools benefit greatly when parents, students, educators and community members work closely together to promote a shared vision of the First Amendment throughout the school culture and across the community.

IV. Translate Civic Education into Community Engagement

A society committed to freedom and justice for all requires citizens with the knowledge, virtues, and skills needed for active engagement in public life.

First Amendment Schools encourage active citizenship by giving students opportunities to translate civic education into community engagement. Active citizens are willing to participate in public life by addressing problems and issues in their communities, our nation, and the world.

First Amendment Schools provide opportunities for students to learn civic virtue and moral character throughout the school culture and across the curriculum. Students are encouraged to demonstrate an active concern for the welfare of others through service learning and civic problem-solving. First Amendment rights are best guarded and civic responsibilities best exercised when citizens are actively engaged in building a more just and free society.

First Amendment Schools 14

A SHARED VISION

These guiding principles are offered as a shared vision for schools seeking to fulfill the promise of freedom under the First Amendment.

Learning about freedom and justice, however important, can never be enough; educating for democratic citizenship must be more than an academic exercise. If we are to sustain and expand the American experiment in liberty, young citizens must acquire the civic skills and virtues needed to exercise their freedom *with* responsibility.

We invite all schools and every citizen to join us in affirming these principles and putting them into action. The time has come for all Americans to work together to renew our shared commitment to the civic principles and virtues vital to democracy, freedom, and the common good.

CHAPTER 15

Sample School District Policies

Davis County School District Policy and Procedures
Davis County, Utah

Wicomico County Board of Education
Salisbury, Maryland

Ramona Unified School District Policy
Ramona, California

Richardson Independent School District
Richardson, Texas

FIRST AMENDMENT TO THE
UNITED STATES CONSTITUTION

The public schools belong to all Americans. As guardians of our constitutional principles, teachers and administrators have a special obligation and responsibility to protect the religious liberty rights of students of all faiths and none, and to ensure that religion and religious conviction are treated with fairness and respect...Every local school district should work with parents and community leaders to develop clear religious liberty policies on student religious expression that reflect the new consensus under current law.

—Final Report of the American
Assembly on Religion in Public Life
March 26, 2000

The four school district policies reproduced below were collected from across the nation and reflect a variety of approaches to religious liberty in public schools. Their inclusion in this guide is not intended as an endorsement of any particular policy, but an illustration of how different communities have addressed these issues. We urge all communities and school districts to develop their own policies and guidelines using the strategies outlined in the guide. Every school system will differ in that they will also need to recognize their state and local laws concerning religious liberty. For additional sample policies on other issues concerning religion and the schools, write to the authors of this guide at The Freedom Forum First Amendment Center at Vanderbilt University.

DAVIS COUNTY SCHOOL DISTRICT POLICY AND PROCEDURES

Davis County, Utah

1. Purpose and Philosophy

1.1. As stated by the national signers of the Williamsburg Charter, the Davis County School Board believes that: "Religious liberty in a democracy is a right that may not be submitted to vote and depends on the outcome of no election. A society is only as just and free as it is respectful of this right, especially toward the beliefs of its smallest minorities and least popular communities."[1]

1.2. The Board also believes in its duty to foster knowledge about, and respect for, the United States Constitution.

1.3. According to the First Amendment of the United States Constitution, "Congress shall make no law respecting the establishment of religion, or prohibiting the free exercise thereof." Consistent with these Constitutional principles, and guidelines issued by the United States Department of Education, the Board recognizes that public schools have two basic and equally important obligations with respect to religion.

1.4. First, schools may not endorse specific religious practices or doctrines, nor may they coerce participation in religious activity. "Among other things, school administrators and teachers may not organize or encourage prayer exercises in the classroom. And the right of religious expression in school does not include the right to have a `captive audience' listen, or to compel other students to participate." Furthermore, school officials "should not permit student religious speech to turn into religious harassment aimed at a student or a small group of students."[2]

1.5. Second, schools may not forbid students acting on their own from expressing their personal religious views or beliefs solely because they are of a religious nature. The Board concurs with the statement that: "Nothing in the First Amendment converts our public schools into religion-free zones, or requires all religious expression to be left at the school house door."[3] Schools may not discriminate against private religious expression by students, but must instead give students the same right to engage in religious activity and discussion as they have to engage in other comparable activity."[4]

1.6. It is the Board's purpose to adhere to these principles and promote mutual understanding and respect for the interests and rights of all individuals regarding their beliefs, values, and customs. Specifically, it is the Board's purpose to have a policy that:

    1.6.1. Foster knowledge and understanding about, and sensitivity toward, religious differences and the role of religion in a diverse, contemporary society;

1.6.2. Allows student and employee[5] religious expression and freedom of speech within the parameters of existing state and federal law;

1.6.3. Supports a climate of academic freedom in which religious ideas and organizations can be discussed in an objective way, for their educational value, with emphasis on the impact of religions on history, literature, art, music, morality, and other key social institutions;

1.6.4. Requires official neutrality on the part of teachers, administrators, other school employees and volunteers regarding religious activity when acting in their official capacities;

1.6.5. Promotes constructive dialogue between schools and community regarding religion;

1.6.6. Encourage educators and all members of the school community to engage in persistent efforts to eliminate prejudice, build trust, work toward consensus, and resolve disputes over religious issues in schools promptly, equitably, sensitively, and with civility at the local level.

2. References

2.1. United States Constitution, First Amendment.

2.2. Utah Constitution, Article X, Section 8.

2.3. Memorandum from Richard Riley, U.S. Secretary of Education, to Superintendents of Schools regarding U.S. Department of Education's Guidance on Religious Expression in Public Schools (Aug. 10, 1995) (Available at the U.S. Department of Education or non the Internet at http://www.ed.gov/Speeches/08-1995/religion.html).

2.4. American Jewish Congress, et al., Religion in the Public Schools: A Joint Statement of Current Law (April 13, 1995) (http://www.ed.gov/Speeches/04-1995/prayer.html).

2.5. President Bill Clinton, Address at James Madison High School, Vienna, Virginia (July 12, 1995) (Transcript available in U.S. Office of the Press Secretary and on the Internet at http://www.ed.gov/PressReleases/07-1995/religion.html) .

2.6. Freedom Forum First Amendment Center, et. al., Religious Liberty, Public Education, and the Future of American Democracy, A Joint Statement of Principles (1995) (http://www.freedomforum.org).

Sample School
District Policies 15

2.7. Finding Common Ground: A First Amendment Guide to Religion and Public Education (Charles Haynes and Oliver Thomas, eds. 1994) (http://www.freedomforum.org).

2.8. Williamsburg Charter Foundation, The Williamsburg Charter (1988).

2.9. Utah Code Ann. §531-13-101. Political and religious doctrine prohibited.

2.10. Utah Code Ann. §531-13-101.1. Maintaining constitutional freedom in the public schools.

2.11. Utah Code Ann. §531-13-101.2. Waivers of participation.

2.12. Utah Code Ann. §531-13-101.3. Expressions of belief-discretionary time.

2.13. Utah Code Ann. §531-11-302. Grounds for exemption from required immunizations.

2.14. Utah Code Ann. §531-11-12. Period of silence.

2.15. Utah Admin. Code R277-105. Recognizing constitutional freedoms in the schools.

2.16. Utah Admin. Code R277-610. Released-time classes for religious instruction.

2.17. 42 U.S.C. §2000bb. Religious Freedom Restoration Act of 1993.

2.18. 42 U.S.C. §2000e. Equal Employment Opportunities Act (Title VII).

2.19. Davis County School District Policy 5S-400. School Attendance and Discipline.

2.20. Davis County School District Policy 5S-401. Safe and Orderly Schools.

2.21. Davis County School District Policy 4I-012. Family Education Rights and Privacy.

2.22. Davis County School District Policy 4I-001. Textbook Adoption and Appeals Procedures.

3. Definitions

3.1. Civility: The attitude of respect for another's belief or views; a method of dialogue and interaction emphasizing reasonableness and sensitivity. Within the context of religious liberty, civility is a civic virtue, a character trait that encompasses respecting the rights of others, including the rights of all citizens to express their beliefs and practice their faith in a law-abiding manner.

3.2. Conscience: A standard based upon learned experiences, a personal philosophy or a system of belief, religious teachings or doctrine, an absolute or external sense of right and wrong which is felt on an individual basis, a belief in an external Absolute, or any combination of the foregoing.[6]

Sample School
District Policies

3.3. Discretionary time: Non-instructional time during which a student is free to pursue personal interests (e.g., free time before and after school, during lunch and between classes or on buses, and private time before and after athletic events or activities).[7]

3.4. Free exercise of religious practice/speech: The right to choose or reject religious, theistic, agnostic, or atheistic convictions and to act upon that choice.[8]

3.5. Harassment: Words, gestures, or actions which threaten, intimidate, coerce, or physically or emotionally abuse someone. In determining whether an activity is harassment, school officials shall consider the totality of the circumstances, including but not limited to: severity or pervasiveness of the conduct, number of students involved, maturity and age of students, the request to stop and the conduct of the futility of such a request, etc.

3.6. Instructional time: Time during which the school is responsible for a student and the student is required to be actively engaged in a learning activity. Such time includes instructional activities in the classroom or study hall during regularly scheduled hours, required school activities outside the classroom, and counseling, private conferences, or tutoring provided by school employees or volunteers acting in their official capacities during or outside of regular school hours.[9]

3.7. Mediation: A structured process in which a neutral facilitator assists parties in a negotiating a voluntary settlement of their dispute.

3.8. Official capacity: The conduct of any school employee or volunteer when performing any authorized school function or tack; i.e., when performing any act under color and by virtue of his/her position. "Official capacity" is also defined as the conduct of any school employee or volunteer when performing official duties, whether before, during, or after regular school hours.

3.9. Official neutrality: School officials and employees while acting in their official capacities shall not use their positions to endorse, promote, or disparage a particular religious, denominational, sectarian, agnostic, or atheistic belief, viewpoint, or practice. Consequently, they are prohibited from doing or saying anything that could be reasonably interpreted as inculcating or inhibiting any religious idea, belief, or practice as defined herein.

3.10. Religion: For purposes of free exercise under this policy, the term religion is generally defined as a specific system of belief or worship encompassing the nature of deity and/or reality and the relationship of human beings to that deity and/or reality.[10] However, the term religion is not limited to orthodox belief systems or practices; an individual's belief does not have to recognize a supreme being[11] or meet any organizational or doctrinal test[12] to be protected under this policy.[13]

3.11. Religious music/non-religious music:

    3.11.1. Religious Music is defined as: 1) Any music that recognizes the existence of a supreme being or deity. "The Messiah," "O Holy Night," "Silent Night," the Kaddish, Kol Nidra, and Maoz Tzur are examples of this music. 2) Any music that is suggestive of or that has become closely associated with religions or religious holidays that may be looked upon as being of a religious nature.

    3.11.2. Non-religious music is defined as seasonal, cultural, or ethnic music such as "Frosty the Snowman," "Jingle Bells," "Winter Wonderland," and "Over the River and Through the Woods."

3.12. Religious symbols: A religious symbol is: 1) Any object that portrays or recognizes the existence or a supreme being or deity. Symbols in this category include The Cross, Star of David, nativity scene, menorah, tablets, chalices, crescent, Buddha, and any other symbols that are part of a religious celebration or ceremony. 2) Any object that is so closely associated with religion or with the celebration of a religious holiday that it is looked upon as being of religious nature. Such objects include the dreydal, Christmas tree, Santa Claus, Lion of Judah, Easter eggs and Easter bunnies.

4. Policy

4.1. It is District policy to comply with existing state and federal law regarding religion and religious expression in public schools. Specifically, it is District policy to: 1) allow students and employees to engage in expression of personal religious views or beliefs within the parameters of current law, and 2) maintain the schools' official neutrality regarding sectarian religious issues: according to the constitutional principle of separation between church and state,[14] the District will neither advance nor inhibit religion.[15]

4.2. It is also District policy to take all reasonable steps to resolve disputes over religious issues in schools promptly, equitably, and with civility at the local level.

5. Student Expression of Personal Religious Beliefs or Views

5.1. Non-discrimination: Schools may not forbid students acting on their own from expressing their personal religious views or beliefs solely because they are of a religious nature. Schools may not discriminate against private religious expression by students, but must instead give students the same right to engage in religious activity and discussion as they have to engage in other comparable activity.

5.2. Freedom to act: While the freedom to believe is absolute, the freedom to act on a belief is not. In order to claim the Free Exercise protections of the First Amendment

15 Sample School
District Policies

and this policy, a person must show that his or her actions 1) are motivated by a sincere religious belief, and 2) have been substantially burdened by school officials or the District.

5.3. Least restrictive means: If an individual can show that his or her actions are motivated by a sincere religious belief and have been substantially burdened by school officials or the District, school officials can still regulate the conduct if they have a compelling interest and pursue such interest the manner least restrictive of the individual's religion.[16]

5.4. Student religious expression during discretionary time: Free exercise of religious practices or freedom of speech by student during discretionary time shall not be denied unless the conduct or speech unreasonably interferes with the ability of the school officials to maintain order and discipline, violates schools rules, impinges on the rights of others, unreasonably endangers persons or property, creates a coercive environment, or violates concepts of civility or propriety appropriate to the school setting.[17]

    5.4.1. Student conduct or speech of a personal religious nature that may not be prohibited unless it violates the standards above, include, but is not limited to:

        5.4.1.1. Reading the Bible or other scriptures;

        5.4.1.2. Saying grace before meals;

        5.4.1.3. Praying with friends in cafeterias, hallways, around flagpoles, or at athletic contests and other extra-curricular activities;

        5.4.1.4. Discussing religious views with other students, or attempting to persuade peers about religious topic, as long as the persuasive speech does not constitute harassment.

5.5. Student religious expression during instructional time: Students participating in school sponsored learning activities, provided and directed by school employees acting in their official capacities, shall not be prohibited from expressing personal religious beliefs or be penalized for so doing, unless the expression unreasonably interferes with the ability of school officials to maintain order and discipline, violates school rules, impinges on the rights of others, unreasonably endangers persons or property, creates a coercive atmosphere, or violate concepts of civility or propriety appropriate to the school setting.[18]

    5.5.1. Student religious conduct or expression that may not be prohibited in homework, classroom discussions, presentations, assignments, or school sponsored activities, unless it violates the standards above, includes but is not limited to:

      5.5.1.1. Submitting homework, artwork, or other assignments with religious content;

      5.5.1.2. Giving class presentations with religious content that are relevant to the curriculum and matter being discussed;

      5.5.1.3. Making religious remarks or asking question about religion in the ordinary course of classroom discussion;

      5.5.1.4. Asking questions of students or school employees regarding their religious beliefs or views.

   5.5.2. Teachers and other school officials should evaluate homework and classroom work with religious content consistent with ordinary academic standards of substance and relevance, as well as other legitimate pedagogical concerns.[19]

   5.5.3. When responding to a student's question about an employee's personal religious beliefs or views, the employee must maintain official neutrality and be careful not to advocate or encourage acceptance or his/her religious belief or perspective (see section 10.2 of this policy).

   5.5.4. While students have the right to give educationally relevant classroom presentations on religious topic or engage in other religious expression during instructional time, they do not have the right to make a captive audience listen to a lengthy sermon, or compel other students to participate in religious exercises. Students should not conduct religious ceremonies or exercises during instructional time. No student should be coerced to participate in such religious activity.[20]

6. Religious Clothing and Apparel

6.1. Because dress is a form of individual expression, any prohibition or regulation of religious clothing or apparel must be done in the least restrictive manner possible to accomplish district and school objectives of maintaining a safe and orderly school environment.[21] School officials should make appropriate exemptions to dress code and reasonably accommodate students who wear hairstyles, clothing, head wear, jewelry, cosmetics, or other apparel as a personal expression of sincerely held religious beliefs.

6.2. Religious attire that should be appropriately accommodated in school includes, but is not limited to:

   6.2.1. Hairstyles;

   6.2.2. Yarmulkes;

Sample School
District Policies

6.2.3. Head scarves or turbans;

6.2.4. Crucifixes, stars of David, CTR rings, and other jewelry;

6.2.5. T-shirts or badges with religious messages or insignia;

6.2.6. Items of ceremonial dress.[22]

6.3. School officials should also be sensitive and appropriately accommodate students who request not to wear certain gym clothes that they regard, on religious grounds, as immodest.

7. Moment of Silence in Classrooms

7.1. In accordance with Utah law[23], teachers may provide for the observance of a period of silence in the classroom each school day. However, teachers and other school officials must maintain official neutrality by neither encouraging nor discouraging prayer or other religious exercise during the moment of silence.[24]

7.2. Under District policy teachers and other school officials may not organize, endorse, or encourage prayer exercises in the classroom.[25] Teachers and other school officials must supervise during this time.

8. Graduation Exercises and Other Extra-Curricular Activities

8.1. Prayers prohibited at graduation: It is District policy to prohibit prayers as an officially scheduled and sanctioned part of graduation exercises.[26]

8.2. Moments of silence: While the District does not endorse or discourage the practice, students may elect to hold a moment of silence as part of graduation ceremonies.[27]

8.2.1. No Prayer: A moment of silence may only be initiated and conducted by students, and shall not be used as a forum for vocal prayer or other religious exercise, but rather as an opportunity for those in attendance at graduation to participate in a quiet moment according to the dictates of their own conscience.[28]

8.2.2. Official neutrality: During a moment of silence and all other activities associated with graduation, school officials shall maintain official neutrality.[29]

8.3. Baccalaureate services: Students who wish to include religious activities, such as prayer, in recognition or celebration of their graduation may organize or attend privately sponsored baccalaureate services. Whether such services are organized or sponsored by students, parents, religious organizations, or community groups, the sponsors may rent District facilities according to the provision of the District's Building Rental Policy (Policy 6F-102).

8.3.1. Under the Building Rental Policy, noncommercial rates apply to religious organizations, parent organizations, or other nonprofit community groups desiring to rent District facilities for baccalaureate services.

8.3.2. School officials may announce the time and place of baccalaureate services, but must mot encourage or discourage student participation in such services. Announcing of all baccalaureate services must be done on the same terms, and school officials must clearly state as part of all announcements that baccalaureate services are privately sponsored and that participation is purely voluntary.

8.4. Prayers by non-students at athletic contests and other extra-curricular events: Consistent with the general policy on school0sanctioned prayers, it is District policy to prohibit prayers initiated or led by coaches, parents, clergy, or other non-students prior to, during, or after athletic contests and other extra-curricular events.[30] Students may pray together at such events consistent with the guidance outlined in Section 5.1 of this policy. Coaches, administrators, and other school officials may be present during student prayers to supervise, but should in no way participate in or encourage prayer exercises. School officials should take steps to prevent any activity from being coercive or harassing.

9. Distribution of Religious Materials on School Grounds

9.1. Non-school sponsored organizations and non-students may only distribute literature or other materials in schools or on school grounds in accordance with reasonable time, place, and manner restrictions imposed by the school.[31]

9.2. Students may distribute literature unrelated to school curriculum or activities only at reasonable times, places, and manners designated by the school.[32]

9.3. Religious tracts, books, or literature may not be singled out for special regulation or prohibition based on content[33], but are subject to reasonable time, place, and manner restrictions imposed by the schools on other non-school related literature.[34]

10. Employee Expression of Personal Religious Beliefs

10.1. Official neutrality: All employees of the Davis County School District must maintain strict neutrality when acting in their official capacities. An employee's rights relating to voluntary religious practices and freedom of speech do not include proselytizing of any student regarding atheistic, agnostic, sectarian, religious, or denominational doctrine while the employee is acting in the employee's official capacity, nor may an

15 Sample School District Policies

employee attempt to use his or her position to influence a student regarding the student's religious beliefs or lack thereof.[35]

10.2. Response to questions: If a student asks an employee about that employee's personal religious beliefs, the employee may choose not to respond out of professional respect for the student's freedom of conscience or personal beliefs. However, while acting in an official capacity, an employee may respond in an appropriate and restrained manner to a spontaneous question from a student regarding the employee's personal religious beliefs or perspectives. Because of the special position of trust held by school employees, employees may not advocate or encourage acceptance of specific religious beliefs or perspectives; but may, by exercising due caution, explain or define personal religious beliefs or perspectives (see section 3.9 of this policy).[36]

10.3. Reasonable accommodation: It is District policy to reasonably accommodate an employee's or prospective employee's religious dress, observance or practice whenever such accommodation can be made without undue hardship on the conduct or the District's business.[37]

11. Volunteers

11.1. The District prohibits discrimination on the basis of religion against any group or individual desiring to volunteer in Davis County Schools.

11.2. Volunteers must maintain strict neutrality regarding religion while performing volunteer work for the schools.

11.3. Volunteers are prohibited from engaging in proselytizing activities or recruiting activities of any type on school grounds or in conjunction with any school activity, and must strictly follow directions given them by school officials.

11.4. Religious apparel is permissible if it is required by a person's religion, is part of the person's ordinary work dress and would not be disruptive of the school environment and does not contain a proselytizing message.

11.5. Volunteers, including those from religious organizations, serving in the schools and interacting directly with student son a regular basis, shall wear a district approved volunteer name tag containing the individual's first and last name, and shall sign a form acknowledging that they understand and will abide by the provisions of this policy.

11.6. School officials are responsible to monitor the behavior and interactions of volunteers while they are serving in schools or participating in school activities. Volunteers who fail to comply with the provisions of this policy shall be asked to leave the school or activity. Ultimate responsibility for enforcement of this policy at the school level rests with the building administrator.

12. Religion in the Curriculum

12.1. Teaching about religion: Religious instruction is the responsibility of parents and religious institutions, but teaching about religion and beliefs of conscience is a legitimate and appropriate part of a complete academic education on the elementary and secondary levels.[38]

12.2. Instructional practices: To ensure that the educational approach to religion is one of academic instruction, not of indoctrination, and that it does not unduly favor religion over non-religion, teachers and school officials shall adhere to the following guidelines:

12.2.1. Study or presentations about religion or other beliefs of conscience must achieve academic educational objectives, and be presented in a balanced manner within the context of the approved curriculum.

12.2.2. The school's approach to religion must be academic, not devotional.

12.2.3. Students may be exposed to any and all religious views and beliefs of conscience, but they should not be coerced to accept any particular view or belief.[39]

12.2.4. The objective study of comparative religions is permissible, but no religious tenet, belief, or denomination may be given inappropriate emphasis; the school may educate about all religions, but may not promote or denigrate any religion or belief of conscience.

12.2.5. Students should be taught to understand a variety of beliefs, and to respect the rights of all people, including the rights of individuals or groups with whom the students may disagree. Teaching about religion and beliefs of conscience should emphasize the role of religion and beliefs of conscience in history and culture, and the importance of religious liberty as a cornerstone of a democratic society.

12.3. Privacy: In accordance with federal and state Family Educational Rights and Privacy laws, school officials shall not solicit private information or explanations from students about their personal religious affiliations, beliefs, or practices, without first obtaining proper parental consent.

13. Religious Music

13.1. Religious music in schools: Seasonally appropriate and sacred religious music may be performed in school, if presented in a balanced, prudent, and objective manner.[40]

13.1.1. Music should be selected on the basis of its musical quality and educational value rather than its religious content.

15 Sample School District Policies

13.1.2. Music performances must achieve secular educational objectives, and be presented in a balanced manner within the context of the approved curriculum.

13.1.3. Teachers should use good judgment and be especially sensitive to the feelings of students who might wish not to participate for religious reasons, and should explore all reasonable alternatives in resolving a student's objection before offering or granting a waiver of participation.

13.2. Performances at religious services: No school employee or student may be required to attend or participate in any religious service, whether in an individual capacity or as a member of a performance group, regardless of where or when the service is held. No penalty may be assessed for failure to attend or perform in such an activity.[41]

13.2.1. Students may voluntarily attend and perform during a religious service as individuals or as members of a group, provided all arrangements are made by students or non-school adults.[42]

13.3. Performance in church-owned facilities: Unless granted an appropriate waiver, students who are members of performing groups such as school choirs may be required to rehearse or otherwise perform in a church-owned or operated facility if the following conditions are met:

13.3.1. The performance is not part of a religious service;

13.3.2. The activity of which the performance is a part is neither intended to further a religious objective nor under the direction of a church official; and

13.3.3. The activity is open to the general public.[43]

13.4. Visits to church-owned facilities: Unless granted an appropriate waiver, students may be required to visit church-owned facilities when religious services are not being conducted if the visit is intended solely for the purpose of pursuing permissible educational objectives such as those relating to art, music, architecture or history.[44]

14. Religious Holidays

14.1. No celebration: Religious and civic holiday such as Easter, Passover, Rosh Hashanah, Yom Kippur, Thanksgiving, Hanukkah, Christmas, Kwanzaa, and Ramadan, offer opportunities to teach about a variety of religious traditions and beliefs of conscience during the school year. While teachers and school officials may teach about religious holidays, they may not celebrate such holidays in school.

14.2. Christmas: Because Christmas is a holiday that may cause particularly strong concerns among some students and members of the community, teachers and school officials should be especially mindful and sensitive to the beliefs of all students during this season.[45] At Christmas the schools should emphasize the positive values of that season that are shared by all people, whether they be of a particular religion or no religion. Thus, values such as peace, goodwill, kindness, unselfishness, giving, and brotherhood are appropriate for recognition at that time, as at any time in the year. During the Christmas season, teachers are encouraged to include discussions or presentations about other religious or cultural winter holidays coinciding with Christmas, such as Hanukkah and Kwanzaa.

14.3. Other holidays: Activities and discussions related to cultural holidays such as Valentine's Day, St. Patrick's Day, and Halloween should be academic in nature. Because these holidays may be viewed by some parents as having religious connotations, requests for excusal in school activities associated with these holidays should be routinely granted.

14.4. Parties: Class parties associated with seasonal holidays are appropriate insofar as they are consistent with the approved curriculum. However, consistent with the District's goal of maximizing instructional time, such parties must not unduly interfere with regular academic activities.

14.5. Teaching about holidays: The significance of holidays, whether religious or secular, may be explained or discussed in an objective manner as part of regular classroom instruction or as questions from students arise, so as to promote a better understanding among all students.[46]

15. Religious Symbols

15.1. During holidays: The display of religious symbols that are part of religious holidays is permitted as a teaching aid or resource, provided such symbols are displayed as an example of the cultural heritage of the holiday, and are temporary in nature.[47] Such holidays include, but are not limited to: Christmas, Kwanzaa, Hanukkah, Ramadan, Easter, Passover, Valentine's Day, St. Patrick's Day, Thanksgiving, and Halloween.

15.2. Diversity of symbols: If any religious symbol is to be part of a display, schools must allow for other religious, cultural or ethnic symbols.[48]

16. Waivers of Participation

16.1. Rights of individuals: While the District acknowledges its obligation to be sensitive and fair toward the personal rights and beliefs of all individuals, merely exposing students to ideas that may offend the religion does not amount to a substantial burden on their religious exercise. Furthermore, it is unconstitutional to allow one person's or one group's religion to determine the curriculum for all others.[49] Consequently, it is District policy to accommodate the legitimate objections of

Sample School
District Policies

individuals by granting waivers of participation when requested or when no other reasonable alternative is possible.[50]

16.2. A parent, a legal guardian of a student, or a secondary student may request a waiver of participation in any portion of the curriculum or school activity which the requesting party believes to be an infringement upon a right of conscience or the exercise of religious freedom in any of the following ways:

16.2.1. It would require participation in a practice that would be offensive to or substantially burdensome on a religion.

16.2.2. It would require participation in a practice forbidden by religious belief or practice, or right of conscience; or

16.2.3. It would bar participation in a practice required by a religious belief or practice, or right of conscience.

16.3. A claimed infringement must rise to a level of belief that the school requirement violates a superior duty which is more than personal preference.

16.4. If a minor student seeks a waiver of participation, the school shall promptly notify the student's parent or legal guardian about the student's choice.

16.5. A parent, guardian, or secondary student requesting a waiver of participation may also suggest an alternative to the school requirement or activity that requires reasonably equivalent performance by the student.

16.6. In responding to a request for a waiver, the school may:

16.6.1. Waive participation by the student in the objectionable curriculum or activity, with no penalty;

16.6.2. Provide a reasonable alternative as suggested by the parent or secondary student, or other reasonable alternative developed in consultation with the requesting party, that will achieve the objectives of the portion of the curriculum or activity for which waiver is sought; or

16.6.3. Deny the request.

16.7. A request for waiver shall not be denied unless school officials determine that requiring the participation of the student is the least restrictive means necessary to achieve a compelling school interest.

16.8. In responding to a request for waiver, the school shall not require a student to accept a substandard or educationally deficient alternative.

17. Waivers of Immunization on Religious Grounds

17.1. General rule: A student may not enter school without a certificate of immunization.

17.2. Exception: A student is exempt from receiving the required immunizations if the student presents to the principal a statement that the student is a bona fide member of a specified, recognized religious organization whose teachings are contrary to immunizations, signed by one of the following persons:

17.2.1. One of the student's parents;

17.2.2. The student's legal guardian;

17.2.3. A legal age brother or sister of a student who has no parent or guardian; or

17.2.4. The student, if of legal age.[51]

18. Release Time

18.1. General rule: Public schools may permit the release of students during school hours for attendance at religious classes taught by religious teachers on private property, but not on public school premises.[52] With respect to released time programs in Davis County, the District practice and procedure is as follows[53]:

18.1.1. Religious classes shall not be held in school buildings or on school property in any way that permits public money or property to applied to, or that requires public employees to become entangled with, any religious worship, exercise, or instruction.

18.1.2. Students shall attend released-time classes during the school day only upon the written request and permission of the student's parent or legal guardian.

18.1.3. Because public schools have a legitimate interest in knowing where their students are during school hours, released-time personnel may transmit regular attendance reports to the public school.[54] However, school personnel may not become entangled with released-time programs by gathering or compiling attendance reports from released-time programs.

18.1.4. Teachers of released-time classes are not to be considered members of the school faculty or to participate as faculty members in any school function.

18.1.5. Schedules of classes for public schools shall not include released-time classes. At the convenience of school, registration forms may contain a space indicating "released-time" designation. Scheduling shall be done on forms and supplies furnished by the religious institution and by personnel employed or engaged by the institution and shall occur off school premises.

18.1.6. Public school publications (i.e., student handbooks, folders, newspapers, etc.) shall not include pictures, reports or records of functions of released-time classes.

18.1.7. Public school teachers, administrators, or other officials shall not request teachers of released-time classes to exercise functions or assume responsibilities for the public school program which would result in a commingling of the activities of the two institutions.

18.1.8. Public school equipment or personnel shall not be used in any manner to assist in the conduct of released-time classes. No connection of bells, telephones, or other devices shall be made between public school buildings and institutions offering religious instruction except as a convenience to the public school in operation of its own program. When any connection of devices is permitted, the pro-rata costs shall be borne by the respective institutions.

18.1.9. Institutions offering religious instruction shall be regarded as private schools completely separate and apart from the public schools.

19. Dispute Resolution

19.1. Importance of alternative dispute resolution: given the divisive, lengthy, and costly nature of civil rights litigation for all parties, when First Amendment conflicts arise[55], it is District policy to take all reasonable steps to resolve disputes over religious issues in schools promptly, equitably, and with civility at the local level.

19.2. School level: Principals and other local school officials shall make every reasonable effort to resolve complaints under this policy at the school level.

19.2.1. Individuals shall file written complaints of religious discrimination with the principal or supervisor. If the complaint involves the principal or supervisor, the complaint may be filed directly with the District's Civil Rights Compliance Officer. Appropriate accommodations should be made for individuals with disabilities or small children unable to write.

19.2.2. As soon as possible, but no later than five (5) working days following receipt of the complaint, the principal or building supervisor shall meet with the complaining party to discuss the complaint and explore possibilities for resolution.

19.3. Mediation: If resolution is not reached at the school level through informal discussions with the principal or supervisor, the complaint will be subject to the following mediation process:

19.3.1. The Civil Rights Compliance Officer shall be contacted and given all relevant information, including copies of written complaints or statements from the parties.

19.3.2. As soon as possible, but no later than five (5) working days following receipt of the complaint, the Compliance Officer will appoint a trained, qualified mediator. The Compliance Officer may appoint an internal (District employee) mediator neutral to the complaint, upon mutual agreement of the parties. If either or both of the parties object to the internal mediator, the Compliance Officer will appoint a mediator from outside the District. If an external mediator is appointed, the District will bear all costs of hiring the mediator.

19.3.3. As soon as possible, but no later than ten (10) working days following the appointment of the mediator, the Compliance Officer will schedule a mediation conference at a neutral site convenient to all parties and the mediator.

19.3.4. The mediator shall earnestly attempt to facilitate a resolution of the complaint. However, the mediator will reserve the right to stop the mediation if it becomes reasonably apparent that a solution cannot be reached or if the parties stop negotiating in good faith.

19.3.5. If resolution is obtained through mediation, the mediator shall forward the complaint, along with the mediator's bill (if an outside mediator), and signed mediation agreement, to the Superintendent of Schools.

19.4. Civil Rights Review Board: If no resolution is reached through mediation, the Compliance Officer shall arrange for an impartial hearing before a Civil Rights Review Board as soon as possible, but not later than ten (10) working days following the close of the mediation.

19.4.1. The Civil Rights Review Board will be a three-person panel consisting of one person with school administration experience, one clergy or religious representative, and one citizen, all of whom must be neutral to the complaint and who have been trained to the impartial hearing officers.

19.4.2. After hearing the complaint and reviewing the totality of the circumstances, the Civil Rights Review Board shall issue a written decision of findings and conclusions, and a written recommendation for resolution, to the Superintendent of Schools as soon as possible, but no later than ten (10) working days following the hearing.

Sample School
District Policies

19.5. Appeals: Any party who disagrees with the decision of the Civil Rights Review Board and/or Superintendent may appeal the decision, in writing, to the Board of Education within ten (10) working days following the date of the decision.

    19.5.1. As soon as possible, but no later than ten (10) working days following the receipt of a timely appeal, the Board of Education shall hold an open hearing to consider the complaint. As soon as possible, but no later than ten (10) working days following the hearing, the Board of Education shall issue a written decision.

19.6. Right to counsel: All parties to a complaint may be represented by legal counsel or other representative of their choosing, and at their own expense, at any stage of this dispute resolution procedure.

20. Monitoring Responsibility and Review

20.1. Monitoring responsibility: The Policy Specialist, and the District Civil Rights Compliance Officer, as designated by the Superintendent of Schools, will be responsible for ensuring compliance with this policy. They will yearly evaluate, among other things: the frequency and nature of complaints under this policy; staff and student compliance with the policy; and staff, student, and parent perceptions of the policy's effectiveness. Results of the evaluation will be used to modify or update the policy as appropriate, with an emphasis on remedying deficiencies.

20.2. Policy review: A committee of administrators, teachers, parents, students, clergy, and attorneys shall be convened annually to review this policy's effectiveness and compliance with applicable State and federal law, and to update the policy accordingly.

21. Policy Dissemination

21.1. A summary of this policy and related materials shall be posted in prominent place in each District facility. A summary of the policy shall also be published in student registration materials, student and employee handbooks, and other appropriate publications as directed by the Superintendent.

Document History
Adopted: January 21, 1997
Policy Effective: February 1, 1997
Revised: August 4, 1998 (Section 11 Volunteers)

[1] Finding Common Ground: A First Amendment Guide to Religion and Public Education (Charles C. Haynes & Oliver Thomas, eds. 1994).

[2] Memorandum from Richard Riley, U.S. Secretary of Education, to Superintendents of Schools regarding U.S. Department of Education's Guidance on Religious Expression in Public Schools (Aug. 10, 1995) (Available at U.S. Department of Education or on the Internet at http://www.ed.gov/PressReleases/07-1995/religion.html).

[3] President Bill Clinton, Address at James Madison High School, Vienna, Virginia (July 12, 1995) (Transcript available in U.S. Office of the Press Secretary or on the Internet at http://www.ed.gov/PressReleases/07-1995/religion.html).

[4] Memorandum from Richard Riley, U.S. Secretary of Education, to Superintendents of Schools regarding U.S. Department of Education's Guidance on Religious Expression in Public Schools (Aug. 10, 1995) (Available at U.S. Department of Education or on the Internet at http://www.ed.gov/PressReleases/07-1995/religion.html).

[5] While this policy addresses expressive rights of both students and employees, the rights of teachers and other school officials are not coextensive with the rights of students. Because school employees are agents of the State of Utah, they are obligated by law to remain neutral with respect to religion while acting in their official capacity. Specifically, school employees must be circumspect in matters of personal religious expression and take care to avoid actions or words that would advance or inhibit religion. For example, courts have held that a teacher does not have the right to sit at his desk and silently read the Bible in front of students during a classroom silent reading period. *Roberts v. Madigan,* 921 F. 2d. 1047 (10th Cir. 1990). In addition, school officials must not do or say anything that could reasonably be construed as encouraging or discouraging prayer or other religious exercise in school.

[6] Utah Admin. Code §R277-105-1 (B)(1996).

[7] Utah Admin. Code §R277-105-1(C)(1996).

[8] Utah Admin. Code §R277-105-1 (E)(1996).

[9] Utah Admin. Code §R277-105-1 (G)(1996).

[10] *Alabama & Coushatta Tribes v. Big Sandy School Dist.,* 817 F.Supp. 1319, 1329 (E.D. Tex. 1993). *See also Welsh v. United States,* 398 U.S. 333, 340 (1970) (defining religion for Free Exercise purposes as any set of beliefs addressing matters of "ultimate concern" occupying a "place parallel to that filled by . . . God in traditionally religious persons."); *Fleishfresser v. Directors of Sch. Dist. 200,* 15 F.3d 680, 688 n. 5 (7th Cir. 1994).

[11] *Torcaso v. Watkins,* 367 U.S. 488 (1961).

[12] *Frazee v. Illinois Dept. of Employment Security,* 489 U.S. 829 (1989); *Alabama & Coushatta Tribes v. Big Sandy Sch. Dist.,* 817 F. Supp. 1319, 1329 (E.D. Tex. 1993); *McGlothin v. Jackson Mun. Separate Sch. Dist.,* 829 F. Supp. 853, 866 n. 19 (S.D. Miss. 1992).

[13] It is District policy to avoid excessive entanglement with religion. Therefore, school officials should not engage in the practice of judging whether a particular belief is truthful, acceptable, logical, consistent, or comprehensible to others. However, it is proper for school officials to determine whether an individual's belief is sincerely religious or a sincere matter of conscience, as opposed to simply a matter of personal preference. *See, e.g., Brown v. Pena,* 441 F. Supp. 1382, 1385 (S.D. Fla. 1977), *aff'd,* 589 F.2d 1113 (5th Cir., 1979); *McGlothin v. Jackson Mun. Separate Sch. Dist.,* 829 F.Supp. 853, 866 n.19 (S.D. Miss. 1992). In reaching such a determination school officials shall consult with relevant individuals (i.e., parents, clergy, etc.) and consider the totality of the circumstances.

[14] *Everson v. Board of Educ.,* 330 U.S. 1 (1947).

[15] School officials may not pray, read scriptures, or do anything else that could be construed by students as encouraging or discouraging acceptance of a particular religious belief or participation in a religious exercise. See §§1.6.4, 3.9, and footnote 5.

[16] In other words, the school must choose a course of action that does not violate the individual's religion if such a course of action is available and feasible for the school.

[17] Utah Code Ann. §53A-13-101.3(2)(b); Utah Admin. Code §R277-105-6 (B).

[18] Utah Code Ann. §53AS-13-101.3(1), Utah Admin. Code R277-105-6 (A).

15 Sample School
District Policies

[19] *See, e.g., Settle v. Dickson County Sch. Bd.,* 53 F.3d. 152 (6th Cir. 1995) (holding that teacher could give 9th grade students a grade of "0"on her proposed research paper covering life of Jesus Christ because student already knew a lot about the subject, and therefore the assignment's objective of having students research an unfamiliar topic would not by accomplished, and also because while assignment called for consulting at least four sources, student submitted the Bible as her sole source of information); *Denooyer v. Livonia Pub. Sch.,* 799 F. Supp. 744 (E.D. Mich. 1992), aff'd 1 F.3d 1240 (1993)(upholding school district's decision to prohibit second grader from showing video of herself singing evangelical proselytizing Christian song in Classroom as part of "show and tell" program because showing of the video tape was inconsistent with program's purpose of teaching children oral communication skills).

[20] Id.; *see also Duran v. Nitsche,* 780 F. Supp. 1048 (E.D. Pa. 1991), *vacated,* 972 F.2d 1331 (3rd Cir. 1992).

[21] According to District and school dress codes, students are prohibited from wearing any gang-related attire, as well as hairstyles, clothing, apparel, or cosmetics that substantially interferes with the work of the school, materially disrupts the educational process, or impinges upon the rights of other students. *See* District Policy #5S-400 § 10 (School Discipline and Attendance Policy): *Tinker v. Des Moines Indep. Sch. Dist.,* 393 U.S. 503 (1969).

[22] See *Cheema v. Thompson,* 67 F.3d 883 (9th Cir. 1995)

[23] Utah Code Ann. §53A-11-12.

[24] Upon holding a classroom moment of silence, teachers should instruct students that they may engage in any quiet activity of their choice. However, teachers should not say or do anything (i.e., folding arms and bowing head, reading scriptures, etc.) that could reasonably be interpreted as encouraging or discouraging prayer or other religious exercise.

[25] Utah Code Ann §53A-13-101.1(3); Utah Admin. Code R277-105-7.

[26] The United States Supreme Court has ruled that it is unconstitutional for clergymen to give prayers at public school graduation ceremonies. *Lee v. Weisman,* 112 S. Ct. 2638 (1992). While the Supreme Court has not yet ruled on the constitutionality of student-led graduation prayers, the lower federal courts are split on the issue. Compare *American Civil Liberties Union of New Jersey v. Black Horse Pike Regional Bd. Of Educ.,* 84 F.3d 1471 (3rd Cir. 1996); *Harris v. Joint Sch. Dist. No. 241,* 41 F.3d 447 (9th Cir. 1994), vacated, 115 S. Ct. 2604 (1995) (ruling that student _led graduation prayers are unconstitutional); with *Ingebretsen v. Jackson Pub. Sch. Dist.,* 88 F.3d 274 (5th Cir. 1996); *Jones v. Clear Creek Indep. Sch. Dist.,* 977 F.2d 963 (5th Cir. 1992), *cert. denied* 113 S. Ct. 2950 (1993); and *Albright v. Board of Educ. Of Granite Sch. Dist.,* 765 F. Supp. 682 (D. Utah 1991) (upholding student-led graduation prayers).

[27] *See Wallace v. Jaffree,* 105 S. Ct. 2479, 2498 (1985) (O'Connor, J., concurring): A state-sponsored moment of silence in the public schools is different from state-sponsored vocal prayers or Bible reading. First, a moment of silence is not inherently religious. Silence, unlike prayer or Bible reading need not be associated with a religious exercise. Second, a pupil who participates in a moment of silence need not compromise his or her beliefs. During a moment of silence, a student who objects to prayer is left to his or her own thoughts, and is not compelled to listen to the prayers or thoughts of others. . . . It is difficult to discern a serious threat to religious liberty from a room of silent, thoughtful school children.

> *See also, Jaffree,* 105 S. Ct. at 2495 ("Although we do not reach the other two prongs of the Lemon test, I note that the 'effect' of a straightforward moment-of-silence statute is unlikely to 'advanc[e]' or inhibi[t] religion.'") (Powell. J., concurring): *School District of Abington Township v. Schempp,* 83 S. Ct. 1560, 1602 ("It has not been shown that . . . the observance of a moment of reverent silence at the opening of class, may not adequately serve the solely secular purposes of the devotional activities without jeopardizing either the religious liberties of any members of the community or the proper degree of separation between the spheres of religion and government.").

> More recently, a federal court in *Bown v. Gwinnett County Sch. Dist.,* 895 F. Supp. 1565, 1579 (N.D. Ga. 1995) noted:

> > Momentary silence simply does not jeopardize either the religious liberties of any members of the community or the proper degree of separation between the spheres of religion and government. Momentary silence does not advance or inhibit religion. Providing this moment of silence for school children does not convey a government message advancing or inhibiting religion.

[28] *See Lundberg v. West Monona Communication Sch. Dist.,* 731 F. Supp. 331, 341 (N.D. Iowa 1989) (holding that school districts' interest in avoiding establishment of religion outweighs students' right to free speech and free exercise and thus prayer at graduation should not be allowed).

[29] Principals, teachers, school board members, and other school officials present on the stand as an official part of graduation ceremonies should not say or do anything (i.e., folding arms and bowing heads, reading scriptures, etc.) that could reasonably be interpreted as encouraging or discouraging prayer or other religious exercise during the moment of silence.

[30] *See Ingebretsen v. Jackson Pub. Sch. Dist.,* 88 F.3d 274 (5th Cir. 1996) (ruling unconstitutional a Mississippi state statute that permitted "invocations, benedictions, or nonsectarian, nonproselytizing student-initiated voluntary prayer during compulsory or noncompulsory school-related student assemblies, student sporting events, . . . and other school-related student events."): *Doe v. Duncanville Indep. Sch. Dist.,* 994 F. 2d 160 (5th Cir. 1993) (striking down coach's custom of leading girls' basketball team in Lord's Prayer before and after practice and games).

[31] *Compare Berger v. Rensselaer Central Sch. Corp.,* 982 F.2d 1160 (7th Cir. 1993), *cert. denied,* 113 S. Ct. 2344 (1933) (striking down school district's practice of allowing the Gideons to distribute Bibles in 5th grade classrooms); with *Peck v. Upshur County Bd. of Educ.,* 941 F.Supp. 1465 (N.D.W.Va. 1996) (upholding district's policy of allowing private citizens to set up tables at designated places in schools to distribute bibles and other religious materials); *Schanou v. Lancaster County Sch. Dist.,* 863 F.Supp. 1048 (D. Neb. 1994), *vacated,* 62 F.3d 1040 (8th Cir. 1995) upholding district's policy of allowing Gideons to distribute Bibles once per year on school grounds, but outside school buildings, in a non-coercive manner).

[32] Federal courts have recently upheld restrictive policies governing the distribution of student materials. For example, the court in *Muller by Muller v. Jefferson Lighthouse School,* 98 F.3d 1530 (7th Cir. 1996) ruled that the following policy of the Racine Unified School District was consistent with the First Amendment and did not violate students' rights to freedom of speech: _

Section 6144.11(Non-School-Sponsored Publications)

Publications produced by school district students without school sponsorship, or handbills, may be distributed and/or sold within the school according to the following procedure.

1. They must include the name of the sponsoring organization and/or individual.

2. A time and place for the distribution must be set cooperatively with the principal.

3. A copy must be given to the principal at least 24 hours before its distribution.

4. The publication shall contain this phrase: "The opinions expressed are not necessarily those of the school district or its personnel."

5. If the principal finds the publication (1) contains libelous . . . or obscene language, (2) may incite (lead) persons to illegal acts, (3) is insulting to any group or individuals, or (4) he/she can reasonably forecast that its distribution to the students will greatly disrupt or materially interfere with school procedures and intrude into school affairs or the lives of others, the principal shall notify the sponsors of the publication that its distribution may not be started, or must stop. The principal shall state the reason for his/her decisions.

Section 6144.12: (Distribution and Displaying Materials)

The written permission of the school principal or the Superintendent of Schools is required before students may distribute or display on designated bulletin boards, materials from other sources outside the school

[33] *See e.g., Clark v. Dallas Indep. Sch. Dist.,* 806 F. Supp. 116 (N.D. Tex. 1992) (striking down district policy that prohibited students from engaging in religious discussions and meetings and from distributing religious materials on district policy before and during school; court found that "a blanket prohibition on high school students' expression of religious views and even proselytizing on campus is unconstitutional and contrary to the purpose of secondary schools.").

[34] For example, a court recently upheld the portions of a school district's literature distribution policy that stipulated the following time, place and manner restrictions:

When any student or students, who as an individual or a group, seek to distribute more than 10 copies of the same written material on one or more days in the school or on school grounds, they must comply with the following procedures:

1. At least 24 hours prior to any distribution of material, the student shall notify the principal of his/her intent to distribute.

2. Material shall be distributed between 7:15 a.m. and 7:45 a.m. and 3:15 p.m. and 3:45 p.m. from a table to be set up by the school for such purposes. The table shall be located at or near the main entrance of the building. No more than two students distributing the same material shall be seated at the table.

Hedges v. Wauconda Community Sch. Dist., 118, 9F.3d 1295, 1296 (7th Cir. 1993). See also *Muller v. Jefferson Lighthouse School,* 98 F3d 1530 (7th Cir. 1996) (upholding district's policy of requiring students wishing to distribute literature on school property to obtain prior approval from school officials); *Harless v. Darr* 937 F. Supp. 1351 (S.D. Ind. 1996) (ruling that district's policy, providing when students wishes to distribute more than 10 copies of written materials on school grounds he must notify principal of intent to distribute at least 48 hours prior to distribution and provided copy of material to be reviewed by Superintendent, was not impermissible prior restraint).

[35] Utah Admin. Code R277-105-8 (A)(1996); *see also Roberts v. Madigan,* 921 F.2d 1047 (10th Cir. 1990), *cert. denied,* 112 S. Ct. 3025 (1992) (upholding school district's directive to fifth grade teacher barring him from reading Bible at his desk during silent reading period in his classroom).

[36] Utah Admin. Code R277-105-8 (B) (1996).

[37] 42 U.S.C. §2000e(j) (1996); *see also Trans World Airlines, Inc. v. Hardison,* 432 U.S. 63 (1977) (holding that TWA was not obligated to accommodation an employee's inability to work Friday nights or Saturdays for religious reasons by allowing a four-day week or paying overtime for shift coverage; the Court stated that "To require [an employer] to bear more than a de minimis cost . . . is an undo

hardship."; *Lee v. ABF Freight System, Inc.,* 22 F.3d 1019, 1023 (10th Cir. 1994) (holding that "The cost of hiring an additional worker or the loss of production that results from not replacing a worker who is unavailable due to religious conflict can amount to undue hardship."); *Brown v. Polk County, Iowa,* 61 F.3d 650 (8th Cir. 1995), *cert. denied,* 116 S. Ct. 1042 (1996) (upholding county's discipline of employee for directing another employee to type his Bible study notes on work time, as such activity created an undue hardship on county business); *Burns v. Southern Pac. Transp. Co.,* 589 F.2d 403, 407 (9th Cir. 1978), *cert. denied,* 439 U.S. 1072 (1979) ("Undue hardship requires more than proof of some fellow-worker's grumbling . . . An employer . . . would have to show actual imposition on co-workers or disruption of the work routine.")

[38] Utah Code Ann. §53A-13-101.1. *See also School Dist. Of Abington Township v. Schempp,* 374 U.S. 203 (1963), where Justice Clark, writing for the Supreme Court, stated:

> It might well be said that one's education is not complete without a study of comparative religion or the history of religion and its relationship to the advancement of civilization. It certainly may be said that the Bible is worthy of study for its literary and historic qualities. Nothing we have said here indicates that such a study of the Bible or of religion, when presented objectively as part of a secular program of education may not be effected consistently with the First Amendment.

[39] 20 U.S.C. § 1232 h; Utah Code Ann. §53A-13-302.

[40] *See Bauchman v. West High,* 900 F.Supp. 254, 268 (D. Utah 1995), *appeal pending* (10th Cir. 1996). Ruling that a high school choir's performance of the songs of "Friends," and "The Lord Bless You and Keep You," both of which contained lyrics referring to the Lord and other religious concepts, did not violate the Establishment Clause or the Free Exercise Clause of the First Amendment, the court reasoned in part:

> Singing of songs is not an "explicit religious exercise," like the graduation prayer was deemed to be by the Supreme Court in Lee v. Weisman or like other prayers and singing in cases cited by plaintiff. . . . Despite references in some songs to "God" and "Lord," as well as language in the songs reflecting a supplication to deity, the songs with religious content are not ipso facto the equivalent of prayers. Neither does the fact that the lyrical source of some songs is scriptural automatically render those songs violative of the Establishment Clause.

[41] Utah Admin. Code R277-105-7 (B).

[42] Utah Admin. Code R277-105-7 (D).

[43] Utah Admin. Code R277-105-7 (C).

[44] Utah Admin. Code R277-105-7 (F).

[45] Teachers and school officials should be mindful that many non-Christians, as well as some Christians (i.e., Jehovah's Witnesses) do not celebrate Christmas and many other holidays.

[46] *See Clever v. Cherry Hill Township Bd. of Educ.,* 838 F. Supp. 929, 939 (D.N.J. 1993) ("If our public schools cannot teach this mutual understanding and respect [about religious symbols and holidays], it is hard to envision another societal institution that could do the job effectively.")

[47] *Florey v. Sioux Falls Sch. Dist.,* 619 F. 2d. 1311 (8th Cir. 1980), *cert. denied,* 449 U.S. 987 (1980).

[48] For example, a teacher may display a Christmas tree together with a Menorah or Star of David, and Santa Claus or a symbol representing Kwanzaa.

[49] *See e.g., Edwards v. Aguillard,* 482 U.S. 578 (1987); *Epperson v. Arkansas,* 393 U.S. 97 (1968); *Brown v. Woodland Joint Unified Sch. Dist.,* 27 F.3d. 1373, 1379 (9th Cir. 1994) ("If an Establishment Clause violation arose each time a student believed that a school practice either advanced or disapproved of a religion, school curricula would be reduced to the lowest common denominator, permitting each student to become a `curriculum review committee' unto himself or herself."); *Fleischfresser v. Directors of Sch. Dist. 200,* 15 F.3d. 680, 690 (7th Cir. 1994) ("If we are to eliminate everything that is objectionable to any [religious group] or inconsistent with any of their doctrines, we will leave public schools in shreds. Nothing but educational confusion and a discrediting of the public school system can result from subjecting it to constant lawsuits.") (*quoting McCollum v. Board of Educ.,* 333 U.S. 203, 235 (1948) (Jackson, J. concurring.)); *Mozert v. Hawkins County Bd. of Educ.,* 827 F.2d 1058 (6th Cir. 1987).

[50] Utah Code Ann. §53A-13-101.2; Utah Admin. Code R277-105-5.

[51] Utah Code Ann. §53A-11-302.

[52] *Zorach v. Clauson,* 343 U.S. 306 (1952); *Lanner v. Wimmer,* 662 F.2d. 1349 (10th Cir. 1981).

[53] Utah Admin. Code R277-610-3.

[54] *Lanner v. Wimmer,* 662 F.2d. 1349, 1358 (10th Cir. 1981).

[55] In a recent federal court opinion, one judge stated:

> Paraphrasing George Orwell, we have sunk to the point at which is becomes one's duty to restate the obvious. What seems obvious to me in disputes like these [First Amendment disputes over religion in schools], deeply enmeshed in social and political policy, are not well handled by the adjudication process. Court Decree, focused on the single goal of pure "non-establishment," supplant decisions based on compromise and consensus which reflect the multifaceted wisdom of the people acting through democratically accountable elected officials and educators.

> *Ingebretsen v. Jackson Pub. Sch. Dist.,* 88 F.3d. 274, 288 (5th Cir. 1996) (Jones, J., dissenting).

15 Sample School
District Policies

WICOMICO COUNTY BOARD OF EDUCATION

Salisbury, Maryland

[Editor's Note: In 1991 the Wicomico County Board of Education adopted a policy establishing guidelines for teaching about religion and advising teachers on how to approach school programs and religious holidays. The adoption of this policy, despite its success and the community's endorsement of it today, was a slow and difficult process. Fortunately, through open discussions between parents, teachers and school administrators, consensus was reached on a policy that all members of the community could support. Parents who felt the policy's original draft represented one portion of the community's religious agenda, eventually were able to support a revised draft which they came to view as a sound policy intended to help the community sensitively address issues of religious liberty.

Wicomico County's success was due to several important factors: a diversified Values Committee which worked steadily on the policy; open community discussions about the proposed policy; and in-service training for teachers after the adoption of the new policy. Dr. Evelyn Blose Holman, then superintendent of schools for Wicomico County, explains that the policy gives the schools guidelines, saving the community from "some of the rancor and debate" that surrounds religious liberty issues.

In order to further promote the goals of the policy, the county intends to adopt new materials for the study about religions, and the Values Committee has drafted a brochure addressing teacher's frequently asked questions in regards to the policy. Clearly, the adoption of such a policy requires hard work and continuing efforts, but as one parent notes, simply the discussions surrounding the policy have been good for the community, helping the county's schools embrace the values articulated in the policy.]

WICOMICO COUNTY'S POLICY: TEACHING ABOUT RELIGION

Preamble

Any discussion of the place of religion in public education must be grounded in the principle of freedom of conscience, particularly as it is embodied in this nation's First Amendment to the Constitution which states that "Congress shall make no law respecting an establishment of religion, or prohibiting the free exercise thereof ..."

This inalienable right to religious liberty depends neither upon political authority nor upon any election but is rooted in the inviolable dignity of each person.

Teaching about religion, then, must adhere to the American experiment which cherishes beliefs that are a matter of conviction rather than coercion. It must foster learning in an atmosphere permeated by the values adopted by the Wicomico County school system: compassion, courtesy, freedom of thought and action, honesty, loyalty, respect for others' rights, responsibility, responsible citizenship, self-respect and tolerance.

While the Supreme Court has prohibited religious indoctrination by the public schools, the court has made clear that teaching *about* religion is permissible under the First Amendment. Operating under the principle that knowledge is preferable to ignorance and recognizing the significant role religion has played in this nation's public life and culture and in the wider arena of world history, the board supports teaching about religious history and tradition where appropriate in the curriculum.

Policy

The board of education endorses teaching *about* religion where the curriculum guides indicate it is appropriate and when the classroom atmosphere encourages both teachers and students to be responsible and to respect the rights of each person.

Such teaching must foster knowledge *about* religion, not indoctrination into religion; it should be academic, not devotional or testimonial; it should promote awareness of religion, not sponsor its practice; it should inform students about the diversity of religious views rather than impose one particular view; and it should promote understanding and respect rather than divisiveness.

Consequently, the board endorses, where appropriate and feasible, the professional development of teachers who wish to learn more about the constitutionally appropriate place of religion in the curriculum. The board also supports the development of new instructional materials that will reflect age-appropriate content and activities for teaching about religion.

Sample School
District Policies

Guidelines

To help school administrators and teachers interpret and apply the Wicomico County Board of Education policy regarding teaching about religion in the schools, the following guidelines have been developed by the Values Committee of the Wicomico County Board of Education in consultation with the First Liberty Institute.

Part 1: Curriculum

A. Religious instruction is the responsibility of parents and religious institutions, but teaching *about* religion is a legitimate part of a complete education on the elementary and secondary levels.

B. Teaching about religion should always operate within the context of First Amendment rights and responsibilities. In order to ensure the activity is constitutional, its purpose and effort should be to educate about rather than promote religion. The activity should also avoid excessive entanglement between the schools and religious organizations.

C. As a part of the curriculum, religious literature, music drama and the arts may be included, provided each is intrinsic to the learning experience in the various fields of study and is presented objectively.

Also, as part of the curriculum, students may be asked to read selections from sacred writings for their literary and historical qualities, but not for devotional purposes.

Part 2: School Programs and Holidays

A. School programs, performances and celebrations will serve an educational purpose. The inclusion of religious music, symbols, art or writings may be permitted if the religious content has an independent educational purpose which contributes to the stated objectives of the approved curriculum.

B. The use of religious symbols, provided they are used only as an example of cultural and religious heritage, is permitted as a teaching aid or resource. These symbols may be displayed only for the length of time that the instructional activity requires.

C. The Supreme Court has made clear that public schools may not sponsor religious celebrations but may teach *about* religion. Secular and religious holidays provide opportunities for educating students about history and cultures, as well as traditions of particular religious groups within a pluralistic society.

However, teachers must exercise special caution and sensitivity whenever discussion about religious holidays occurs. Presentation of materials dealing with religious holidays must be accurate, informed and descriptive. Focus should be on the origins, history and generally agreed-upon meanings of the holidays. Since teachers will need to be aware of the diversity of religious beliefs in their classroom and in the county at large, they will need to be particularly sensitive to the rights of religious minorities as well as those who hold no religious belief. Respect for religious diversity in the classroom requires that teachers be fair and balanced in their treatment of religious holidays. Teachers may not use the study of religious holidays as an opportunity to proselytize or to inject religious beliefs into the discussions. Teachers can teach through attribution, i.e., by reporting that "some Buddhists believe ..."

D. On the elementary level, natural opportunities arise for discussion of religious holidays while studying different cultures and communities; in the secondary level, students of world history or literature will have opportunities to consider the holy days of religious traditions.

E. Teachers need to be aware of the major religious holidays of all the represented religions in their classrooms so as to avoid, as much as possible, creating an undue burden on students who choose not to attend school on those days.

Part 3: Scheduling

A. School scheduling should reasonably accommodate religious observances in the community. The yearly school calendar should minimize conflicts with the religious holidays of all faiths.

B. The Wicomico School calendar shall continue to recognize national, state, school and community observances. Special days beyond those specified on the calendar may be accommodated as reasonably as possible, with students being asked to make up assignments or examinations without loss of status or penalty.

Part 4: Procedures

A. Recognizing the importance of religious liberty and freedom of conscience, school administrators and teachers will allow students to be excused, where it is feasible, from activities that are contrary to religious beliefs. Students are responsible for notifying school officials in advance and arranging for make-up work. Students and/or staff members wishing to be excused from activities that are contrary to their religious beliefs may make that request of the appropriate teacher or supervisor, within a reasonable time period to allow accommodations to be made.

B. This policy holds for all lectures, programs and performances presented within the school during normal school hours. It is the responsibility of teachers and school officials to notify, whenever relevant, outside speakers and performers of Wicomico County's policy and its guidelines.

15 Sample School
District Policies

C. Disciplinary questions that relate to violations of this policy by teachers or administrators will be resolved through the already established procedures of the board.

D. Recognizing that no guidelines can give exhaustive treatment of this issue, the Superintendent may choose to refer disputes about implementation of this policy to an appropriate committee.

RAMONA UNIFIED SCHOOL DISTRICT POLICY

Ramona, California

Recognition of Religious Beliefs and Customs

Preamble

Any discussion of the place of religion in public education must be grounded in the principles of religious liberty, or freedom of conscience, particularly as embodied in this nation's First Amendment to the Constitution, which states that "Congress shall make no law respecting an establishment of religion, or prohibiting the free exercise thereof...". This inalienable right to religious liberty depends neither upon political authority nor upon any election but is rooted in the inviolable dignity of each person.

Statement of Purpose

The board of education endorses teaching about religion where the curriculum guides indicate it is appropriate and when the classroom atmosphere encourages both teachers and students to be responsible and to respect the rights of each person.

Such teaching must foster knowledge *about* religion, not indoctrination into religion; it should be academic, not devotional or testimonial; it should promote awareness of religion, not sponsor its practice; it should inform students about the diversity of religious views rather than impose one particular view; and it should promote understanding of different religious views as well as respect for the rights of persons who hold such views.

Right and Responsibility of Students/Staff

Students have the right to pray individually or in groups or to discuss their religious views with their peers so long as they are not disruptive. Because the Establishment Clause does not apply to purely private speech, students enjoy the right to read religious literature, pray before meals and before tests, and discuss religion with other student listeners as long as the listeners do not feel coerced or harassed. However, the right to engage in voluntary prayer does not include, for example, the right to have a captive audience listen or to compel other students to participate.

Teachers and school administrators, when acting in those capacities, are representatives of the state, and, in those capacities, are themselves prohibited from encouraging or soliciting student religious or anti-religious activity. Similarly, when acting in their official capacities, teachers may not engage in religious activities with their students. However, teachers may engage in private religious activity during duty free and noncontractual hours.

As a general rule, students may express their religious viewpoints in the form of reports, both oral and written, homework and artwork. Teachers may not reject or correct such submissions simply because they include a religious symbol or address religious themes. Likewise, teachers may not require students to modify, include or excise religious views in their assignments, if germane. These assignments should be judged by ordinary academic standards of substance, relevance, appearance, and grammar. As noted, however, teachers should not allow students to use a captive, classroom audience to proselytize or conduct religious activities.

Students have the right to distribute religious literature to their schoolmates, subject to those reasonable time, place, and manner or other constitutionally acceptable restrictions imposed on the distribution of all non-school literature. Thus, a school may confine distribution of all literature to a particular table at particular times. It may not single out religious literature for burdensome regulation.

Student participation in before- or after-school religious events on campus is permissible. School officials, acting in an official capacity, may neither discourage nor encourage participation in such events.

Students have the right to speak to and attempt to persuade their peers about religious topics just as they do with regard to political topics. But school officials should intercede to stop student speech if it turns into religious harassment aimed at a student or small group of students.

Student religious clubs in secondary schools are permitted to meet and to have equal access to campus media to announce their meetings. Teachers may not actively participate in club activities and "non-school persons" may not control or regularly attend club meetings.

School Calendars

The school calendar should be prepared so as to minimize conflict with the religious holidays of all faiths. Where conflicts are unavoidable, care should be taken to avoid tests, special projects, introduction of new concepts, and other activities that would be difficult to make up on religious holidays. Students are expected to make up missed assignments without loss of status or penalty.

Religion in Curriculum and Instruction

Students may be taught *about* religion, but public schools may not teach religion. As the U.S. Supreme Court has said repeatedly, "[I]t might well be said that one's education is not complete without a study of comparative religion, or the history of religion and its relationship to the advancement of civilization." It would be difficult to teach art, music, literature, and most social studies without considering religious influences.

The history of religion, comparative religion, the Bible or other religious texts as literature (either as a separate course or within some other existing course) are all permissible public school subjects. It is both permissible and desirable to teach objectively about the role of religion in the history of the United States and other countries.

As a part of the curriculum, religious literature, music, drama, and the arts may be included, provided each is intrinsic to the learning experience in the various fields of study and is presented objectively.

Also, as part of the curriculum, students may be asked to read selections from sacred writings for their literary and historical qualities, but not for devotional purposes. The approach to religion shall be one of instruction, not one of indoctrination. The purpose is to educate, not convert. The focus shall be on the study of what all people believe and must not be on teaching a student what to believe.

At all levels, the study of religious music as part of a musical appreciation course, as a musical experience, as part of a study of various lands and cultures is to be encouraged. Seasonally appropriate religious music may be studied during the season when interest is highest. In all public school programs and study, care must be taken to avoid presentation of the music as a celebration of a particular religion or religious holiday and to ensure that there is no bias shown for or against any religion or non-religion.

Schools may teach civic virtues, including honesty, good citizenship, sportsmanship, courage, respect for the rights and freedoms of others, respect for persons and their property, civility, the virtues of moral conviction, tolerance and hard work. Although schools may teach *about* the role religion may play in character and values formation, schools may not invoke religious authority.

Religious Symbolism

Religious messages on T-shirts and the like may not be singled out for suppression. Students may wear religious attire, such as yarmulkes and head scarves, and they may not be forced to wear gym clothes that they regard, on religious grounds, as immodest.

The use of religious symbols that are a part of religious holidays at the appropriate times of the year are permitted as teaching aids or as resources, provided such symbols are displayed as examples of the broad cultural and religious heritage of the celebration and are limited to a brief or temporary period of instruction.

School Ceremonies and Activities

School officials may not mandate, organize, or encourage prayer at graduation or other school activities or dedications, nor may they organize a religious baccalaureate ceremony. The school district may rent facilities under the School Communities Facilities to

Sample School
District Policies

community groups who wish to sponsor such events. At certain occasions at which it is appropriate to set a solemn tone, a time of silence may be appropriate.

Parents' Rights to Excuse Students for Religious Reasons

Students will be excused, when feasible, from lessons/activities which their parents find objectionable for religious reasons. Alternative assignments will be substituted.

RICHARDSON INDEPENDENT SCHOOL DISTRICT GUIDELINES FOR RELIGIOUS PRACTICES

Richardson, Texas

Religious Practices
  Grades K-12
Equal Access Act
  Limited Open Forum
  Grades 7-12

Richardson Independent School District 2000-2001

To the RISD Staff:

This handbook is designed to serve as a guide for all of us concerning the religious policies we must follow. These policies, revised during the 1999-2000 school year by a task force comprised of school patrons, religious leaders, and school staff members, are in alignment with court rulings and support an approach of neutrality, inclusion, and respect within our culturally diverse community.

The handbook includes:
  Mission Statement
  Principles Relating to Religious Practices
  Religious Practices
    Revised or new sections are:
      Religious Content in the Instructional Setting
      Religious Music
      Baccalaureate
  Limited Open Forum Policies
  Complaint Procedure (revised)
  Sample Complaint Form (new)

In response to the federal Equal Access Act, the Board of Trustees created a Limited Open Forum for all students in secondary schools. The second part of this handbook defines the guidelines, rules, and regulations associated with the Limited Open Forum, followed by the complaint procedure and sample form.

It is important that you read thoroughly the guidelines and familiarize yourself with them. I am so grateful for the commitment and willingness exhibited by the task force to support our RISD community in this worthy endeavor. I also want you to be aware that these guidelines are being reviewed on a continual basis by this broad-based task force to ensure that we find a common ground when dealing with religious issues.

Sincerely,
Carolyn Bukhair
Superintendent of Schools

Mission Statement

The Richardson Independent School District recognizes that two of its educational goals are to advance the students' knowledge and appreciation of the role that religious heritage has played in the social, cultural, and historical development of civilization, and to develop the students' understanding and toleration of religious differences in America.

Principles Relating to Religious Practices

In accomplishing the mission statement's goals, the District may permit studies about religion but may not sponsor the practices of religion.

The First Amendment of the United States Constitution states:

> "Congress shall make no law respecting an establishment of religion,
> or prohibiting the free exercise thereof…"

The U.S. Supreme Court has interpreted the First Amendment as requiring the state to maintain a wholesome neutrality in its interaction with religion in our pluralistic democratic society. The United States Court of Appeals for the Fifth Circuit, which has jurisdiction over Texas, has developed five guidelines based on Supreme Court doctrine for determining the appropriateness and/or legality of any specific school-sponsored activity. *First,* the activity must be one that accomplishes the Richardson Independent School District's legislative purpose, namely education. *Second,* the activity's principal or primary effort must neither advance nor inhibit religion. *Third,* the activity must not require or encourage excessive involvement with religion on the part of the District. *Fourth,* the activity must not give the appearance of an endorsement of religion by the District or its employees. And *fifth*, the activity must not coerce students to participate in a religious activity [*Jones v. Clear Creek ISD,* 977 F.2d 963 (Fifth Circuit, 1992)].

While the District may not sponsor or endorse religion, it recognizes the right of each student and school employee to the free exercise of religion, subject to the provisions of this handbook. Further, under the newly enacted Texas Religious Freedom Restoration Act, the District must establish a compelling purpose when it substantially burdens a person's free exercise of religion and must show that the means it uses to accomplish the purpose is the least restrictive way of doing so.

The provisions set forth in this handbook reflect the decisions reached by the U.S. Supreme Court and the U.S. Court of Appeals for the Fifth Circuit, as well as Texas state law.

No religious belief or nonbelief shall be promoted by the Richardson Independent School District, and none shall be disparaged. The Richardson Independent School District shall encourage all students and staff members to appreciate and be tolerant of each other's religious views. The District shall utilize every opportunity to foster understanding and mutual respect among students and parents regarding race, culture, economic background, and religious belief. Fostering high ideals, consideration for others, moral standards, patriotism, justice, and basic values such as love, compassion, family ties, peace, honesty, and goodwill toward all persons is not in conflict with the principles of religious liberty and government neutrality toward religion. The District shall make constructive contributions to the well-being of the community by sharing with families the responsibility of preparing students for participation in a pluralistic society.

Following are specific provisions based upon the preceding principles and federal and state law. This list is not meant to be all inclusive. These provisions, as well as issues not covered in this handbook, should be interpreted in accordance with the preceding principles.

Religious Practices

Prayer

The following shall apply:

1. The District shall permit private, voluntary prayer or meditation by individuals. Such activity shall not be disruptive or interfere with the rights of others.

2. The District and its employees shall not lead, compose, sponsor, encourage, suggest, or provide the means for the recitation of prayers in school facilities during school hours or before, during, or after any school-sponsored public athletic or extracurricular event.

3. The District shall not permit the recitation of student-initiated public prayers as part of an organized class, team, or school-sponsored activity [*Ingebretsen v. Jackson Public School District, Fifth Circuit, 1996, Doe v. Santa Fe ISD*, Fifth Circuit, 1999]. However, nothing prohibits students from engaging in voluntary private individual or group prayer that does not occur under the sponsorship or involvement of the District or its employees [*Doe v. Duncanville ISD*, Fifth Circuit, 1995]. Thus, a student or group of students may elect to say a private prayer not under school sponsorship before lunch or before an athletic contest.

4. School personnel, while representing the District, shall not audibly pray with or in the presence of their students. However, district employees shall treat voluntary student private prayer with respect.

Sample School
District Policies

Religious Texts

The following shall apply:

1. The reading from religious texts during instructional time shall be permitted for instructional and literary purposes. The readings shall not be used for promoting religious beliefs or for devotional purposes.

2. The District shall permit the private, voluntary reading of religious texts by students as long as it does not interfere with the educational process. As district representatives and public employees, Richardson ISD employees must remain neutral in matters involving religion and avoid any action that has the effect of advancing religious beliefs at school.

3. The distribution of religious literature by an individual student in the District shall be permitted as long as the distribution does not interfere with the educational process and complies with other District policies [see EFA and FMA].

4. The distribution of religious literature on campus or at school sponsored activities by District employees shall be prohibited.

Religious Content in the Instructional Setting

The following shall apply:

1. Curriculum content pertaining to religion may be presented as part of a secular program of education. Such content may not be taught with the intent of promoting or denigrating any particular religion.

2. The study of religious observances may be included in the curriculum as an opportunity for teaching about religions. Recognition of and information about such holy days shall focus on their educational aspects. Such study serves the academic goals of educating students about history and cultures, as well as fostering among students understanding and mutual respect within a pluralistic society.

3. The use of religious symbols is permitted as a teaching aid or resource, provided such symbols are used as examples of cultural and religious heritage. Their display and use shall be limited to the specific teaching activity and shall not be used for devotional or proselytizing purposes.

4. Student papers and presentations on religious topics are permitted as part of a secular program of instruction. Students may express their opinions about religion in the form of homework, artwork, and other assignments provided they fulfill the purposes of the classroom assignment. Students work containing religious content should be evaluated by ordinary academic standards of substance and relevance and in accordance with other legitimate pedagogical concerns of the teacher and the school.

At all grade levels, the classroom teacher is responsible for setting guidelines to ensure that the content of all student papers and presentations is relevant to the curriculum. At the elementary level, teachers will make special effort to anticipate and prevent situations in which the religious content of a student presentation is likely to offend, confuse, or cause discomfort to impressionable students.

Parent Religious Objection
Upon written parental request, parents are entitled to an exemption under state law for their child from the classroom or other school activity that conflicts with their religious or moral beliefs, provided that the purpose is not to avoid a test or to prevent the student from taking a subject for the semester.

Religious Attire
Dress required by religious customs shall be permitted. If a student's dress could cause a safety hazard in a particular activity, an alternative activity shall be substituted for that student. District personnel may wear religious symbols provided that the symbols do not serve to advance religious beliefs in a way to jeopardize the district's neutrality toward religion.

Religious Observances
The following shall apply:

1. The cultural and historical aspects of religious holy days and their meaning may be taught, but such holy days may not be recognized with religious observances by school personnel.

2. The District calendar should be prepared to minimize conflicts with religious observances of all faiths.

3. Students shall be excused from class for religious observances and shall not be penalized or deprived of reasonable make-up opportunities for such observances [see FDD]. Excusal includes travel days to and from the observance. District employees who are absent for religious observance shall be granted leave without pay unless they wish to use their unused personal business leave for this purpose [see DEC (Regulation)].

Religious Symbols as Decorations
Religious symbols may not be displayed in school as decorations and may be displayed only on a temporary basis as part of the academic program [see also *Religious Attire* in this handbook].

Religious Music
Religious music may be performed by district bands, choirs, and orchestras as part of an academic program of instruction. When planning and presenting performances that include religious music, District personnel must make all reasonable efforts to provide a balanced

presentation of secular and religious music from a variety of traditions throughout the course of the school year.

Students may present a musical work with a religious theme in class or as part of a special performance, variety, or talent show, etc., as long as such selections are consistent with the purpose or theme of the assignment or presentation.

Student selections are permitted based upon ordinary academic standards and relevance in accordance with other legitimate pedagogical concerns of the teacher and school.

Rental of District Facilities by Religious Organizations

The District facilities may be rented for purposes of religious worship or religious teaching by religious organizations or groups only if such facilities are made available under the District's general policies applicable to nonschool organizations or groups. In this context, the policy shall permit the use of such facilities by staff and students acting as private individuals. In all circumstances, District facilities may be used for religious activities only if the activities…

> …are outside normal school hours;
> …are not promoted or encouraged by the District; *and*
> …do not require the expenditure of public funds.

Baccalaureate Services

Baccalaureate, as a religious service, is not sponsored or organized by the District. However, individual schools may sponsor a secular graduation celebratory event. Attendance at such an event shall be optional and voluntary. The event, including the farewell address, shall be motivational and celebratory in character. The event is to be initiated and planned by students in coordination with a faculty advisor who shall assure that the event complies with District policies.

Commencement Ceremonies

Commencement is a secular celebration of the culmination of study leading to graduation. School personnel may not invite clergy to lead invocation and/or benediction or to present an address at school commencement ceremonies. School personnel may permit the graduating class to choose whether to have an invocation and/or benediction at graduation so long as the invocation/benediction is to be given by a student volunteer, is nonproselytizing, and is nonsectarian.

Special Programs or Events

Content of school-sponsored programs and events shall be secular in purpose and effect and shall not promote or denigrate any particular religion. Such programs or events shall reflect a sensitivity to religious diversity within a pluralistic society. Students shall be excused without penalty from participation in such events if participation is in conflict with their religious beliefs.

Other Programs or Student Events

For local provisions on the content of school-sponsored programs as it relates to neutrality in religious matters see FM (Local).

Guidelines for Visitors

Visitors who represent or act as proponents of a religious, political, or philosophical viewpoint shall be allowed only as invited guests of a specific student or small number of students, provided that such visits are consistent with general school policies regarding visitors.

The visitation privileges shall not include the right to establish a situation whereby visitors shall attempt to influence students other than the invitors as to a particular religious, political, or philosophical viewpoint.

This policy is designed not to interfere with the students' right to maintain personal relationships or to restrain free speech, but to prohibit visitors from using such visits as a platform for proselytizing religious beliefs to students. Visitors must also refrain from any conduct that implies, directly or indirectly, school support for or endorsement of a religious message or a religious viewpoint.

Student Religious Groups

Student religious groups may not be school sponsored and District employees may not participate in their affairs. However, such groups may be granted access to the secondary school campus and to school media under the terms of the federal equal access act discussed in the section *"Limited Open Forum Policies for Noncurriculum-Related Student Groups"* in this handbook.

Limited Open Forum Policies for Noncurriculum-Related Student Groups

Curriculum-related groups and clubs may be sponsored and promoted by the school.
This section does not apply to such curriculum-related groups and clubs.

For purposes of the Federal Equal Access Act, the Board has created a limited open forum at the District's secondary schools so that noncurriculum-related student groups may meet on school premises during noninstructional time [see District policy FM and FM (Local)]. As interpreted by the U. S. Supreme Court in *Board of Education of Westside Community Schools v. Mergens,* a noncurriculum-related student group means that the group is not related to the school curriculum because the subject matter is not taught, the subject matter does not relate to the curriculum in general, participation is not required for a course, or participation does not convey academic credit. Each secondary school principal shall set aside noninstructional time before or after actual classroom instruction begins or ends for meetings of noncurriculum-related student groups. This time period includes an activities period when instruction is not occurring.

Sample School
District Policies

Student Requests for Access to the Campus

Students in secondary grades (7-12) wanting to meet on school premises shall file a written request with the campus principal. That request shall contain a brief statement of the group's purposes and goals, a list of the group's members, and a schedule of its proposed meeting times. The noncurriculum-related student group must agree to have a monitor (a District employee who is appointed by the principal) who will attend all meetings and activities for custodial purposes. Requests shall be approved by the principal and Superintendent subject to the availability of suitable meeting space and without regard to the religious, political, philosophical, or other content of the speech likely to be associated with the group's meetings. The District and its personnel may not limit the rights of noncurricular-related student groups that are not of a specific size (no minimum).

Staff Participation

Noncurriculum-related student groups must be studentinitiated, voluntary, and student-led. The District and its employees are prohibited from sponsoring meetings of noncurricular-related student groups and may be present at religious meetings only in a nonparticipatory capacity. The District and its personnel are prohibited from influencing the form or content of prayer or other religious activity or from requiring any person to participate in prayer or other religious activity at a meeting of a student religious group.

Monitors

A "monitor" is defined as a District employee appointed by the principal who attends all meetings and activities of noncurriculum-related student groups. No employee of the District may be required to accept appointment as a monitor if the purpose of the organization is contrary to the beliefs of the employee. District monitors shall be present at religious meetings only in a nonparticipatory capacity.

Notice of Meetings

Notice of meetings of noncurriculum-related groups may only be posted in a central area(s) designated by the principal. Such notices may only include the name of the noncurriculum group, date, time, and location of the meeting and a statement that the group is non-school sponsored. Posting of meeting notices in other parts of the building not approved by the principal or announcements on the public address system regarding meetings are prohibited.

Involvement of Non-School Persons

Non-school persons only may attend or make presentations at meetings of noncurriculum-related groups with approval of the principal. The principal reserves the right to limit the number of times a non-school person(s) may attend a meeting of the group.

Recognition of Student Groups

Noncurriculum-related student groups may be recognized in the school yearbook, provided the recognition is in a section of the yearbook that is separate from curriculum-related groups and is clearly delineated for noncurriculum-related student groups.

Nondiscrimination

Noncurriculum-related student groups may not abridge the constitutional rights of any person, nor discriminate against any person on the basis of race, color, religion, sex, national origin, or disability.

Rules for Meetings

Meetings of noncurriculum-related student groups granted access to the school during noninstructional time must conform to the provisions listed in this handbook and are subject to the following additional rules:

1. The principal or designee shall assign the specific space to be used for the meeting and shall approve in writing the use of the space to the initiating student(s). A yearly calendar of meetings shall be submitted in advance to the principal or designee for approval and the monitor shall keep a log of all such meetings.

2. Notices of meetings shall conform to the notice requirement in the previous section and shall state that such meetings are nonschool-sponsored. Organizations shall identify the nature of their group in all publicity.

3. The meeting shall be voluntary and initiated by a student enrolled in that school.

4. The meeting shall not be sponsored by the District or its employees. District monitors shall be present at religious meetings only in a nonparticipatory capacity.

5. The meeting shall not materially and substantially interfere with the orderly conduct of educational activities within the school.

6. The meeting shall not require expenditure of public funds beyond the incidental cost of providing the space for student-initiated meetings.

7. The meeting shall not result in additional or special student transportation provided at District expense.

8. The cost of repair of any damage to District property, as well as to teachers' and students' property, incurred during such meetings shall be borne by the person(s) responsible and may result in denial of future access to the building.

9. Nothing in this section shall be construed to limit the authority of the school principal to maintain order and discipline on school premises, to protect the well-being of students and faculty, and to assure that attendance of students at meetings is voluntary.

Violations

Failure of a noncurriculum-related student group to comply with applicable rules may result in its loss of rights to meet on school premises. The principal shall report rule violations to the Superintendent.

Sample School
District Policies

After a fair determination of the facts concerning rule violations, the Superintendent may decide to suspend the noncurriculum-related student group's rights to meet on school premises for the balance of the school year or some lesser time period, depending upon the seriousness of the violations.

If a determination to suspend a group occurs during the last six-week reporting period of the school year, the suspension may be extended through the end of the first semester of the next school year. Suspensions or warnings imposed by the Superintendent may be appealed to the Board in accordance with District policy [see FNG (Local)].

Religious Practices Complaint Procedure

The Religious Practices Complaint Procedure provides a venue for channeling and resolving complaints that arise under the provisions of the RISD Guidelines for Religious Practices. The procedure is designed to operate expeditiously and equitably.

General Provisions

- As defined in RISD policy FNG (Legal), the term "parent" means a person standing in parental relation, but does not include a person as to whom the parent-child relationship has been terminated or a person not entitled to possession of or access to a child under a court order.

- The term "student" means a person who is enrolled in the Richardson school district.

- For purposes of this procedure, "days" shall mean school days.

- The term "Religious Practices Advisory Committee" means a committee of parents and community members appointed by the RISD Superintendent.

Level One

Level One is the first step in the "Religious Practices Complaint Procedure" and, as such, includes processes for complaints that originate either within a particular school or at the district level.

School Level Complaint

A student or parent who has a **complaint regarding religious practices occurring in the school that the student attends** shall schedule a conference with the school principal within fifteen (15) days of the time the student or parent knew of the event or series of events causing the complaint. The principal shall schedule a conference with the student or parent within ten (10) days of the request for the conference. The student or parent shall secure a Religious Practices Complaint Form from the principal and submit the completed complaint form to the principal at the conference. Within ten (10) days following the conference, the principal shall communicate a written response to the student or parent.

District Level Complaint

A student or parent who has **a complaint regarding religious practices occurring in the district as a whole** shall schedule a conference with the Executive Director, Extended Programs, or designee within fifteen (15) days of the time the student or parent knew of the event or series of events causing the complaint. The Executive Director, Extended Programs, or designee shall schedule a conference with the student or parent within ten (10) days of the request for the conference. The student or parent shall secure a Religious Practices Complaint Form from the principal of the school the student attends and submit the completed form to the Executive Director, Extended Programs, or designee at the conference. Within ten (10) days following the conference, the Executive Director, Extended Programs or designee shall communicate a written response to the student or parents.

Level Two

If the outcome at Level One is not to the student's or parent's satisfaction, the student or parent may present, within fifteen (15) days of receiving the written response, an appeal to the Religious Practices Advisory Committee. In addition to submitting the completed Religious Practices Complaint Form at the time of the appeal, the student or parent shall describe in writing why they have appealed the Level One decision. The Committee shall schedule an informal conference within fifteen (15) days of the filing of the appeal. During the conference, both the Level One administrator and the student and/or parent may make a presentation to the Committee, subject to reasonable time limits set by the Committee chair. The conference is not subject to the Texas Open Meetings Act.

Within ten (10) days following the conference, the Committee shall prepare a written response to be submitted as a recommendation to the Superintendent. Copies of the written response shall be delivered to the Level One administrator and to the student or parent.

The Superintendent shall review the recommendation and accompanying documents in light of the *RISD Guidelines for Religious Practices.* The Superintendent shall advise the parties of a final decision within thirty (30) days.

Level Three

If the outcome at Level Two is not to the student's or parent's satisfaction, the student or parent may submit to the Superintendent a written request to place the matter on the agenda of the next regular Board meeting. The Superintendent shall inform the student or parent of the date, time, and place of the meeting.

The procedures to be followed at the Level Three hearing are delineated in the section "Hearing" in RISD Board Policy FNG (Local), page 2 of 3.

Appeal from the Board to the Texas Commissioner of Education shall be prescribed by Texas state law, regulations, and procedures. The student or parent shall be so advised. Nothing shall preclude the student or parent from any legal remedy in state or federal court.

Sample School
District Policies

RISD Religious Practices Complaint Form

In processing a complaint regarding religious practices at the school or district level, a student or parent must complete this form and submit it to the appropriate administrator within the required timeline as described in the Religious Practices Complaint Procedure (see *RISD Guidelines for Religious Practices*). The form must also be filed within the stipulated timelines for appeals (see reverse side).

Name_____ Phone_____

Address _____ City, Zip _____

I am a *(check one)*: ☐ Parent   ☐ Student

Student's school: _____ Grade level _____

Explain below in detail what your complaint is and what relevant provision or provisions of the *RISD Guidelines for Religious Practices* are implicated. Attach an additional sheet if necessary.

Describe below what solution or remedy you propose to resolve your complaint. Be as specific as you can. Attach an additional sheet if necessary.

Complainant's signature _____ Date _____

During the complaint process, student and parent personally identifiable information is protected from disclosure to third parties under the terms of the Family Educational Rights and Privacy Act (FERPA). Appeal from the Board to the Texas Commissioner of Education shall be prescribed by Texas state law, regulations, and procedures. The student or parent shall be so advised. Nothing shall preclude the student or parent from any legal remedy in state or federal court.

Appendix A:
Contact Information
for Organizations
Signing Consensus
Statements

APPENDIX A: CONTACT INFORMATION FOR ORGANIZATIONS SIGNING CONSENSUS STATEMENTS

American Academy of Religion

825 Houston Mill RD NE
Atlanta, GA 30329-4246
Phone 1 (404) 727-3049
Fax 1 (404) 727-7959
aar@aarweb.org
www.aar-site.org

American Association of School Administrators

1801 North Moore Street
Arlington, VA 22209-1813
Phone (703) 528-0700
Fax (703) 841-1543
webmaster@aasa.org
www.aasa.org

American Center for Law and Justice

P.O. Box 64429
Virginia Beach, VA 23467
Phone (757) 226-2489
Fax (757) 226-2836
www.aclj.org

American Federation of Teachers

555 New Jersey Avenue, NW
Washington, DC 20001
Phone (202) 879-4400
online@aft.org
www.aft.org

American Jewish Committee

Jacob Blaustein Building
165 East 56 Street
New York, NY 10022
Phone (212) 751-4000
Fax (212) 838-2120
PR@ajc.org
www.ajc.org

American Jewish Congress

Stephen Wise Congress House
15 East 84th Street
New York, NY 10028
Phone (212) 879-4500
Fax (212) 249-3672
www.ajcongress.org

Americans United for Separation of Church and State

518 C Street, N.E.
Washington, D.C. 20002
Phone (202) 466-3234
Fax (202) 466-2587
americansunited@au.org
www.au.org

Anti-Defamation League

823 United Nations Plaza
New York, NY 10017
Phone (212) 490-2525
www.adl.org

Association for Supervision and Curriculum Development

1703 North Beauregard Street
Alexandria, VA 22311-1714
Phone (703) 578-9600 or
1 (800) 933-ASCD
Fax (703) 575-5400
www.ascd.org

Baptist Joint Committee on Public Affairs

200 Maryland Ave., N.E.
Washington, DC 20002
Phone (202) 544-4226
Fax (202) 544-2094
bjcpa@bjcpa.org
www.bjcpa.org

Carnegie Foundation for the Advancement of Teaching

555 Middlefield Road
Menlo Park, CA 94025
Phone (650) 566-5100
Fax (650) 326-0278
clyburn@carnegiefoundation.org
www.carnegiefoundation.org

Catholic League for Religious and Civil Rights

450 Seventh Ave
New York, NY 10123
Phone (212) 371-3191
Fax (212) 371-3394
www.catholicleague.org

Central Conference of American Rabbis

355 Lexington Avenue
New York, NY 10017
Phone (212) 972-3636
info@ccarnet.org
www.ccarnet.org

Christian Coalition

499 So. Capitol Street SW
Suite 615
Washington, DC 20003 USA
Phone (202) 479-6900
Fax (202) 479-4260
www.cc.org

Christian Educators Association International

Post Office Box 41300
Pasadena, CA 91114
Phone (626) 798-1124
Fax (626) 798-2346
info@ceai.org
www.ceai.org

Christian Legal Society

4208 Evergreen Lane, Suite 222
Annandale, VA 22003
Phone (703) 642-1070
Fax (703) 642-1075
CLSHQ@clsnet.org
www.christianlegalsociety.org

Coalition for the Community of Reason

6 Peele Place
Charleston, SC 29401
Phone (843) 577-0637
Fax (843) 953-1410
facilitator@communityofreason.org

Council on Islamic Education

P.O. Box 20186
Fountain Valley, CA 92728-0186
Phone (714) 839-2929
Fax (714) 839-2714
info@cie.org
www.cie.org

Church of Jesus Christ of Latter-day Saints

50 East North Temple Street
Salt Lake City, Utah 84150
Phone 801-240-1000
www.lds.org

Department of Education of the United States Conference of Catholic Bishops

3211 4th Street, N.E.,
Washington, DC 20017-1194
Phone (202) 541-3000
www.usccb.org

First Amendment Center

1207 18th Avenue South
Nashville, TN 37221
Phone 615-727-1600
Fax 615-727-1319
news@freedomforum.org
www.firstamendmentcenter.org

General Conference of Seventh-day Adventists

12501 Old Columbia Pike
Silver Spring, MD 20904-6600
Phone (301) 680-6306
www.adventists.org

Islamic Society of North America

PO Box 38
Plainfield, IN 46168
Phone 317-839-8157
Fax 317-839-1840
www.isna.net

National Association of Elementary School Principals

1615 Duke Street
Alexandria, VA 22314
Phone (800) 38-NAESP [800-386-2377]
or (703) 684-3345
naesp@naesp.org
www.naesp.org

National Association of Evangelicals

1001 Connecticut Avenue, NW
Suite 522
Washington, DC 20036
Phone (202) 789-1011
Fax (202) 842-0392
oga@nae.net
www.nae.net

National Association of Secondary School Principals

1904 Association Drive
Reston, VA 20191-1537
Phone (703) 860-0200
nassp@principals.org

National Conference for Community and Justice

475 Park Avenue South, 19th Floor
New York, NY 10016-6901
Phone (212) 545-1300
Fax (212) 545-8053
www.nccj.org

National Council for the Social Studies

3501 Newark Street, NW
Washington, DC 20016
Phone (202) 966-7840
Fax (202) 966-2061
www.ncss.org

National Council of Churches of Christ in the USA

Room 850, 475 Riverside Drive
New York, NY 10115
Phone (212) 870-2227
Fax (212) 870-2030
news@ncccusa.org
www.ncccusa.org

National Education Association

1201 16th Street, NW
Washington, DC 20036
Phone (202) 833-4000
www.nea.org

National PTA

330 N. Wabash Avenue
Suite 2100
Chicago, IL 60611
Phone 312-670-6782 or
800-307-4PTA (4782)
Fax 312-670-6783
info@pta.org
www.pta.org

National School Boards Association

1680 Duke Street
Alexandria, VA 22314
Phone 703-838-6722
Fax 703-683-7590
info@nsba.org
www.nsba.org

People for the American Way

2000 M Street, NW, Suite 400
Washington, DC 20036
Phone: 202-467-4999
or 800-326-7329
pfaw@pfaw.org
www.pfaw.org

Phi Delta Kappa

408 N. Union St., P.O. Box 789
Bloomington, IN 47402-0789
Phone 800-766-1156 or 812-339-1156
Fax 812-339-0018
www.pdkintl.org

Union of American Hebrew Congregations

633 Third Avenue
New York, NY 10017-6778
Phone 212-650-4227
www.uahc.org

Union of Orthodox Jewish Congregations of America

333 7th Ave., 19th Fl.
New York, NY 10001
Phone 212-563-4000
www.ou.org

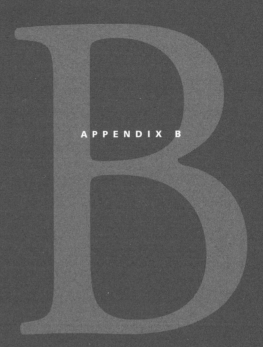

The Williamsburg Charter

FIRST AMENDMENT TO THE
UNITED STATES CONSTITUTION

APPENDIX B:
THE WILLIAMSBURG CHARTER

This introduction to the Williamsburg Charter is taken from Articles of Faith, Articles of Peace: The Religious Liberty Clauses and the American Public Philosophy. Hunter, James Davison and Os Guinness, eds. Washington: The Brookings Institution, 1990.

The Williamsburg Charter was written and published expressly to address the dilemmas, challenges, and opportunities posed by religious liberty in American public life today. Beginning in the fall of 1986, the charter was drafted by representatives of America's leading faiths—Protestant, Catholic, Jewish, and secularist, in particular. It was revised over the course of two years in close consultation with political leaders, scholars from many disciplines, and leaders from a wide array of faith communities. Named after Williamsburg in honor of the city's role as the cradle of religious liberty in America, it was presented to the nation in Williamsburg on June 25, 1988, when the first 100 national signers signed it publicly on the occasion of the 200th anniversary of Virginia's call for the Bill of Rights.

The stated purpose of the charter is fourfold: to celebrate the uniqueness of the First Amendment religious liberty clauses; to reaffirm religious liberty—or freedom of conscience—for citizens of all faiths and none; to set out the place of religious liberty within American public life; and to define the guiding principles by which people with deep differences can contend robustly but civilly in the public arena.

There are three main sections in the charter: first, a call for a reaffirmation of the first principles that underlie the religious liberty in American experience; second, a call for a reappraisal of the course and conduct of recent public controversies; and third, a call for "reconstitution" of the American people, in the sense of this generation reappropriating the framers' vision and ideals in our time.

Numerous individual points could be highlighted in a document that has much to say on current issues in law and society—the place accorded to naturalistic faiths, the delineation of the relationship of the two religious liberty clauses, the mention of the menace of the modern state, the insistence on the danger of "semi-establishments," and so on. But the two principal themes of the charter center on the importance of religious liberty as America's "first liberty," and on the religious liberty clauses as the "golden rule" for civic life. These themes—the inalienable right and the universal duty to respect that right—are developed in various ways, ranging from exposition of first principles to contemporary guidelines, but the overall effect is a powerful restatement of a critical aspect of America's public philosophy.

Summary of Principles

Congress shall make no law respecting an establishment of religion, or prohibiting the free exercise thereof ...

The Religious Liberty clauses of the First Amendment to the Constitution are a momentous decision, the most important political decision for religious liberty and public justice in history. Two hundred years after their enactment they stand out boldly in a century made dark by state repression and sectarian conflict. Yet the ignorance and contention now surrounding the clauses are a reminder that their advocacy and defense is a task for each succeeding generation.

We acknowledge our deep and continuing differences over religious beliefs, political policies and constitutional interpretations. But together we celebrate the genius of the Religious Liberty clauses, and affirm the following truths to be among the first principles that are in the shared interest of all Americans:

1. Religious liberty, freedom of conscience, is a precious, fundamental and inalienable right. A society is only as just and free as it is respectful of this right for its smallest minorities and least popular communities.

2. Religious liberty is founded on the inviolable dignity of the person. It is not based on science or social usefulness and is not dependent on the shifting moods of majorities and governments.

3. Religious liberty is our nation's "first liberty," which undergirds all other rights and freedoms secured by the Bill of Rights.

4. The two Religious Liberty clauses address distinct concerns, but together they serve the same end — religious liberty, or freedom of conscience, for citizens of all faiths or none.

5. The No Establishment clause separates Church from State but not religion from politics or public life. It prevents the confusion of religion and government which has been a leading source of repression and coercion throughout history.

6. The Free Exercise clause guarantees the right to reach, hold, exercise or change beliefs freely. It allows all citizens who so desire to shape their lives, whether private or public, on the basis of personal and communal beliefs.

7. The Religious Liberty clauses are both a protection of individual liberty and a provision for ordering the relationship of religion and public life. They allow us to live with our deepest differences and enable diversity to be a source of national strength.

8. Conflict and debate are vital to democracy. Yet if controversies about religion and politics are to reflect the highest wisdom of the First Amendment and advance the best interests of the disputants and the nation, then *how* we debate, and not only *what* we debate, is critical.

9. One of America's continuing needs is to develop, out of our differences, a common vision for the common good. Today that common vision must embrace a shared understanding of the place of religion in public life and of the guiding principles by which people with deep religious differences can contend robustly but civilly with each other.

10. Central to the notion of the common good, and of greater importance each day because of the increase of pluralism, is the recognition that religious liberty is a universal right. Rights are best guarded and responsibilities best exercised when each person and group guards for all others those rights they wish guarded for themselves.

We are firmly persuaded that these principles require a fresh consideration, and that the reaffirmation of religious liberty is crucial to sustain a free people that would remain free. We therefore commit ourselves to speak, write and act according to this vision and these principles. We urge our fellow citizens to do the same, now and in generations to come.

THE WILLIAMSBURG CHARTER

Keenly aware of the high national purpose of commemorating the bicentennial of the United States Constitution, we who sign this Charter seek to celebrate the Constitution's greatness, and to call for a bold reaffirmation and reappraisal of its vision and guiding principles. In particular, we call for a fresh consideration of religious liberty in our time, and of the place of the First Amendment Religious Liberty clauses in our national life.

We gratefully acknowledge that the Constitution has been hailed as America's "chief export" and "the most wonderful work ever struck off at a given time by the brain and purpose of man." Today, two hundred years after its signing, the Constitution is not only the world's

oldest, still-effective written constitution, but the admired pattern of ordered liberty for countless people in many lands.

In spite of its enduring and universal qualities, however, some provisions of the Constitution are now the subject of widespread controversy in the United States. One area of intense controversy concerns the First Amendment Religious Liberty clauses, whose mutually reinforcing provisions act as a double guarantee of religious liberty, one part barring the making of any law "respecting an establishment of religion" and the other barring any law "prohibiting the free exercise thereof."

The First Amendment Religious Liberty provisions epitomize the Constitution's visionary realism. They were, as James Madison said, the "true remedy" to the predicament of religious conflict they originally addressed, and they well express the responsibilities and limits of the state with respect to liberty and justice.

Our commemoration of the Constitution's bicentennial must therefore go beyond celebration to rededication. Unless this is done, an irreplaceable part of national life will be endangered, and a remarkable opportunity for the expansion of liberty will be lost.

For we judge that the present controversies over religion in public life pose both a danger and an opportunity. There is evident danger in the fact that certain forms of politically reassertive religion in parts of the world are, in principle, enemies of democratic freedom and a source of deep social antagonism. There is also evident opportunity in the growing philosophical and cultural awareness that all people live by commitments and ideals, that value-neutrality is impossible in the ordering of society, and that we are on the edge of a promising moment for a fresh assessment of pluralism and liberty. It is with an eye to both the promise and the peril that we publish this Charter and pledge ourselves to its principles.

We readily acknowledge our continuing differences. Signing this Charter implies no pretense that we believe the same things or that our differences over policy proposals, legal interpretations and philosophical groundings do not ultimately matter. The truth is not even that what unites us is deeper than what divides us, for differences over belief are the deepest and least easily negotiated of all.

The Charter sets forth a renewed national compact, in the sense of a solemn mutual agreement between parties, on how we view the place of religion in American life and how we should contend with each other's deepest differences in the public sphere. It is a call to a vision of public life that will allow conflict to lead to consensus, religious commitment to reinforce political civility. In this way, diversity is not a point of weakness but a source of strength.

I. A time for reaffirmation

We believe, in the first place, that the nature of the Religious Liberty clauses must be understood before the problems surrounding them can be resolved. We therefore affirm both their cardinal assumptions and the reasons for their crucial national importance.

With regard to the assumptions of the First Amendment Religious Liberty clauses, we hold three to be chief:

1. The Inalienable Right

Nothing is more characteristic of humankind than the natural and inescapable drive toward meaning and belonging, toward making sense of life and finding community in the world. As fundamental and precious as life itself, this "will to meaning" finds expression in ultimate beliefs, whether theistic or non-theistic, transcendent or naturalistic, and these beliefs are most our own when a matter of conviction rather than coercion. They are most our own when, in the words of George Mason, the principal author of the Virginia Declaration of Rights, they are "directed only by reason and conviction, not by force or violence."

As James Madison expressed it in his Memorial and Remonstrance, "The Religion then of every man must be left to the conviction and conscience of every man; and it is the right of every man to exercise it as these may dictate. This right is in its nature an unalienable right."

Two hundred years later, despite dramatic changes in life and a marked increase of naturalistic philosophies in some parts of the world and in certain sectors of our society, this right to religious liberty based upon freedom of conscience remains fundamental and inalienable. While particular beliefs may be true or false, better or worse, the right to reach, hold, exercise them freely, or change them, is basic and non-negotiable.

Religious liberty finally depends on neither the favors of the state and its officials nor the vagaries of tyrants or majorities. Religious liberty in a democracy is a right that may not be submitted to vote and depends on the outcome of no election. A society is only as just and free as it is respectful of this right, especially toward the beliefs of its smallest minorities and least popular communities.

The right to freedom of conscience is premised not upon science, nor upon social utility, nor upon pride of species. Rather, it is premised upon the inviolable dignity of the human person. It is the foundation of, and is integrally related to, all other rights and freedoms secured by the Constitution. This basic civil liberty is clearly acknowledged in the Declaration of Independence and is ineradicable from the long tradition of rights and liberties from which the Revolution sprang.

2. The Ever Present Danger

No threat to freedom of conscience and religious liberty has historically been greater than the coercions of both Church and State. These two institutions—the one religious, the other political—have through the centuries succumbed to the temptation of coercion in their claims over minds and souls. When these institutions and their claims have been combined, it has too often resulted in terrible violations of human liberty and dignity. They are so combined when the sword and purse of the State are in the hands of the Church, or when the State usurps the mantle of the Church so as to coerce the conscience and compel belief. These and other such confusions of religion and state authority represent the misordering of religion and government which it is the purpose of the Religious Liberty provisions to prevent.

Authorities and orthodoxies have changed, kingdoms and empires have come and gone, yet as John Milton once warned, "new Presbyter is but old priest writ large." Similarly, the modern persecutor of religion is but ancient tyrant with more refined instruments of control. Moreover, many of the greatest crimes against conscience of this century have been committed, not by religious authorities, but by ideologues virulently opposed to traditional religion.

Yet whether ancient or modern, issuing from religion or ideology, the result is the same: religious and ideological orthodoxies, when politically established, lead only too naturally toward what Roger Williams called a "spiritual rape" that coerces the conscience and produces "rivers of civil blood" that stain the record of human history.

Less dramatic but also lethal to freedom and the chief menace to religious liberty today is the expanding power of government control over personal behavior and the institutions of society, when the government acts not so much in deliberate hostility to, but in reckless disregard of, communal belief and personal conscience.

Thanks principally to the wisdom of the First Amendment, the American experience is different. But even in America where state-established orthodoxies are unlawful and the state is constitutionally limited, religious liberty can never be taken for granted. It is a rare achievement that requires constant protection.

3. The Most Nearly Perfect Solution

Knowing well that "nothing human can be perfect" (James Madison) and that the Constitution was not "a faultless work" (Gouverneur Morris), the Framers nevertheless saw the First Amendment as a "true remedy" and the most nearly perfect solution yet devised for properly ordering the relationship of religion and the state in a free society.

There have been occasions when the protections of the First Amendment have been overridden or imperfectly applied. Nonetheless, the First Amendment is a momentous decision for religious liberty, the most important political decision for religious liberty and public justice in the history of humankind. Limitation upon religious liberty is allowable only where the State has borne a heavy burden of proof that the limitation is justified—not by any ordinary public interest, but by a supreme public necessity—and that no less restrictive alternative to limitation exists.

The Religious Liberty clauses are a brilliant construct in which both No establishment and Free exercise serve the ends of religious liberty and freedom of conscience. No longer can sword, purse and sacred mantle be equated. Now, the government is barred from using religion's mantle to become a confessional State, and from allowing religion to use the government's sword and purse to become a coercing Church. In this new order, the freedom of the government from religious control and the freedom of religion from government control are a double guarantee of the protection of rights. No faith is preferred or prohibited, for where there is no state-definable orthodoxy, there can be no state-punishable heresy.

With regard to the reasons why the First Amendment Religious Liberty clauses are important for the nation today, we hold five to be pre-eminent:

1. **The First Amendment Religious Liberty provisions have both a logical and historical priority in the Bill of Rights.** They have logical priority because the security of all rights rests upon the recognition that they are neither given by the state, nor can they be taken away by the state. Such rights are inherent in the inviolability of the human person. History demonstrates that unless these rights are protected our society's slow, painful progress toward freedom would not have been possible.

2. **The First Amendment Religious Liberty provisions lie close to the heart of the distinctiveness of the American experiment.** The uniqueness of the American way of disestablishment and its consequences have often been more obvious to foreign observers such as Alexis de Tocqueville and Lord James Bryce, who wrote that "of all the differences between the Old world and the New, this is perhaps the most salient." In particular, the Religious Liberty clauses are vital to harnessing otherwise centrifugal forces such as personal liberty and social diversity, thus sustaining republican vitality while making possible a necessary measure of national concord.

3. **The First Amendment Religious Liberty provisions are the democratic world's most salient alternative to the totalitarian repression of human rights and provide a corrective to unbridled nationalism and religious warfare around the world.**

4. **The First Amendment Religious Liberty provisions provide the United States' most distinctive answer to one of the world's most pressing questions in the late-twentieth century.** They address the problem: How do we live with each other's deepest differences? How do religious convictions and political freedom complement rather than threaten each other on a small planet in a pluralistic age? In a world in which bigotry, fanaticism, terrorism and the state control of religion are all too common responses to these questions, sustaining the justice and liberty of the American arrangement is an urgent moral task.

5. **The First Amendment Religious Liberty provisions give American society a unique position in relation to both the First and Third worlds.** Highly modernized like the rest of the First World, yet not so secularized, this society—largely because of religious freedom—remains, like most of the Third World, deeply religious. This fact, which is critical for possibilities of better human understanding, has not been sufficiently appreciated in American self-understanding, or drawn upon in American diplomacy and communication throughout the world.

In sum, as much if not more than any other single provision in the entire Constitution, the Religious Liberty provisions hold the key to American distinctiveness and American destiny. Far from being settled by the interpretations of judges and historians, the last word on the First Amendment likely rests in a chapter yet to be written, documenting the unfolding drama of America. If religious liberty is neglected, all civil liberties will suffer. If it is guarded and sustained, the American experiment will be the more secure.

II. A time for reappraisal

Much of the current controversy about religion and politics neither reflects the highest wisdom of the First Amendment nor serves the best interests of the disputants or the nation. We therefore call for a critical reappraisal of the course and consequences of such controversy. Four widespread errors have exacerbated the controversy needlessly.

1. The Issue Is Not Only What We Debate, But How

The debate about religion in public life is too often misconstrued as a clash of ideologies alone, pitting "secularists" against the "sectarians" or vice versa. Though competing and even contrary worldviews are involved, the controversy is not solely ideological. It also flows from a breakdown in understanding of how personal and communal beliefs should be related to public life.

The American republic depends upon the answers to two questions. By what ultimate truths ought we to live? And how should these be related to public life? The first question is personal, but has a public dimension because of the connection between beliefs and public virtue. The American answer to the first question is that the government is excluded from giving an answer. The second question, however, is thoroughly public in character, and a public answer is appropriate and necessary to the well-being of this society.

This second question was central to the idea of the First Amendment. The Religious Liberty provisions are not "articles of faith" concerned with the substance of particular doctrines or of policy issues. They are "articles of peace" concerned with the constitutional constraints and the shared prior understanding within which the American people can engage their differences in a civil manner and thus provide for both religious liberty and stable public government.

Conflicts over the relationship between deeply held beliefs and public policy will remain a continuing feature of democratic life. They do not discredit the First Amendment, but confirm its wisdom and point to the need to distinguish the Religious Liberty clauses from the particular controversies they address. The clauses can never be divorced from the controversies they address, but should always be held distinct. In the public discussion, an open commitment to the constraints and standards of the clauses should precede and accompany debate over the controversies.

2. The Issue Is Not Sectarian, But National

The role of religion in American public life is too often devalued or dismissed in public debate, as though the American people's historically vital religious traditions were at best a purely private matter and at worst essentially sectarian and divisive.

Such a position betrays a failure of civil respect for the convictions of others. It also underestimates the degree to which the Framers relied on the American people's religious convictions to be what Tocqueville described as "the first of their political institutions." In America, this crucial public role has been played by diverse beliefs, not so much despite disestablishment as because of disestablishment.

The Founders knew well that the republic they established represented an audacious gamble against long historical odds. This form of government depends upon ultimate beliefs, for otherwise we have no right to the rights by which it thrives, yet rejects any official formulation of them. The republic will therefore always remain an "undecided experiment" that stands or falls by the dynamism of its non-established faiths.

3. The Issue Is Larger Than the Disputants

Recent controversies over religion and public life have too often become a form of warfare in which individuals, motives and reputations have been impugned. The intensity of the debate is commensurate with the importance of the issues debated, but to those engaged in this warfare we present two arguments for reappraisal and restraint.

The lesser argument is one of expediency and is based on the ironic fact that each side has become the best argument for the other. One side's excesses have become the other side's arguments; one side's extremists the other side's recruiters. The danger is that, as the ideological warfare becomes self-perpetuating, more serious issues and broader national interests will be forgotten and the bitterness deepened.

The more important argument is one of principle and is based on the fact that the several sides have pursued their objectives in ways which contradict their own best ideals. Too often, for example, religious believers have been uncharitable, liberals have been illiberal, conservatives have been insensitive to tradition, champions of tolerance have been intolerant, defenders of free speech have been censorious, and citizens of a republic based on democratic accommodation have succumbed to a habit of relentless confrontation.

4. The Issue Is Understandably Threatening

The First Amendment's meaning is too often debated in ways that ignore the genuine grievances or justifiable fears of opposing points of view. This happens when the logic of opposing arguments favors either an unwarranted intrusion of religion into public life or an unwarranted exclusion of religion from it. History plainly shows that with religious control over government, political freedom dies; with political control over religion, religious freedom dies.

The First Amendment has contributed to avoiding both these perils, but this happy experience is no cause for complacency. Though the United States has escaped the worst excesses experienced elsewhere in the world, the republic has shown two distinct tendencies of its own, one in the past and one today.

In earlier times, though lasting well into the twentieth century, there was a de facto semi-establishment of one religion in the United States: a generalized Protestantism given dominant status in national institutions, especially in the public schools. This development was largely approved by Protestants, but widely opposed by non-Protestants, including Catholics and Jews.

In more recent times, and partly in reaction, constitutional jurisprudence has tended, in the view of many, to move toward the de facto semi-establishment of a wholly secular understanding of the origin, nature and destiny of humankind and of the American nation. During this period, the exclusion of teaching about the role of religion in society, based partly upon a misunderstanding of First Amendment decisions, has ironically resulted in giving a dominant status to such wholly secular understandings in many national institutions. Many secularists appear as unconcerned over the consequences of this development as were Protestants unconcerned about their de facto establishment earlier.

Such de facto establishments, though seldom extreme, usually benign and often unwitting, are the source of grievances and fears among the several parties in current controversies. Together with the encroachments of the expanding modern state, such de facto establishments, as much as any official establishment, are likely to remain a threat to freedom and justice for all.

Justifiable fears are raised by those who advocate theocracy or the coercive power of law to establish a "Christian America." While this advocacy is and should be legally protected, such proposals contradict freedom of conscience and the genius of the Religious Liberty provisions.

At the same time there are others who raise justifiable fears of an unwarranted exclusion of religion from public life. The assertion of moral judgments as though they were morally neutral, and interpretations of the "wall of separation "that would exclude religious expression and argument from public life, also contradict freedom of conscience and the genius of the provisions.

Civility obliges citizens in a pluralistic society to take great care in using words and casting issues. The communications media have a primary role, and thus a special responsibility, in shaping public opinion and debate. Words such as public, secular and religious should be free from discriminatory bias. "Secular purpose," for example, should not mean "non-religious purpose" but "general public purpose." Otherwise, the impression is gained that "public is equivalent to secular; religion is equivalent to private." Such equations are neither accurate nor just. Similarly, it is false to equate "public" and "governmental." In a society that sets store by the necessary limits on government, there are many spheres of life that are public but non-governmental.

Two important conclusions follow from a reappraisal of the present controversies over religion in public life. First, the process of adjustment and readjustment to the constraints and standards of the Religious Liberty provisions is an ongoing requirement of American democracy. The Constitution is not a self-interpreting, self-executing document; and the prescriptions of the Religious Liberty provisions cannot by themselves resolve the myriad confusions and ambiguities surrounding the right ordering of the relationship between religion and government in a free society. The Framers clearly understood that the Religious Liberty provisions provide the legal construct for what must be an ongoing process of adjustment and mutual give-and-take in a democracy.

We are keenly aware that, especially over state-supported education, we as a people must continue to wrestle with the complex connections between religion and the transmission of moral values in a pluralistic society. Thus, we cannot have, and should not seek, a definitive, once for all solution to the questions that will continue to surround the Religious Liberty provisions.

Second, the need for such a readjustment today can best be addressed by remembering that the two clauses are essentially one provision for preserving religious liberty. Both parts, No establishment and Free exercise, are to be comprehensively understood as being in the service of religious liberty as a positive good. At the heart of the Establishment clause is the prohibition of state sponsorship of religion and at the heart of Free Exercise clause is the prohibition of state interference with religious liberty.

No sponsorship means that the state must leave to the free citizenry the public expression of ultimate beliefs, religious or otherwise, providing only that no expression is excluded from, and none governmentally favored, in the continuing democratic discourse.

No interference means the assurance of voluntary religious expression free from governmental intervention. This includes placing religious expression on an equal footing with all other forms of expression in genuinely public forums.

No sponsorship and no interference together mean fair opportunity. That is to say, all faiths are free to enter vigorously into public life and to exercise such influence as their followers and ideas engender. Such democratic exercise of influence is in the best tradition of American voluntarism and is not an unwarranted "imposition" or "establishment."

III. A time for reconstruction

We believe, finally, that the time is ripe for a genuine expansion of democratic liberty, and that this goal may be attained through a new engagement of citizens in a debate that is reordered in accord with constitutional first principles and considerations of the common good. This amounts to no less than the reconstitution of a free republican people in our day. Careful consideration of three precepts would advance this possibility:

1. The Criteria Must Be Multiple

Reconstitution requires the recognition that the great dangers in interpreting the Constitution today are either to release interpretation from any demanding criteria or to narrow the criteria excessively. The first relaxes the necessary restraining force of the Constitution, while the second overlooks the insights that have arisen from the Constitution in two centuries of national experience.

Religious liberty is the only freedom in the First Amendment to be given two provisions. Together the clauses form a strong bulwark against suppression of religious liberty, yet they emerge from a series of dynamic tensions which cannot ultimately be relaxed. The Religious Liberty provisions grow out of an understanding not only of rights and a due recognition of faiths but of realism and a due recognition of factions. They themselves reflect both faith and skepticism.

They raise questions of equality and liberty, majority rule and minority rights, individual convictions and communal tradition.

The Religious Liberty provisions must be understood both in terms of the Framers' intentions and history's sometimes surprising results. Interpreting and applying them today requires not only historical research but moral and political reflection.

The intention of the Framers is therefore a necessary but insufficient criterion for interpreting and applying the Constitution. But applied by itself, without any consideration of immutable principles of justice, the intention can easily be wielded as a weapon for governmental or sectarian causes, some quoting Jefferson and brandishing No establishment and others citing Madison and brandishing Free exercise. Rather, we must take the purpose and text of the Constitution seriously, sustain the principles behind the words and add an appreciation of the many-sided genius of the First Amendment and its complex development over time.

2. The Consensus Must Be Dynamic

Reconstitution requires a shared understanding of the relationship between the Constitution and the society it is to serve. The Framers understood that the Constitution is more than parchment and ink. The principles embodied in the document must be affirmed in practice by a free people since these principles reflect everything that constitutes the essential forms and substance of their society—the institutions, customs and ideals as well as the laws. Civic vitality and the effectiveness of law can be undermined when they overlook this broader cultural context of the Constitution.

Notable, in this connection is the striking absence today of any national consensus about religious liberty as a positive good. Yet religious liberty is indisputably what the Framers intended and what the First Amendment has preserved. Far from being a matter of exemption, exception or even toleration, religious liberty is an inalienable right. Far from being a sub-category of free speech or a constitutional redundancy, religious liberty is distinct and foundational. Far from being simply an individual right, religious liberty is a positive social good. Far from denigrating religion as a social or political "problem," the separation of Church and State is both the saving of religion from the temptation of political power and an achievement inspired in large part by religion itself. Far from weakening religion, disestablishment has, as an historical fact, enabled it to flourish.

In light of the First Amendment, the government should stand in relation to the churches, synagogues and other communities of faith as the guarantor of freedom. In light of the First Amendment, the churches, synagogues and other communities of faith stand in relation to the government as generators of faith, and therefore contribute to the spiritual and moral foundations of democracy. Thus, the government acts as a safeguard, but not the source, of freedom for faiths, whereas the churches and synagogues act as a source, but not the safeguard, of faiths for freedom.

The Religious Liberty provisions work for each other and for the federal idea as a whole. Neither established nor excluded, neither preferred nor proscribed, each faith (whether transcendent or naturalistic) is brought into a relationship with the government so that each is separated from the state in terms of its institutions, but democratically related to the state in terms of individuals and its ideas.

The result is neither a naked public square where all religion is excluded, nor a sacred public square with any religion established or semi-established. The result, rather, is a civil public square in which citizens of all religious faiths, or none, engage one another in the continuing democratic discourse.

3. The Compact Must Be Mutual

Reconstitution of a free republican people requires the recognition that religious liberty is a universal right joined to a universal duty to respect that right.

In the turns and twists of history, victims of religious discrimination have often later become perpetrators. In the famous image of Roger Williams, those at the helm of the Ship of State forget they were once under the hatches. They have, he said, "One weight for themselves when they are under the hatches, and another for others when they come to the helm." They show themselves, said James Madison, "as ready to set up an establishment which is to take them in as they were to pull down that which shut them out." Thus, benignly or otherwise, Protestants have treated Catholics as they were once treated, and secularists have done likewise with both.

Such inconsistencies are the natural seedbed for the growth of a de facto establishment. Against such inconsistencies we affirm that a right for one is a right for another and a responsibility for all. A right for a Protestant is a right for an Orthodox is a right for a Catholic is a right for a Jew is a right for a Humanist is a right for a Mormon is a right for a Muslim is a right for a Buddhist—and for the followers of any other faith within the wide bounds of the republic.

That rights are universal and responsibilities mutual is both the premise and the promise of democratic pluralism. The First Amendment, in this sense, is the epitome of public justice and serves as the Golden Rule for civic life. Rights are best guarded and responsibilities best exercised when each person and group guards for all others those rights they wish guarded for themselves. Whereas the wearer of the English crown is officially the Defender of the Faith, all who uphold the American Constitution are defenders of the rights of all faiths.

From this axiom, that rights are universal and responsibilities mutual, derives guidelines for conducting public debates involving religion in a manner that is democratic and civil. These guidelines are not, and must not be, mandated by law. But they are, we believe, necessary to reconstitute and revitalize the American understanding of the role of religion in a free society.

First, those who claim the right to dissent should assume the responsibility to debate: Commitment to democratic pluralism assumes the coexistence within one political community of groups whose ultimate faith commitments may be incompatible, yet whose common commitment to social unity and diversity does justice to both the requirements of individual conscience and the wider community. A general consent to the obligations of citizenship is therefore inherent in the American experiment, both as a founding principle ("We the people") and as a matter of daily practice.

There must always be room for those who do not wish to participate in the public ordering of our common life, who desire to pursue their own religious witness separately as conscience dictates. But at the same time, for those who do wish to participate, it should be understood that those claiming the right to dissent should assume the responsibility to debate. As this responsibility is exercised, the characteristic American formula of individual liberty complemented by respect for the opinions of others permits differences to be asserted, yet a broad, active community of understanding to be sustained.

Second, those who claim the right to criticize should assume the responsibility to comprehend: One of the ironies of democratic life is that freedom of conscience is jeopardized by false tolerance as well as by outright intolerance. Genuine tolerance considers contrary views fairly and judges them on merit. Debased tolerance so refrains from making any judgment that it refuses to listen at all. Genuine tolerance honestly weighs honest differences and promotes both impartiality and pluralism. Debased tolerance results in indifference to the differences that vitalize a pluralistic democracy.

Central to the difference between genuine and debased tolerance is the recognition that peace and truth must be held in tension. Pluralism must not be confused with, and is in fact endangered by, philosophical and ethical indifference. Commitment to strong, clear philosophical and ethical ideas need not imply either intolerance or opposition to democratic pluralism. On the contrary, democratic pluralism requires an agreement to be locked in public argument over disagreements of consequence within the bonds of civility.

The right to argue for any public policy is a fundamental right for every citizen; respecting that right is a fundamental responsibility for all other citizens. When any view is expressed, all must uphold as constitutionally protected its advocate's right to express it. But others are free to challenge that view as politically pernicious, philosophically false, ethically evil, theologically idolatrous, or simply absurd, as the case may be seen to be.

Unless this tension between peace and truth is respected, civility cannot be sustained. In that event, tolerance degenerates into either apathetic relativism or a dogmatism as uncritical of itself as it is uncomprehending of others. The result is a general corruption of principled public debate.

Third, those who claim the right to influence should accept the responsibility not to inflame: Too often in recent disputes over religion and public affairs, some have insisted that any evidence of religious influence on public policy represents an establishment of religion and is therefore precluded as an improper "imposition." Such exclusion of religion from public life is historically unwarranted, philosophically inconsistent and profoundly undemocratic. The Framers' intention is indisputably ignored when public policy debates can appeal to the theses of Adam Smith and Karl Marx, or Charles Darwin and Sigmund Freud but not to the Western religious tradition in general and the Hebrew and Christian Scriptures in particular. Many of the most dynamic social movements in American history, including that of civil rights, were legitimately inspired and shaped by religious motivation.

Freedom of conscience and the right to influence public policy on the basis of religiously informed ideas are inseverably linked. In short, a key to democratic renewal is the fullest possible participation in the most open possible debate.

Religious liberty and democratic civility are also threatened, however, from another quarter. Overreacting to an improper veto on religion in public life, many have used religious language and images not for the legitimate influencing of policies but to inflame politics. Politics is indeed an extension of ethics and therefore engages religious principles; but some err by refusing to recognize that there is a distinction, though not a separation, between religion and politics. As a result, they bring to politics a misplaced absoluteness that idolizes politics, "Satanizes" their enemies and politicizes their own faith.

Even the most morally informed policy positions involve prudential judgments as well as pure principle. Therefore, to make an absolute equation of principles and policies inflates politics and does violence to reason, civil life and faith itself. Politics has recently been inflamed by a number of confusions: the confusion of personal religious affiliation with qualification or disqualification for public office; the confusion of claims to divine guidance with claims to divine endorsement; and the confusion of government neutrality among faiths with government indifference or hostility to religion.

Fourth, those who claim the right to participate should accept the responsibility to persuade: Central to the American experience is the power of political persuasion. Growing partly from principle and partly from the pressures of democratic pluralism, commitment to persuasion is the corollary of the belief that conscience is inviolable, coercion of conscience is evil, and the public interest is best served by consent hard won from vigorous debate. Those who believe themselves privy to the will of history brook no argument and need never tarry for consent. But to those who subscribe to the idea of government by the consent of the governed, compelled beliefs are a violation of first principles. The natural logic of the Religious Liberty provisions is to foster a political culture of persuasion which admits the challenge of opinions from all sources.

Arguments for public policy should be more than private convictions shouted out loud. For persuasion to be principled, private convictions should be translated into publicly accessible claims. Such public claims should be made publicly accessible for two reasons: first, because they must engage those who do not share the same private convictions, and second, because they should be directed toward the common good.

Renewal of first principles

We who live in the third century of the American republic can learn well from the past as we look to the future. Our Founders were both idealists and realists. Their confidence in human abilities was tempered by their skepticism about human nature. Aware of what was new in their times, they also knew the need for renewal in times after theirs. "No free government, or the blessings of liberty," wrote George Mason in 1776, "can be preserved to any people, but by a firm adherence to justice, moderation, temperance, frugality, and virtue, and by frequent recurrence to fundamental principles."

True to the ideals and realism of that vision, we who sign this Charter, people of many and various beliefs, pledge ourselves to the enduring precepts of the First Amendment as the cornerstone of the American experiment in liberty under law.

We address ourselves to our fellow citizens, daring to hope that the strongest desire of the greatest number is for the common good. We are firmly persuaded that the principles asserted here require a fresh consideration, and that the renewal of religious liberty is crucial to sustain a free people that would remain free. We therefore commit ourselves to speak, write and act according to this vision and these principles. We urge our fellow citizens to do the same.

To agree on such guiding principles and to achieve such a compact will not be easy. Whereas a law is a command directed to us, a compact is a promise that must proceed freely from us. To achieve it demands a measure of the vision, sacrifice and perseverance shown by our Founders. Their task was to defy the past, seeing and securing religious liberty against the terrible precedents of history. Ours is to challenge the future, sustaining vigilance and broadening protections against every new menace, including that of our own complacency. Knowing the unquenchable desire for freedom, they lit a beacon. It is for us who know its blessings to keep it burning brightly.

Signers of the Williamsburg Charter

Representing Government

President Jimmy Carter
President Gerald R. Ford
Chief Justice William H. Rehnquist
Chief Justice Warren E. Burger, retired
Secretary of Education William J. Bennett
Senator Dennis DeConcini, D-Arizona; Trustee; Bicentennial Commissioner
Senator Robert Dole, R-Kansas, Minority Leader, U.S. Senate
Senator Mark O. Hatfield, R-Oregon; Trustee
Senator Daniel Patrick Moynihan, D-New York; Trustee
Senator Ted Stevens, R-Alaska; Trustee; Bicentennial Commissioner
Representative James Wright, Speaker, U.S. House of Representatives
Representative Representative Robert Michel, R-Illinois, Minority Leader,
    U.S. House of Representatives
Representative Don Bonker, D-Washington; Trustee
Representative James Slattery, D-Kansas; Trustee
Governor Michael S. Dukakis, Chairman, Democratic Governors Association
Mr. Charles Z. Wick, Director, United States Information Agency
Ms. Pamela Plumb, President, National League of Cities

Members of the Drafting Committee

Mr. William Bentley Ball, Attorney, Ball, Skelly, Murren & Connell
Dr. Os Guinness, Executive Director, The Williamsburg Charter Foundation
Mr. Nat Hentoff, Columnist, The Washington Post and Village Voice, and Staff Writer,
    The New Yorker
Dean Kelley, Director, Religious and Civil Liberties Division of the National Council
    of Churches
Pastor Richard Neuhaus, Director, Center for Religion and Society
Mr. George S. Weigel, Jr., President, The James Madison Foundation

Academic Consultants

Professor Robert N. Bellah, University of California at Berkeley
Professor Peter L. Berger, Boston University
Professor Robert A. Destro, U.S. Civil Rights Commission
Professor Edward Gaffney, Jr., Loyola Law School
Dr. William A. Galston, The Roosevelt Center
Professor James Davison Hunter, University of Virginia
Professor George M. Marsden, Duke University
Professor David Martin, The London School of Economics
Professor William Lee Miller, University of Virginia

Mr. A. James Reichley, The Brookings Institution
Professor William Van Alstyne, Duke University School of Law
Professor Robert Wuthnow, Princeton University

Representing Political Parties
Mr. Frank Fahrenkopf, Jr., Chairman, Republican National Committee
Mr. Paul Kirk, Jr., Chairman, Democratic National Committee

Representing the Commission on the Bicentennial of the U.S. Constitution
Mr. Frederick K. Biebel
Representative Lindy Boggs, D-Louisiana
Dr. Mark W. Cannon, Executive Director
The Honorable Lynne V. Cheney
Representative Philip Crane, R-Illinois
Mr. William J. Green
Reverend Edward Victor Hill
Senator Edward M. Kennedy, D-Massachusetts
Mrs. Betty Southard Murphy
Dr. Thomas H. O'Connor
Mrs. Phyllis Schlafly
Mr. Obert C. Tanner
Senator Strom Thurmond, R-South Carolina
Mr. Ronald H. Walker
Judge Charles E. Wiggins

Representing the Commonwealth of Virginia
Governor Gerald Baliles
Senator Paul Trible
Senator John Warner
Representative Herbert H. Bateman
Representative Thomas Jerome Bliley, Jr.
Representative Rick C. Boucher
Representative Stan Parris
Representative Owen Bradford Pickett
Representative Norman Sisisky
Representative D. French Slaughter, Jr.
Representative Frank R. Wolf
Mayor John Hodges, Williamsburg
Professor A.E. Dick Howard, Chairman, Virginia Commission on the Bicentennial
    of the United States Constitution
Mr. Charles R. Longsworth, President, Colonial Williamsburg Foundation
Dr. Paul Verkuil, President, College of William and Mary

Representing American Communities of Faith

Mr. Edward L. Ericson, Former President, American Ethical Union

Bishop Charles H. Foggie, African Methodist Episcopal Zion Church

His Eminence Archbishop Iakovos, Primate of the Greek Orthodox Church of North and South America; Trustee

Very Reverend Leonid Kishkovsky, President-elect, National Council of Churches

Rabbi Gilbert Klaperman, President, Synagogue Council of America

Archbishop John L. May, President, U.S. Catholic Conference; Trustee

Reverend Patricia A. McClurg, Past President, National Council of Churches

Imam Warith Deen Muhammad, Muslim American Community Assistance Fund

Elder Dallin H. Oaks, Apostle, Church of Jesus Christ of Latter-Day Saints

Dr. Adrian Rogers, President, Southern Baptist Convention

Mr. John Lewis Selover, Chairman, Christian Science Board of Directors

Bishop Rembert Stokes, President, Council of Bishops, African Methodist Episcopal Church

Rev. Leon H. Sullivan, Pastor, Zion Baptist Church, Philadelphia; Trustee

Metropolitan Theodosius, Orthodox Church of America

Dr. John H. White, President, National Association of Evangelicals

Professor Elie Wiesel, Nobel Laureate

Mr. Neil Wilson, World President, Seventh-day Adventists

Bishop Seigen H. Yamaoka, Buddhist Church of America

Representing Organizations Concerned with Religion and Public Life

Dr. Arie R. Brouwer, General Secretary, National Council of Churches; Trustee

Reverend John Buchanan, Chairman, People for the American Way

Dr. James C. Dobson, President, Focus on the Family

Dr. Robert P. Dugan, Jr., Director of Public Affairs, National Association of Evangelicals; Trustee

Mr. James Dunn, Executive Director, Baptist Joint Committee

Mr. Samuel Ericsson, Executive Director, Christian Legal Society

Reverend Thomas Gallagher, Secretary for Education, U.S. Catholic Conference

Rabbi Joshua O. Haberman, President, Foundation for Jewish Studies

The Honorable Philip M. Klutznick, Honorary President, B'nai B'rith; Trustee

Mr. Norman Lear, Founding Chairman, People for the American Way

Dr. Robert Maddox, Executive Director, Americans United for Separation of Church and State

Mr. Tom Neumann, Executive Vice-President, B'nai B'rith International

Mr. Michael A. Pelavin, Chairman, National Jewish Community Relations Council

Mr. Samuel Rabinove, Legal Director, American Jewish Committee

Mr. Jerry P. Regier, President, Family Research Council

Ms. Jacqueline Wexler, President, National Conference of Christians and Jews

Representing Business

Mr. Howard F. Ahmanson, Jr., President, Fieldstead & Company

Mr. Andrew Athens, President, Metron Steel Corporation; Trustee

Mr. Richard T. Baker, Former Chairman, Ernst & Whinney; Trustee

Mr. Dennis W. Bakke, President, Applied Energy Services; Trustee

Mr. Robert J. Brown, President, B&C Associates; Trustee

Mr. Philip B. Chenok, President, American Institute of Certified Public Accountants

Mr. Donald K. Cliffor, Jr.

Ambassador Holland Hanson Coors, President's Special Representative for the
   National Year of the Americas; Trustee

Mr. T. J. Dermot Dunphy, President, Sealed Air Corporation

Mr. William J. Flynn, Chairman and Chief Executive Officer, Mutual of America;
Chairman, "First Liberty" Summit Committee; Trustee

Ms. Mary Falvey Fuller, Chairman and President, Falvey Motors, Troy, Michigan; Trustee

Dr. Thomas S. Haggai, Chairman and President, IGA, Inc.; Trustee

General David C. Jones, Former Chairman, Joint Chiefs of Staff; Trustee

Mr. William S. Kanaga, Chairman, U.S. Chamber of Commerce; Trustee

Mr. Harvey Kapnick, Chariman & President, Chicago Pacific Corporation

Mr. George S. Kovats, The Stewardship Foundation

Mr. Henry Luce III, President, The Henry Luce Foundation; Trustee

Mr. William E. MacDonald, Chairman and Chief Executive Officer (Retired),
   Ohio Bell; Trustee

Mr. J. Willard Marriott, Jr., Chairman, Marriott Corporation; Trustee

Mrs. Forrest E. Mars, Jr.; Trustee

The Honorable Alonzo L. McDonald, Chairman, The Avenir Group, Inc. and
Chairman,   The Williamsburg Charter Foundation

Mr. Luis G. Nogales, President, ECO, Inc.; Trustee

The Honorable Charles H. Percy, Charles Percy & Associates; Trustee

Mr. Dudley Porter, Trustee, Maclellan Foundation

Mr. Edmund Pratt, Jr., President, Business Roundtable

Mrs. Linda Gosden Robinson, President and Chief Executive Officer,
   Robinson, Lake, Lerer & Montgomery; Trustee

Mr. Donald Seibert, Former Chairman, J.C. Penney Company, Inc.

Mr. Michael L. Stefanos, President, Dove Bar International; Trustee

Mr. Frank D. Stella, Chairman and Chief Executive Officer, F.D.
   Stella Products Co.; Trustee

Mr. Michael T. Timmis, Vice-Chairman, Talon, Inc.; Trustee

Sidney Topol, Chairman, Scientific-Atlanta; Trustee

Mr. Alexander B. Trowbridge, President, National Association of Manufacturers

Mrs. Anne Wexler, Chairman, Wexler, Reynolds, Harrison & Schule; Trustee

Mr. C. Davis Weyerhaeuser; Founder and Trustee, the Stewardship Schule; Trustee

Mr. Edward Lee White, Jr., President, Cecil B. Day Foundation

Representing Education and Public Policy
Dr. Thomas A. Bartlett, Chancellor, University of Alabama
Dr. Derek Bok, President, Harvard University
Dr. Ernest Boyer, President, The Carnegie Foundation for the Advancement of Teaching
Dr. John Brademas, President, New York University
Mr. Richard T. Burress, Associate Director, The Hoover Institution; Trustee
Dr. James E. Cheek, President, Howard University
Mr. Edward Crane, President, Cato Institute
Mr. Christopher DeMuth, President, American Enterprise Institute
Mr. Edwin Feulner, President, The Heritage Foundation
Ms. Mary Hatwood Futrell, President, National Education Association
Dr. George Gallup, Jr., President, Gallup Poll; Trustee
Mr. David Gardner, President, University of California
Mr. William Gorham, President, Urban Institute
Mr. Samuel Husk, Chairman, Education Leadership Consortium
Professor Barbara Jordan, Lyndon B. Johnson School of Public Affairs,
    University of Texas at Austin
Dr. Ernest Lefever, President, Ethics and Public Policy Center
Dr. Bruce K. MacLaury, President, The Brookings Institution; Trustee
Dr. Robert M. O'Neil, President, University of Virginia
Dr. Frank H. T. Rhodes, President, Cornell University
Mr. Albert Shanker, President, American Federation of Teachers
Dr. Thomas A. Shannon, Director, National School Boards Association
Mrs. Manya Ungar, President, National Congress of Parents and Teachers

Representing Labor Unions
Mr. Lane Kirkland, President, AFL-CIO
Mr. Howard D. Samuel, President, Trade and Industrial Department, AFL-CIO

Representing Law
The Honorable Mark A. Constantino, U.S. District Judge
Mr. Robert MacCrate, President, American Bar Association
Mr. Walter L. Sutton, President, National Bar Association
The Honorable Robert H. Wahl, President, American Judges Association

Representing the Media
Mr. Ben Armstrong, Executive Director, National Religious Broadcasters
Mr. Robert Brunner, Chairman, Radio-Television News Directors Association
Mr. Walter Cronkite
Ms. Patricia Diaz Dennis, Federal Communications Commissioner
Mr. Edward O. Fritts, President and Chief Executive Officer, National Association
    of Broadcasters; Trustee

Mr. David R. Gergen, Editor, U.S. News & World Report; Trustee

Mr. Wallace Jorgenson, Chairmen of the Joint Boards, National Association
   of Broadcasters

Mr. John Seigenthaler, President, American Society of Newspaper Editors

Representing Medicine

Dr. William S. Hotchkiss, President, American Medical Association

Dr. C. Everett Koop, U.S. Surgeon General

Representing Minorities and Ethnic Groups

Madame Nien Cheng, Author

Ms. Suzanne Shown Harjo, Executive Director, National Congress of American Indians

Dr. Benjamin Hooks, Executive Director, NAACP

Dr. John E. Jacob, President and Chief Executive Officer, National Urban League

Dr. Kyo Jhin, Chairman, Asian-American Voter's Coalition

Dr. Vernon E. Jordan, Jr., Former President, Urban League

Mrs. Coretta Scott King, President, Martin Luther King, Jr. Center
   for Non-Violent Social Change; Trustee

Ms. Beverly LaHaye, President, Concerned Women for America

Mr. Pluria W. Marshall, Chairman, National Black Media Coalition

Mr. Oscar Moran, President, League of United Latin American Citizens

Mr. Raul Yzaguirre, President, National Council of La Raza

Representing Senior Citizens

Mr. Horace B. Deets, Executive Director, American Association of Retired Persons

Representing Voluntary Organizations

Mr. William Aramony, President, United Way of America; Trustee

Mr. Andrew S. Miller, National Commander, Salvation Army

Mr. Richard F. Schubert, President, American Red Cross

Mr. Carmi Schwartz, Executive Vice President, Council of Jewish Federations

Representing Youth

Mr. David W. Bahlmann, National Director, Camp Fire, Inc.

Mrs. Frances Hesselbein, National Executive Director, Girl Scouts of the U.S.A.

Mr. Fritz Kidd, Student Chairman, National Association of Student Councils

Mr. Ben H. Love, Chief Scout Executive, Boy Scouts of America

Mr. Tony Ortiz, National Honor Society, Century III Leaders

Mr. Grant Shrum, President, 4-H National Council

Other Organizations and Individuals

Mrs. Susan Garrett Baker, founding member of the Committee for
Food and Shelter; Trustee

The Honorable Stuart E. Eizenstat, Partner, Powell, Goldstein, Frazer & Murphy; Trustee

Mr. Joe Gibbs, Head Coach, Washington Redskins; Trustee

The Honorable Robert S. McNamara, Former President, World Bank; Trustee

The Honorable Robert S. Strauss, Partner, Akin, Gump, Strauss, Hauer & Feld; Trustee

Ms. Kathleen Kennedy Townsend, Chairman, Maryland Special Initiative for
Community Service; Trustee

Subject Index

FIRST AMENDMENT TO THE
UNITED STATES CONSTITUTION

SUBJECT INDEX

Index

Publication No. 01-F09 REV / 5k BL / 12-02